Fiction in the Archives

Pardon Tales and Their Tellers in Sixteenth-Century France

The Harry Camp Lectures at Stanford University

The Harry Camp Memorial Fund was established
in 1959 to make possible a continuing series
of lectures at Stanford University on topics bearing on
the dignity and worth of the human individual.

Fiction in the Archives

PARDON TALES AND THEIR TELLERS IN SIXTEENTH-CENTURY FRANCE

Natalie Zemon Davis

1987

STANFORD UNIVERSITY PRESS

Stanford, California

Stanford University Press
Stanford, California

© 1987 by the Board of Trustees of the
Leland Stanford Junior University

Printed in the United States of America

Library of Congress Cataloging-in-Publication Data

Davis, Natalie Zemon, 1928–
  Fiction in the archives.

    Bibliography: p.
    Includes index.
    1. French prose literature—16th century—History
and criticism.   2. Pardon—France—History—16th
century.   3. Storytelling—France—History—16th
century.   4. Criminal justice, Administration of—
France—History—16th century.   5. Fiction—Technique.
6. Criminals' writings, French—History and criticism.
I. Title.
PQ613.D38   1987   848'.308'09   87-17951
ISBN 0-8047-1412-6 (alk. paper)

For

LAWRENCE STONE

historian par excellence and

storyteller, too

Preface

For years I have been reading sixteenth-century letters of remission for crimes, dutifully taking notes on names and acts, while chuckling and shaking my head as though I had the *Decameron* in my hands. To begin with, I was especially searching out people from the Lyonnais, but my eye would be caught by a transvestite riot in Languedoc or a family homicide in Picardy. Then I was given the happy responsibility of writing a review of Emmanuel Le Roy Ladurie's *Montaillou*. Examining the Inquisition sources behind that splendid study, I realized that one could find in these full and uninterrupted narratives some evidence for the storytelling skills of Pyrenean villagers in the early fourteenth century. I called my review "The Storytellers of Montaillou" and promised myself one day to make such an analysis of documents from my own century.

When Stanford University invited me to give the Harry Camp Lectures for 1985–86, I thought, "Here is my chance." By now, my sleuthing on the Martin Guerre case had complicated my goals. In my book on that subject, I had been able to describe how the judge and the law clerk structured the events after the impostor was dead, but what of the villagers' memories? What cultural resources did they use to order departures and returns, identities and complicities, and how could you get evidence for their forms of recital?

So back to the archives for collecting letters of remission from many parts of France. If I were not going to concentrate on a distinctive regional style, then at least I could detect the range of nar-

vii

rative techniques and motifs found in several provinces. And back to sixteenth-century legal texts and Renaissance novellas. A cultural analysis of pardon texts would have to understand the rules for their creation. I could hope that historians of the law and of crime would savor with me the storytelling features of their documents, while perhaps critic/scholars would find here an interesting model for the production of literature.

As I began to write up my material, links between violence, storytelling, and pardon seeking cropped up everywhere. They appeared in the sixteenth century, where connections between riot and ritual, which I had noted in an earlier publication, now seemed important not merely because events had happened that way but also because people of the time told about them that way. And they appeared in the twentieth century, where despite major differences from the Old Regime in values, law, and judicial procedure, similar motifs surface in crime reports and similar quarrels break out about accepting responsibility and seeking rightful excuse.

"Listen to this," I would say to my husband as he was fixing breakfast and I was reading the *New York Times*, "here's a man sentenced for the beating death of his mother when she refused to make him meatballs for Thanksgiving dinner. . . . Here's an uninvited guest shooting another young man at a party 'when everyone was dancing.' . . . Here's a father who wants his son to accept the death penalty to atone for murder." Meanwhile, letters to the editor were debating how "self-defense" should be understood in Bernhard Goetz's shooting in the subway, and Jean Harris told us, in her book published from prison, that she never intended the death of the man she loved, that she does not know how he was killed.

My study stays squarely within its sixteenth-century bounds, but I hope readers will share my sense of its wider resonance, both for perceiving recurrent connections between history, literature, and law and for reading pardon tales and crime stories of the present.

Given first in January 1986 as the Harry Camp Lectures at Stanford University, *Fiction in the Archives* was also presented as the 1986 Whidden Lectures at McMaster University. I am appreciative not only of the honor of these invitations, but also of the lively questioning and suggestions from my audiences. The John Simon Guggenheim Memorial Foundation provided funds to support my re-search, and, once in the archives, I was much assisted by the staff of the Archives Nationales, the Archives de la Préfecture de la Police at Paris, the Archives Départementales du Rhône, and the Archives d'Etat de Genève. I want particularly to thank Barbara Roth at the last institution.

The argument of this book was also presented in brief to several intellectual communities, whose responses helped in the early formulation and reformulation of the project: the Toronto Semiotic Circle; the Center for the Humanities of Wesleyan University; the History Departments of Johns Hopkins University, Georgetown University, Case Western Reserve University, Hofstra University, and the University of Edinburgh; and the Centre de Recherches Historiques of the Ecole des Hautes Etudes en Sciences Sociales. Alfred Soman gave me excellent guidance on how to track down materials in the registers of the Parlement of Paris and the Paris Police Archives and responded with his characteristic generosity to questions about the workings of French criminal justice, both early in my work and at its end. Bernard Lescaze helped me to follow the pardon trail in Geneva. The manuscript of the lectures was read by Stephen Greenblatt, Joan W. Scott, and Thomas A. Green, and their suggestions were invaluable in writing the final version of the book. Numerous friends provided ideas and bibliography, including John M. Beattie, Philip Berk, Joan deJean, Carla Hesse, Madeleine Jeay, Jean-Philippe Labrousse, François Rigolot, Peter Sahlins, Marcia Cantor Stubbs, Stephen D. White, and Froma Zeitlin. Dean Dabrowski was indefatigable in tracking down books and in other secretarial help, and Ellen Smith of Stanford University Press gave astute attention to copy editing the finished manuscript. None of these counselors should be held responsible, however, for any defects in the final product, but only its author.

As for my husband, Chandler Davis, I hope he will pardon me for countless interruptions to hear one more bloody tale or to discuss one more interpretation, even though I have no excuse and do not promise to mend my ways.

Contents

Illustrations

Fiction in the Archives

Pardon Tales and Their Tellers in Sixteenth-Century France

Introduction

et me begin with an archival text: François, by the grace of God king of France, let it be known to all those present and to come that we have received the humble supplication of Thomas Manny, poor plowman, aged about 36, living in Sens, Saying that he had been joined in marriage with one Claudine Guyart, by whom he had had one child. And although the said supplicant had always treated and governed her honestly and well and was himself of good renown and honest conversation, nonetheless his ill-advised wife had behaved herself with lewdness and wickedness and had caught the disease known as the great pox. The supplicant, very displeased, had her cared for and cured. But then, together with the chambermaid who had tended her during her illness, she left for the house of Jean Baston, a tavern-keeper living outside Saint Anthony's gate, where she stayed for two days till he was told about it by a bath-house girl named Symonette. Together with Thomas Geneteau the mason and Pierre Numbiliers, a royal sergeant, he went to Baston's, found her hiding in the cellar, and took her back to his house, he promising not to beat her or outrage her, which in fact he did not do, and she promising to conduct herself well.

But after five or six days she broke her promise, stole whatever she wanted from the house and departed without his knowing for the house of a blacksmith named Graffiquart at Saint Anthony's gate. There she stayed for about eight days until a *fille de joie* named Jacquette came upon the supplicant in front of his house and said that if he would buy her a drink, she would tell him where his wife was, and he promised he would.

Soon after, on a Sunday morning in June 1529, the supplicant went with the royal sergeants Jean Collart and Pierre Hofflart over to Graffiquart's house. They ordered him to open the door, which he did, and they went right in and found his wife in a little bed with some man, who managed to

1

flee naked out the back door. They brought his wife back to the supplicant's house, and he reprimanded her and punished her with a broom, but after three days she was gone again. About three weeks later he was informed she was in the house of a certain Edmé Choppin. He went there to see her, but instead was met by his wife's sister Katherine, who threw a stone at his head and made him bleed heavily.

And since then, in July, the supplicant betook himself to a meadow near Sens, where he found his wife working with several other people, including her *paillard* [that is, her rascally sex-partner]. He reproached her for her faults, but everyone made fun of him. Full of shame, he took a wooden pitchfork, hit his wife on the shoulders saying she was wicked to be with her paillard in front of everyone, and brought her back home. That same night about nine o'clock, the paillard came to his house with a couple of other men, threw big stones at the windows, and shouted that he should send her out, calling him "cuckold" and other insults.

On the feast of Mary Magdalene fifteen days later, the said paillard came back to the house with his two companions, and, swearing and blaspheming the name of the Lord, he gave the supplicant three or four big slaps on his face and said he would kill him. One of them took a little ax from under his robe and tried to strike him on the head, but the supplicant put out his arm and was hit there. To get away, he fled to a neighbor's house, but then, all aroused and frightened at the outrage done him, he came out holding a stone in his hand. On the way back, he saw the paillard and his companion following him and, more afraid than ever, hurried toward his house. In front of it he met his wife and, swearing and in hot anger, said to her, "Must I die for a whore?" As he spoke, he hit her on the head with the stone. She fled before him, and he struck her two or three times with a table-knife he always wore, but does not know exactly where he got her.

Whereupon fearing the rigor of Justice, he left the scene, and heard afterward that because of his blows and by lack of good care . . . his wife died. The supplicant was then taken prisoner in Sens, where held in captivity . . . he is in danger of finishing his life miserably.

Since the homicide came about because of "hot anger" and since otherwise Thomas Manny has been a person "of good life and honest conversation," in August 1530, the king instructs the bailiff of Sens to release him from prison without further trial, without penalty, and without infamy.[1]

Whenever I read these royal letters of pardon and remission—and the French archives are full of them—I marvel at the literary qualities of these texts, or, I might say, their "fictional" qualities, by which I mean the extent to which their authors shape the events of a crime into a story.[2] Thomas Manny's story has less suspense in it than many other requests for royal grace—the reader knows from the first mention of the lascivious wife who the victim is likely to be—but the events move to a climax through the husband's trials and humiliations and his ever stronger sexual language: the cured pox; the bath-house girl and the "fille de joie" from whom he gets not intercourse but information; the "paillard"; and the final outburst, "Faut-il que je meure pour une putain?" And the unrepentant wife is called for by her lover and slain by her husband on Mary Magdalene's day.

When I was a student, we were ordinarily taught as scientific historians to peel away the fictive elements in our documents so we could get at the real facts. We had to correct for Thomas Manny's special pleading if we wanted to discover the actual events of July 22, 1529. What is the "documentary value" of letters of remission? a recent study asked, and concluded that some from the fourteenth and fifteenth centuries were "a tissue of counter-truths."[3] Nonetheless, there are many important ways that historians have used and can continue to use the letters without too much worry about their literary construction. They have been precious sources for studies of holiday customs, of violence and revenge in different social milieus and age groups, of attitudes toward and images of the king and other social and cultural norms.[4] We can readily see how Thomas Manny's tale provides interesting particulars about wife beating and small-town prostitution.

I would like to take a different tack. I want to let the "fictional" aspects of these documents be the center of analysis. By "fictional" I do not mean their feigned elements, but rather, using the other and broader sense of the root word *fingere*, their forming, shaping, and molding elements: the crafting of a narrative. In the current debate about the relation of the "real" and the "historical" to the "fictional," I think we can agree with Hayden White that the world does not just "present itself to perception in the form of well-made stories, with central subjects, proper beginnings, middles, and ends." And in the diverse efforts to define the character of historical narrative, I think we can agree with Roland Barthes, Paul Ricoeur, and Lionel Gossman that shaping choices of language, detail, and order are needed to present an account that seems to both writer and reader true, real, meaningful, and/or explanatory.[5]

By the categories of Renaissance rhetoricians and literary theorists, the letter of remission was a mixed genre: a judicial supplication to persuade the king and courts, a historical account of one's past actions, and a story. In all three there was a role for crafting and shaping. As the sixteenth-century rhetorician Daniel d'Augé observed, in drawing on Aristotle, judicial speech is one of the three kinds of oratory—deliberative, demonstrative, and legal; it needs "artifice" just like the others. The verb *feindre* itself was used in the literary exchange of that time to mean "create," rather than merely to dissemble; its fruit was "fiction." To be sure, fictive creation had its most appropriate expression in poetry or a story, not in history, which was increasingly praised (though not always practiced) as a truth which was "bare" and "unadorned." But the artifice of fiction did not necessarily lend falsity to an account; it might well bring verisimilitude or a moral truth. Nor did the shaping or embellishing of a history necessarily mean forgery; where that line was to be drawn was one of the creative controversies of the day. To look for the "fictive" aspects of a letter of remission would not by sixteenth-century definition inevitably be a quest for fraud.[6]

In my twentieth-century enterprise I have been much helped by what literary specialists have shown us about how narratives are put together, but my historian's eye will not focus on morphologies of the tale, on production from a universal grammar, or on arrangements of functions, "indices," and propositions that might be found in any time or place. Rather I am after evidence of how sixteenth-century people told stories (albeit in the special case of the pardon tale), what they thought a good story was, how they accounted for motive, and how through narrative they made sense of the unexpected and built coherence into immediate experience. I want to see how their stories varied according to teller and listener and how the rules for plot in these judicial tales of violence and grace interacted with wider contemporary habits of explanation, description, and evaluation. My method here will in part resemble that recommended by Barbara Herrnstein-Smith, attending closely to the means and settings for producing the stories and to the interests held by both narrator and audience in the storytelling event. But I will also be conceiving of "structures" existing prior to that event in the minds and lives of the sixteenth-century participants: possible story lines determined by the constraints of the law and approaches to narrative learned in past listening to and telling of stories or derived from other cultural constructions.[7]

After exploring the crafting of the tales, I will circle back to their fidelity to "real events," or at least to the same events as recounted by others, and ask what relation truth-telling had to the outcome of the stories and what truth status they enjoyed in society at large. The concerns of the social and political historian will crop up here, too—not as isolated motifs collected from many tales, but as steps in a narrative or a narrative transaction. You will not read any quantitative estimates of, say, the kinds of weapons people used in sixteenth-century homicide, but you will hear how people described putting weapons into play. You will not read analyses of political crimes per se, but you will be asked to consider the importance of the king as a frame for all pardon tales and their role in enhancing his sovereignty. Finally, I will be inquiring how these self-interested recitals by people with bloody hands compare with printed crime accounts and with stories by literary figures such as Marguerite de Navarre and Noël du Fail, authors who might want the king's readership, but who did not need his pardon. In an age when the *conte* and the *nouvelle* employed many concrete details as marks of their reality and often claimed to be retelling actual events, what resemblance did they bear to fictions in the archives?

Why then choose the letters of remission? Because they are one of the best sources of relatively uninterrupted narrative from the lips of the lower orders (and indeed from others, too) in sixteenth-century France. Letters and memoirs from peasants and artisans are rare. Marriage contracts, wills, and other contracts are plentiful and tell us much about the actions, plans, and sensibilities of men and women who could not even sign their names at the bottom, but the documents themselves are dominated by notarial sequences and formulae.[8] Letters of remission were also collaborative efforts, as we will see, but they gave much greater scope to the person to whom the notary was listening. Depositions and records of interrogations in criminal cases are extant for certain jurisdictions in the sixteenth century and are valuable indications of the way people recounted events. But witnesses were supposed to confine themselves to what they had seen or heard of a crime, and their stories often lack a beginning and an end. For example, in Lyon in 1546, two barber's journeymen and a chambermaid attest to the plans of their mistress to poison their master. They report what their mistress said to them about the poison, their actions to reveal the plot, and the encounter between husband and wife; but they can say little about motive except the wife's remark to a customer who asked her why she looked glum ("I have no occasion to be cheerful since I am badly treated"), and they do not tell how the affair turned out.[9]

As for the accused in criminal prosecutions, their testimony was ordinarily directed at every moment by the judge. Read the testimony of Lyon printing worker Galiot Thibout and think how different it would be if he were petitioning for pardon:

> And who are those whom the Printers call Forfants? [a judge demanded of Galiot in a trial of 1565].
> Responds that that's what one calls the people who beat them up and work for lower wages and with apprentices.
> And those who are called Griffarins or Compagnons?
> Responds that they are people of his sort.
> And what does the word Griffarin signify?
> Responds that he doesn't know unless it's because of some banquets they give together and money they put in a box to support their poor. . . .
> And what day and what time was the fight among the Printers of Lyon when one of them was killed?
> Responds that the fight was during Lent one Sunday after supper and a man named Aymé was killed.
> And how was he killed?
> Responds in fighting, but he didn't see the blows, but just heard about it. . . .
> And hasn't he been at other fights and where and when?
> Responds that no, except one time against the papists who wanted to kill them.

The story of this Griffarin worker was chopped up into many questionings, some under torture, and was pulled together in a single narrative only by the jurist who recommended he be executed for the homicide of a Forfant.[10]

By a letter of remission (once it had been ratified by a court of law), the king's grace prevented a person from being so executed and also prevented or limited the royal confiscation of goods that accompanied such a penalty, or—to quote the formula—"pardoned the act . . . and remitted every penalty, fine, and corporal, criminal, and civil injury which might be incurred as a result of it . . . and restored to the supplicant his good name and reputation and his goods."[11] Incorporated into the king's command was a narrative, as the supplicant wanted it told. It is the creation and character of this pardon tale which is our subject—or, I should say, of these pardon tales, for they are myriad, more than enough for Scheherazade's thousand and one nights.

ONE

The Time of Storytelling

 letter of remission entered a life ordinarily in connection with a death.[1] Pardon tales were mostly about homicides, claimed to be unpremeditated, unintentional, in self-defense, or otherwise justifiable or excusable by French law. Remissions can also be found for bearing false witness, theft, receiving stolen goods, defloration of a virgin, taking part in a tax riot, resisting royal officers, and heresy, but these are the exceptions in the sixteenth century. In principle, though not always in practice, remission was reserved for crimes where the offender had been or could be sentenced to death.[2]

The supplicant asked for grace in two situations. Like Thomas Manny, he might have been imprisoned immediately in the wake of the victim's death and then been advised by a relative, an attorney, or a judge, or realized on his own that his was a good case for a remission.[3] The request sometimes went out soon after the arrest; sometimes while the case was making its deliberate way through the lower courts, the supplicant "in danger of finishing his life miserably in prison" before the trial was done; sometimes after he had been condemned to execution and heavy fines.[4]

Often, however, the killer fled, perhaps directly from the scene of the crime: peasant Pierre Guillot left his bleeding wife in their Orléanais barn—"thinking she had fainted, [I] asked the women to revive her and returned to plow my fields, but fearing something might happen . . . [I] got on one of my horses and rode away."[5] Other times the guilty party waited for days or weeks while the vic-

7

tim nursed his wounds, probably compensating him and his angry family with a payment, and then when death occurred, "fearing the rigors of justice," fled out of the jurisdiction, the region, and sometimes even out of the kingdom of France.[6] (The small number of royal sergeants and other police, the slowness of communication, and the absence of routine extradition made it quite possible to take refuge.) The scholar-publisher Etienne Dolet described in a poem his getaway after he had killed a painter on New Year's Eve 1536: helped by friends, he left Lyon before dawn. Through the frosty mountains and valleys of Auvergne he went in tempestuous weather, then by rowboat swiftly down the Allier, into the Loire as Dolet insisted the boatman break the ice floes with his oars, then from Orléans on horseback to Great Paris. "To retire to the king was my one resolve."[7]

What Dolet needed to get from the king was an order to a royal notary to draw up a letter of remission. Few people in Dolet's predicament went directly to his majesty, but in principle everyone seeking a pardon had to get a "command," a *jussio,* from an officer of the royal chancellery: from the chancellor himself or a master of requests in the Grand Chancellery in Paris or following the king's suite, or from one of the Little Chancellery offices associated with the sovereign courts at Paris, Bordeaux, Rouen, Toulouse, and elsewhere.[8] Here then was an early telling of one's pardon tale. For important personages or at least those with important connections now was a time for intervention. The learned Guillaume Budé and Marguerite de Navarre herself talked to the king on Dolet's behalf in 1537, and in 1567 the Reformed Church of Lyon sent its solicitor to court to win grace for a simple swordcutler who had killed his adulterous wife.[9] Meanwhile those fortunate enough to be in prison when the king made a Joyous Entry into a town (his first appearance there after his coronation) would have been interviewed by the royal almoner; if their cases were found suitable for pardon—and here royal mercy was at its most capacious, able to extend to "whatever crimes they had committed"—the king would direct them to ask for a letter of remission.[10]

Then the story was told to a royal notary and his clerks, sometimes by the supplicant, sometimes by relatives—"ses parens et amys charnelz"—and sometimes by an attorney. In early 1536, when Pierre Ungnart, a journeyman from a burg in Picardy, sought

1. A 1548 letter of remission, copied for the Chancellery archives, with the face of Henri II. Archives Nationales, JJ258A, 216^r.

pardon for his Twelfth-Night homicide after taking refuge across the border in Flanders, he presumably initiated the process by a dictated letter, returning only when things got under way.[11]

Once the formal letter of remission had been drawn up, it had to be read (as did all royal letters) before the chancellor or one of his representatives, such as a keeper of the seals, and perhaps be discussed by a master of requests. If the hearing was before the Grand Chancellery, the king himself might be among the listeners, and he was certain to be there on Good Friday, a day set aside for remitting death penalties "in honor and reverence for the passion of Our Lord."[12] The supplication was looked at a last time so that the chancellery officers could be sure that the offense recounted was a remissible one—a deliberate ambush was not supposed to be considered, but neither was a mere peccadillo—and especially that the excuse set forth was one of the acceptable ones. Then the letter would be signed and sealed in green wax with silken threads and, once it had been paid for, delivered into the hands of the supplicant.[13]

The cost of a letter of remission in the 1530's and 1540's was more than two months' wages for an unskilled laborer, more than a month's salary for a printer's journeyman, and most of a chambermaid's dowry. From 6 livres, it rose to more than 10 livres in the 1550's. By 1563, despite the protests of the Third Estate, it could cost as much as 11 livres, an increase that could not be blamed only on inflation; and beyond this there might be payments for an attorney or for "gifts," licit and illicit, to smooth the way.[14] To be sure, when a supplicant was too "poor and miserable," the king gave the letter gratis or at a reduced rate. People from families in the lower orders either obtained this added grace or somehow scraped together the needed funds—we find one artisan lending to another "to help him obtain his grace"—for they are very numerous among petitioners.[15] The obstacle to asking for the king's pardon was not so much poverty by itself, but isolation, being cut off from a network of information and support during a time of trouble.

Having one's parchment in hand was not the end of it, however: it needed ratification (*entérinement*) by a royal court, either the higher court in the regional jurisdiction (the *bailliage* or *sénéchaussée*) where the crime had occurred or the Parlement, which was the supreme court for that jurisdiction. In principle the process had to be started within a year of the sealing and, by the last part of the century, within three months.[16] One presented oneself humbly to the judges, bare-headed, on one's knees and with imploring hands (see illustration 3). The kin of one's victim were supposed to be there, too, if they were nearby. The letter was read aloud, and one swore it contained the truth and begged to avail oneself of the king's grace. Soon after, the judges asked questions and encouraged a long recital of answers to see whether they conformed both to the story one had told the king and to information collected during one's trial or flight. And then, ordinarily as a prisoner,[17] one waited anywhere from a few weeks to many months, while relatives of the deceased had their chance to claim that the letter of remission was full of loopholes and lies, while local witnesses were questioned about the matter and about one's past "good life and conversation," and while the king's attorney formulated his opinion.[18]

If the story of unpremeditated or justifiable homicide (or whatever else the claim might be) still seemed acceptable after this investigation, then the letter was ratified, often with the proviso that the supplicant pay a sum to the victim's family or fund prayers for the victim's soul or make a donation to the poor. In a small number of cases, the supplicant was ordered to stay away for a year or two from the town or village where the killing had occurred; a few were required to serve in the king's army during their time of banishment.[19] But one could go back eventually to one's former life, pardoned and "restored to good fame and reputation."

Seeking mercy rather than justice had its risks. The supplicant had, after all, freely confessed to committing the act; there was no chance now to claim he had really been somewhere else, even if there had been no witnesses to the homicide. If the letter of remission were dismissed rather than ratified—and we will consider in the next chapter how often and why this might happen—then he would have to go through the rigors of a criminal trial, unless this had already taken place, or suffer execution or a long banishment or the galleys for life, plus heavy fines (see Appendix C).

On the other hand, taking the path of remission had some signal advantages within the context of the French law of homicide and French criminal procedure. Sixteenth-century French law did not make a conceptual distinction between "murder" and "manslaughter" with their separate penalties, as would happen soon in England, or between "homicide involontaire" and "homicide volontaire" with their subdivisions and special penalties, which would crystallize in France only in Napoleon's Penal Code.[20] Rather, homicide was treated under a single rubric, as in the text of jurist Jean Papon, "for which the ordinary punishment is death." (This grouping may be due in part to the long-enduring belief, supported by Deuteronomy 21 and cited in legal texts, that any shedding of blood—from parricide to a slaying by chance—aroused the wrath of God and had somehow to be atoned for.) Within this general frame, cases were then sorted out in which the judge could be more moderate in his sentence and in which the king could offer his pardon. "The youth, the age, the dignity" of the person who had committed the act were to be considered by the judge (so advised the 1538 *Guydon des Practiciens*, citing Roman law); the killer's ignorance of what he or she had done and the circumstances surrounding it were to be remembered as well.[21] Papon spelled out thirteen extenuating circumstances, starting with two where homicide was permitted and readily pardonable—avenging the adultery of one's wife or daughter and killing in self-defense—and going on to others where homicide was not permitted, but might be pardonable, such as killing during a game or in drunkenness or in a sudden quarrel.*

But whatever the situation, if an accusation had been brought and

*Jean Papon's eleven "cases" where homicide was not permitted, but could be remitted and pardoned by the king, are as follows: homicide by accident, "par cas fortuit"; homicide by imprudence, without thinking or intending evil, as a carpenter who without fraud ("sans dol") puts up a building and a piece of it falls off on a passerby; homicide of a thief or aggressor entering one's house in the night; homicide committed in a tourney by chance or imprudence or without evil intent; homicide committed by a person without discretion and thus presumed to be without fraud and malice or ill-will, namely, those who kill while sleeping or drunk ("surprins de vin et yvre"), who are mad ("furieux"), or who are too young to have discretion, that is, a child up to the age of seven or slightly older; homicide coming out of a "sudden quarrel," remissible because of the anger; homicide in connection with the arrest of persons who resist (Papon adds that if it is impossible to take someone alive, the homicide can go unpunished, and it is customary not to resort to the prince for grace; however, as we will see, there were disputed cases where the sergeants had to petition for mercy); homicide during a tennis game or a ball game by vehemence of the action and without intention to kill; homicide committed by a person who is "rare and excellent," and whose death will be a great loss to the kingdom, such as a remarkable weapon-maker, a painter, a physician, or a surgeon (Papon warns that one must use this warily); homicide committed by an old man who previously has lived a life without quarrel and contention; and homicide that has remained twenty years without accusation or prosecution (*Trias Iudiciel du Second Notaire* [Lyon, Jean de Tournes, 1575], pp. 466–71).

2. A composite portrait of male homicides being committed at night. From Jean Milles de Souvigny, *Praxis Criminis Persequendi* (Paris, 1541).

a person had been found to commit a homicide, a judge had to give a penalty:

> He who while sleeping has put another to death . . . must he be punished? [asked the *Guydon des Practiciens*].
> He must be punished for the case, though not so grievously as if he had committed it maliciously . . . for *non est excusatio in peccatis*.[22]

The Parlement of Paris could and did lower the death penalties of some homicide appellants to, say, whipping and banishment or the galleys; but it could not simply free a person who had killed someone in legitimate self-defense, even though (as one criminal lieutenant complained) this was "permitted by divine, civil, and natural law" and should not need grace from the Prince. The Parlement's justice could stretch only to urging the defendant to ask the king for pardon and to ratifying that pardon if it came.[23]

The king alone had the power to remit, then, but he could do it in at least thirteen situations, each one offering possible story lines for a supplicant. Furthermore, that story had a better chance of being taken seriously by ratifying judges when it arrived in a letter of remission. In the French criminal procedure—judicial inquiry, interrogation by a judge or judges, formal confrontation with witnesses, and interrogation under torture if sufficient testimony and other indications warranted it[24]—the accused might never be able to establish before the court the justifiable or excusable nature of the crime. (Dyer's journeyman Thomas Guerin explained he had not been able to give a true recital during his trial for deflowering a virgin because of his "fear of the judicial procedure, his youth, and his not taking things seriously enough.")[25] In contrast, the judicial review of the royal pardon *started* with the supplicant's story; it set the frame for all the questioning and comparing of testimony that followed. And the letter of remission came to the judges from an important reader who had found the story at least plausible—namely, the king. If the ratification hearings went smoothly, the supplicant would not be subject to the anxiety of formal confrontation with and challenging of witnesses, and questioning under torture was even less likely.[26] A fugitive who had got a remission letter and then surrendered as a voluntary prisoner for the ratification process might never undergo the "extraordinary procedure" (as it was called) of the secret criminal trial.

This legal picture suggests the guidelines for remission narratives. They were usually to save a person's life, but they were very different from the old "neck-riddle" of the condemned prisoner who got his judges to promise to free him if they could not figure it out. Neck-riddles were like Samson's riddle to the Philistines; they had improbable or inconsequent answers.[27] Rather than confounding king and magistrates, remission narratives had to persuade them and establish a story that would win out over competing versions.

Let us now examine more carefully their authors. Every letter of remission had at least two persons, and often more, involved in its composition. A royal notary and his clerks prepared a draft with the supplicant or with the supplicant's agent and then recorded the letter on its final parchment. Royal notaries or secretaries (as they were also called) made up the elite of the world of scribes, possessors of a lucrative royal office, which could pass from father to son or uncle to nephew and bring with it ennoblement. Rather than just recording the contracts and wishes of private persons, they reported in "all truth and loyalty" what the king had resolved and commanded. As the chancellor could be compared to the Biblical Melchizedek "giving out Grace and Remissions of Crimes," so the royal secretaries could be compared to the prophets.[28] Numbering 119 in the first half of the sixteenth century, they were up to 200 by 1589. Many of them were grouped in Paris; some worked in Toulouse or Rouen or in other cities where there were chancellery offices associated with the Parlements; some were distributed in centers like Orléans and Lyon; still others went with the court when it traveled, perhaps complaining that they had "to write standing up, on the corner of the queen's coffer."[29]

By and large the king's notaries were not active literary figures: if the historian Jean Du Tillet had his years as secretary in the Little Chancellery of Paris, still the names that we see at the bottom of letters of remission (De Courlay, Olier, Juvyneau, Deslandes, Sanyan, Aurillot, to give a few) are rarely found on the title pages of printed books. Even less is this the case for the clerks that did much of the actual writing in the secretaries' offices. Just the same, through family, through patronage, and through their own libraries, many royal secretaries had ties to the liberal arts. They were advised to

15

read Cicero and Politian for their instruction, and on their shelves, along with such books and with legal texts, could sometimes be found the great story collections: the fifteenth-century Burgundian *Cent Nouvelles Nouvelles* and Boccaccio's *Decameron*.[30] Surely they ought to have been able to recognize a good tale when they heard it.

As for the letter of remission, the royal notary who drew it up was responsible for the wording of the introduction and conclusion. He would have learned the formulas as a young man and might well have a Chancellery style book in his office for his own clerks to check:

François, etc. Be it known to all present and to come. We have received the humble supplication of A, poor young plowman, responsible for wife and children, living in such and such a place, saying that, etc.

After the second "et cetera," the style book instructs, "let the case be put down as it happened."[31] The secretary or his clerk might fatten the preamble with other facts which made the supplicant appear more pitiful—"poor simple miller," "poor disabled widow," "burdened with five children including two stepdaughters ready to marry," "burdened with seven children, including six girls, one of whom is engaged"[32]—or which made the supplicant more significantly connected—"man of arms in our royal troops under the charge of our very dear and esteemed cousin the Marquis de Saluces."[33]

The major secretarial contribution came in the concluding formulas. Here were compressed the arguments that the supplicant's story was expected to document in order to elicit royal grace and mercy rather than the rigor of justice:

That the said case has come about out of *chaude colle* [sudden violent anger, literally "hot bile"] and after drinking and the said deceased was the aggressor. That what the supplicant did was in defending himself. And that in all other situations he has always governed himself honestly and well, and is a man of good life and conversation, without ever having been reproved, attainted, or convicted of any other vile action ["vilain cas"] . . . or done anything worthy of blame. We wish to impart to him our grace and mercy.[34]

Some seekers after that grace and mercy had also talked to a lawyer or attorney about their predicament, especially better-off supplicants who had money for the fee. Anyone might need a solicitor to deliver a message to a royal secretary, pick up letters from the chancellery, or send a preliminary request for ratification to a judge.[35] And some supplicants had counsel with them when they asked for entérinement: peasants Pierre Guyon and Pierre Peroussel and courier Christofle Farfannchy were by themselves when they got down on their knees before the Sénéchaussée of Lyon, but boatman Jean Bas and clerk Pierre Rambaud had attorneys at their side. The person seeking pardon had to tell about what had happened "from his own mouth," as was prescribed for all criminal actions by the 1539 edict of Villers-Cotterêts, but occasionally lawyers added a plea for mercy (or against mercy, if they were speaking for the victim's kin).[36]

The question that interests us here, however, is the role of men of the law in the initial creation of the story, that is, the letter of remission. They might be consulted at an early stage on substantive points for the pardon—say, on such matters as weapons (one had to indicate that the instrument with which the deceased was killed was worn every day for one's craft or was lying handily on the table, and not specifically put on for an anticipated encounter with an enemy) or the state of mind of the dying person (it helped to say that the victim had had time for final sacraments or had been heard to pardon the killer or take on the blame or urge his or her kin not to prosecute). Occasionally a lawyer may have helped draft the supplication itself before it went to the royal notary. In 1553 an attorney of Tours, imprisoned for misdeeds with court records, got into more trouble when he tried to change the words on his parchment letter of remission to accord with "the draft which had been made by his Counsel" ("suivant la minute qu'en avoit fait son Conseil"). When we find such a draft in the family papers of two notable brothers of the Gascon town of Mauvezin in the early seventeenth century, both of them fugitives for a homicide, it is already equipped with formulas that suggest a counselor's hand.[37]

Once men of the law are mixed up in shaping a story, we are, of course, dealing with persons who have important connections with French literary traditions. Even the solicitors and attorneys (soliciteurs, praticiens, procureurs), described by one judge as "not trained in Philosophy and good letters, given over to the mere Practice of soliciting," had in fact tried out their youthful skills in ribald and satirical cases made up at Twelfth Night and Mardi Gras by their confraternity of the Basoche and had often acquired small book collections over the years.[38]

As for the advocates, they were university trained. Whether pleading cases before the courts, as they did in the vigor of adulthood (Avocats plaidoyants), or playing the consulting role, as they did as older men (Avocats consultants), they cared almost as much about good letters as about Roman law. Legal rhetoric was their business, learned perhaps from the forensic rules of the fourteenth-century Guillaume de Breuil or from Cicero's *Orations* and other classical models; learned surely from listening as young lawyers (Avocats écoutants) to the pleas of their elders and from taking their own turn at carnival cases. By the end of the century the most admired of the advocates' pleas were being published, including those for ratification of a pardon. They were in French, the language of most plaidoyers long before the edict of Villers-Cotterêts required that all justice be conducted in the vernacular.[39] Some lawyers went on to other kinds of writing—poems, political tracts, histories, and stories—and many more had libraries with romances and collections of tales shelved in with the law books, devotional works, and humanist texts.[40] In short, when a lawyer was approached by a supplicant about a letter of remission, he was likely to be interested in it as a story, not just as a legal problem. As Judge Jean Papon said about a 1532 letter of remission, it was indeed "well narrated" ("bien narré").[41]

The first author of the story, however, was the supplicant, and I will suggest a little later what evidence allows us to hear his or her voice the primary one in a collective endeavor. As a group, the petitioners ranged from seigneurs to shepherds, from notaries, lawyers, and priests[42] to many people who had rarely held a book in their hands.* The unlearned among them did not come to their request for pardon innocent of storytelling skills. The times for such narration were several: at the *veillées*, or evening gatherings in city and countryside, where romances were read aloud, stories told, and

---

*From the hundreds of remissions read for this study, I selected some 164 male pardons, dating from 1523 through 1568, for detailed examination of narrative strategy, language, characterization, and motif. Though no effort was made at "scientific sampling," I sought social and geographical range as well as texts that would illustrate effectively the interest and stylistic range of the letters. The social distribution of the 164 males in this privileged group of supplicants is as follows: peasants, 48; artisans, 56; merchants, 17; lawyers, notaries, sergeants, and other officers of justice, 19; priests and students, 6; gentlemen and seigneurs, 18. As for the letters of remission for women, all that were found (pardons involving 42 female supplicants) were given detailed examination (see Chapter 3, n. 22). My storytelling pool is twice that of the *Decameron*.

guessing games played amid flirting, spinning, and the mending of tools; at work, when slack moments or the noise of shop activity permitted it; and while making good cheer at the dinner table or in the tavern. Local events were often made into songs, passing through the neighborhood to the comfort or discomfort of their subjects. And, of course, in this society where the old were expected to inform the young about their family, people told their life histories. Indeed, a fatal fight among some tailors in Brie started over supper at an inn, when one of them was recounting his past and along the way said something insulting about another's father.[43]

An especially important preparation for telling about one's misdeeds was, of course, confession—for most people an annual affair when one "did one's Easter duty." Every Lent the pulpits rang with admonitions to examine one's conscience. How many individuals reviewed their lives ahead of time by the recommended grid of the Ten Commandments and the Seven Deadly Sins or came to confession with notes we will never know. But it is clear from a sixteenth-century confessors' *Summa* by Brother Jean Benedicti that penitents were narrating their sins one by one as they happened, rather than clumping them under moral headings, that they were bringing in chatty details ("babil," "caquet," "propos impertinens"), rather than sticking to what the clergy thought relevant, and that they were laying the blame elsewhere, rather than admitting "C'est moy"—"It is I." To make matters worse, they were seeking remission of their sins without being ashamed, that is, they were confessing "as if they were telling a story" ("comme s'ils racont[oient] une histoire").[44]

When it came to preparation for seeking royal letters of remission, there was no precise equivalent to Lenten preaching, though an annual sermon on "Thou shalt not kill" might give examples of accidental or excusable homicide.[45] Nonetheless, general information about the legal paths to pardon seems to have been quite widely distributed throughout the countryside, as necessary to villagers as information about dowry customs was to any wife. One could learn details from popular *nouvelles* about the husband who, thinking he has beaten his wife to death, is advised by his neighbors to flee, "for if you're taken by the rigorous justice in this town, you're finished." One could learn details from local persons who had won grace in the past and from rural notaries and sergeants. So in a hamlet in Rouergue, when Jeanne Galzy killed a man who allegedly stole her husband's shirt, she could seek advice from that husband, for he was a local sergeant. So a suspect in a Beauvaisis village asked a sergeant what to do after his pitchfork was found next to the body of a man with whom he had been quarreling about trespassing pigs: "If you feel guilty," the sergeant said, "don't let anyone put a hand on you, but if you're not guilty, then don't leave, for flight will render you guilty." In the cities, one would have observed the king's special grace at a time of an Entry, and indeed we see persons fleeing after a homicide to surrender themselves to prison in a town on the king's itinerary.[46]

A report from witnesses of a parricide in a small town in the Or-léanais in 1565 illustrates how ready at hand such knowledge could be. A quarrel broke out between the hatter Emé Guy and his son Jean, when the former threatened to evict the latter because of his dissipation, and Jean retorted that he would leave that minute if his parents would just give him his clothes. The angry father approached to beat him, and the son hit him with his sword. Bleeding on the ground, the father said, "Flee, flee, my son! I forgive you my death." The mother repeated the sentiment. Unable to move, Jean was immediately arrested and questioned, and his answer, given without benefit of counsel, shows the kernel of a story which might have grown into a remission request: "he had not tried to kill his father; his father's anger alone had been the cause, for he had precipitated himself on to the sword which [Jean] had taken up only to avoid his father's wrath."[47]

The would-be supplicant arrived at the royal notary's office, then, with a story in mind and, in the case of a literate person, perhaps with a draft. One school of historical interpretation would assume that the minute a learned agent of the state puts his hand to another's words, they are so remade and reshuffled that their original form is effaced. But periods and political encounters differ. Several features of the sixteenth-century situation pushed the secretary and his clerks to make the body of the letter of remission—the "let-the-case-be-put-down-as-it-happened" after the preamble—be close to the recital of the pardon seeker. First was the very concept of the request for grace: it was to evoke a personal exchange, a subject's voice speaking to the king and the merciful king responding. The state itself had an interest in a letter that went beyond a notary's formulations.

Second was the reality that faced the supplicant after the letter was sealed. To get the remission ratified, we remember, the supplicant's oral testimony before the judges had to "conform" to the written parchment as well as to other information taken about the case. So important was this evaluation to the criminal judge Jean Imbert that he urged the questioning of the supplicant as soon as possible after his request for ratification, "so that no one tells him what to say" ("à fin qu'on ne luy face le bec").[48] The simplest way to achieve some conformity was for the royal secretary to reflect, where the document allowed it, the supplicant's own language and ordering of events. Montaigne himself talked of how hard it was to reproduce a studied and memorized speech, especially when one's life hung in the balance.[49] Imagine how difficult it would be for an unlearned person in that situation to recite a story not in his or her own words.

So far I have come upon only two instances where records allow me to compare the two tellings.[50] One is the account of the Lyon swordcutler Claude Dater of killing his wife for committing adultery with a priest, given first for a letter of remission in July 1567, then given again four months later to the criminal lieutenant of Geneva, to which city he repaired after his letter was ratified at Lyon. The letter is longer than the Geneva response (see Appendix B), but the story is told in the same segments: his return home in the early evening; his neighbors apprising him that his wife had been found alone with a priest with his clothes open ("débraillé"); his failure to catch the priest, who (in Boccaccio-like fashion) was hiding in a trunk; and his meeting his wife on the stairs, where in anger ("de colere"), he gave her two blows of his sword. The ability to provide vivid detail in the remission letter is shown also in the Geneva testimony, where the "loud noise" of his neighbors becomes the ironic shout "Go up, go up, you'll find swell housekeeping in your place" ("Montez, montez, vous trouverez beau mesnage chez vous").[51]

The second example comes from Pierre Marion, a peasant in Champagne in 1611, who had killed an alleged witch while getting her to lift a spell from his sick wife. Here it turns out that the peasant was a better storyteller than in his letter of remission, amplifying in a lively fashion as the Paris judges tried to push him to admit that he had "massacred a woman . . . who could not defend herself." But there is still overlapping of phrases and feelings in the two accounts; and they conform in the overall relation of what happened, beginning with the wife's uncured illness being diagnosed as bewitchment, moving to Marion's enticement of the witch to his house and his hitting her, and ending with the witch dying at the very instant that the wife recovered from her spells.[52]

In short, these two cases suggest that the royal notary had on the whole followed the standard prescription "to take down faithfully what is said,"[53] and that the "fictive," the "literary" quality of the account need not derive from an educated secretary, but could come in part from the speaker.

Let us try to visualize a telling and recording in the presence of the secretary and his clerks. Among the first duties of all notaries was "to listen diligently," while the royal secretary was especially instructed to use terms appropriate to his subject matter—grave for weighty events, familiar for familiar ones.[54] The secretary might start out by reminding the supplicant

that he must set forth the events truthfully, as they happened, without putting in anything that he cannot prove and without keeping silent about anything that could come out through witnesses.[55]

As the secretary or his clerk then went on to write down "the-case-as-it-happened," certain transformations were made. The speaker's regional dialect, if he or she had one, was turned into French (less of a change, to be sure, that if it had gone into Latin).* The speaker's first person "I" was turned into the third person of the "supplicant," to whom the king is listening and whom he will pardon in the last sentences of the letter.

But the direct quotations were often kept: "Must I die for a whore?" or "Don't hit him with the cutting-edge, but just with the flat" ("Ne frappes point du taillant mais seulement du plat") or "Is it

---

*Emmanuel Le Roy Ladurie makes the valid observation in his important study of the eighteenth-century tale *Jean-l'ont-pris* by Jean-Baptiste Castor Fabre that this tale is especially useful because it is in Occitan: "where the archives of social history (notaries' records, etc.) are in French, the regional literature represents the only cultural monument in which an author can express himself in the language of the local people" (*Love, Death and Money in the Pays d'Oc*, trans. Alan Sheridan [New York, 1982], Preface). The letters of remission do lose in proximity to regional expression and the affects of the mother tongue, but they gain in proximity to the remembered experience of the individual, with all its specificity, and to more immediate and fully stated cultural understandings than can be found in archetypical folktales. A number of the motifs I will describe are absent from Stith Thompson's extensive *Motif-Index of Folk Literature*, rev. ed. (Bloomington, Ind., 1955–58).

up to me to prepare dinner when I've come from far away and have worked all day and you do nothing but grumble?" or, in the Gascon in which it was shouted, "Traitors, traitors, take those oxen to the fields."[56] (On the other hand, the content of blasphemous oaths was usually suppressed; as with Thomas Manny and the paillard, it was simply stated that swearing occurred. Repeating them to the king would compound the dishonor to the Lord.) Some royal notaries substituted their own legalese here and there for the supplicant's words: Thomas Manny probably didn't "remonstrate" ("remonstroit") with his wife, but rather told her "she was doing wrong"; Pierre Marion certainly did not characterize the medical remedies for his wife as "frustratoires," but rather (as he said in his testimony before the judges) found that "tout cela ne servait de rien." But many secretaries made their recording quite colloquial. In any case, the supplicant had the chance to revise everything once a clerk had made a clean copy, either hearing it read aloud or reading it himself. Only then would the final version be made.[57]

The resulting letters of remission have a variety about them that seems impossible to attribute merely to the talents of a limited number of notarial hands.[58] When the learned Etienne Dolet tells a story to get pardoned for printing heretical books, he sounds different from the plowman Thomas Manny. Manny is satisfied to assert his good husbandly behavior in the past; Dolet gives a glowing little picture of his life from his student days to his current efforts to maintain his family and "support good letters." Manny does not speculate about the motives of his wife's lover or reflect on his own feelings, though they come out clearly enough; Dolet claims that jealous master printers have incited the Inquisition against him and talks of the "curiosity . . . ordinarily felt by lovers of letters" to know things they may want to refute. Manny does not add to the remission formulas on the king's grace; Dolet puts words into the king's mouth about divine mercy.[59]

When two Lyon policemen try to get pardoned for the homicide of a man they were chasing to arrest, they cast the same events differently, the captain trying to lay the blame on the sergeant and vice versa. When a peasant mother asks for pardon for her son, a young Chartres linenmaker imprisoned and condemned to death in 1525, we hear her hand-wringing even more than his excuses. She ascribes all her son's troubles to his wife's leaving him for a priest and to his taking up with some good-for-nothing archers in the king's infantry. Though she makes plausible connection between these events and his subsequent actions—among other things, he abducted a chambermaid—her description of her son's shame and disquiet is so strong that it would have been devastating for a sixteenth-century artisan to say it about himself.[60] In these cases, the royal notary seems to have "listened diligently," done the required transformations, but not remade the events into his own narrative.

As for the lawyers' presence in the letters, it is harder to specify, for we do not know how often they were consulted by supplicants. An attorney's hand probably excised some of the scenes in an orgy recounted in 1541 by Guillaume Fournier, a Lyon "gentleman" who sought a second letter of remission as a "tonsured cleric." The dead man is no longer heard insulting Fournier as a "town lily . . . who says he is a gentleman," but the story still moves from gaming and dining with a prostitute to a drinking contest in which the killer accuses the victim of putting salt in his wine.[61] Back in the late fifteenth and early decades of the sixteenth century, advocates had narrated such events before the courts, interspersing them with points of law, principle, or morality, but the edict of Villers-Cotterêts as well as shifts in rhetorical taste were cutting back their role as expositors of the *facts* of a criminal case. A good story could still loosen the lawyer's tongue, but even better was organizing the events thematically so as to make a legal argument, or painting a general picture of the state of criminal justice.[62] In 1546, when an advocate was pleading to the Parlement of Paris on behalf of a seigneur's remission, he talked not of the *fait particulier*, but of how the supplicant had served as captain in the king's army for twenty years and how his letter had already been ratified by the Sénéchaussée of Anjou. In 1594, when the celebrated lawyer Claude Expilly asked the Parlement of Grenoble to ratify the letter of remission of a certain Angelon Platel, he devoted one sentence to his client's homicide (it was due to the fatal stubbornness of the deceased and committed only in self-defense). It was the king's clemency that was the subject of Expilly's oration, elaborated on in a Plutarchan "rhetoric of quotations" very pleasing to late sixteenth-century judges: Ovid was cited along with Scriptures, Ronsard was quoted along with Roman law.[63] However interested Expilly might have been in a criminal narrative, he left it to Angelon Platel, an unknown person from an Alpine village, to tell his story by himself.

The Time of Storytelling

What to conclude, then, about the authorship of the letter of remission? It emerges from an exchange among several people about events, points of law, and chancellery style. All the authors have some connections with narrative traditions, literary and/or oral, but the remission setting, with a faithful secretary and consulting attorney, privileges the account of the person asking for pardon. Even the monarch has an interest in the petitioner's voice being the predominant one. The notary gives the document its frame and writes the king and the supplicant into the narrative, but collaborative product though it is, the letter of remission can still be analyzed in terms of the life and values of the person saving his neck by a story.

Up to now I have been talking about the times when pardon tales were told and establishing the historical context for their composition. In beginning our systematic exploration of the stories, I want to ask what kind of time they gave to themselves. Did they draw upon wider historical contexts or events beyond the immediate lives of the actors to account for what happened, to justify motive or give coherence to the actions? Was the date when an insult was shouted or a knife suddenly drawn important beyond the need for juridical precision?

Let us listen to a Gentleman's Tale, the 1536 supplication of Charles de Villelume of a seigniorial family in the Bourbonnais.[64] It moves from one misadventure to another over many years. He begins in 1518, when he was only eighteen. Visiting a peasant household, he made a lascivious gesture toward the wife and her washing fell across his knees. She answered that she would rather be ridden ("chevaulchée") by the friar who was with him. Next he tells how a priest sought his aid in retaining his appointment to a priory, which was being challenged by another priest. Being a "young gentleman desiring to be of service to everyone by good zeal" ("jeune gentilhomme desirant faire service à ung chacun et par bon zelle"), he seized the priory against the wishes of the local judge, kissed and had others kiss the relics, rang the bells, and argued with the local inhabitants shouting outside. Later, when "assemblies" were organized against him, he hit the competing priest and some of the neighbors with a stick to disperse them "in terror and fear." His next "service" was to a village confraternity celebrating Pentecost. Some of the brothers begged him to help stop a fight with a seigneur and two priests who were trying to dance with the women, even though it was an age-old custom of the locality not to dance with women on that holy day. When he arrived, so he says, they were starting to kill one of the priests, and to avoid such "scandal," he told them instead to take off all the man's clothes and whip him, which he proceeded to help them do.

The next episode involved his own efforts to keep control of a property given him by his uncle, a local prévôt, who said he had it by the feudal right of *mainmorte* (an unfree tenant dying without an heir). A peasant named Le Maignan claimed it belonged to him and, supported by another seigneur, engaged in a quarrel with our supplicant in which cattle were hidden, crops seized, and any number of men assembled with clubs, crossbows, and harquebuses. Finally, after the supplicant broke into his uncle's granaries and diverted his uncle's carts of grain to his own house, he was made a prisoner and tried. Because he had not killed or mutilated anyone in actions due more to "youthfulness" ("jeunesse") than to malice, the king gave Charles de Villelume an Easter pardon, provided he pay 10 livres for prayers for the dead.

This text reads to us as though it were written by Cervantes, a parody of the romances of chivalry that would have been recounted around Charles de Villelume's fireplace.[65] It contains no reference to the "historic crisis" in values and functions of the country gentlemen in the reign of François Ier or any reflection on the other rural conflicts which make the historian itch to use it as an illustrative document in a graduate seminar. It does not refer to the fact that in the 1520's the Bourbonnais was passing from a feudal duchy under the Bourbons to the domain of the French king and that the royal prisons in Moulins where he was "in danger of finishing his life miserably" were new to the region.[66] The story is not presented in a frame of historical time; the supplicant is "a gentleman desiring to be of service" and the nephew of a gentleman, and that explains everything.

Now this was not an inevitable way of thinking about one's personal adventures and mishaps. In the fourteenth and fifteenth centuries, when pardons were given for participating in the uprising of the Jacquerie, urban tax revolts, and other kinds of political disturbance, there is a convergence between historical time and the time of the story:

On the first day of March 1381, when there occurred the commotion of the people in our good town of Paris, a great quantity of common folk in high feeling passed before the supplicant's house on the rue Saint Denis, and because of the great noise and tumult he came to the door to see what it was, and as they passed, noting that they were taking along with them everyone they found, he went with them to the Paris Halles, where he saw that they were pulling down a wooden gallows at the sign of the Swan . . . though he didn't get mixed up in it in any way, but just watched.

And the narrative goes on through the riot to end with the supplicant's turning over to the authorities a pearl rosary which he had "found" when the crowd pushed into the Church of Saint Jacques.[67]

Similarly, a priest's story from the days of the Jacquerie in 1358 begins with the assemblies of the peasant communes in Champagne, in whose view all the curés were traitors and especially the supplicant, about whom they said "he had sold the bells of Blacy to the nobles." He tells of how he participated in one of their meetings only for fear of his life, but now the nobles mistrust him and he dare not go back to his parish.[68] A more substantive connection between historical events and remission events is established by a peasant from a village in the Ile-de-France in 1417. He accounts for his statements about the king, not by simple fear or by being swept along by a crowd, but by his reaction to the troubled times of the Hundred Years' War:

The supplicant has always been our obedient little subject and a good plowman, who has never got mixed up with anything but farming. But because of the wars for the past ten years . . . he was so trodden down and damaged that he lost most of his livelihood, his sense, and his memory. And out of distress, he several times said insulting words about our person and the government of our kingdom . . . namely . . . that "there was nothing but shit on our Council" and that "the king is mad."[69]

During the first half of the sixteenth century, there were also some occasions when political or historical events framed a remission tale in an explanatory or interpretive way. Such was the case with the Sire de Saint-Vallier, implicated in Duke Charles de Bourbon's treacherous alliance with the emperor against his own king. Saint-Vallier's supplication of 1527 began not only with his innocent wedding invitation to the duke, but with Bourbon's genuine grievances against François Ier.[70] Another historical context was drawn upon in a Plague Story by a rural priest of Auvergne. Having killed his sacristan in a fight over a contaminated shroud, he opened his request, "In the parish of Montaigut last year, 1524, there was a great mortality of parishioners."[71] Royal edicts and ordinances could also set some tales in motion. A sergeant's plea started with the announcing in Lyon of the king's prohibition against anyone carrying weapons. The sergeant was thus primed to react to the unfortunate craftsman dancing with a dagger at his side. A fisherman's request cited an edict forbidding the entrance of Genoese silks into France by the Saône river. He had reported a smuggler who had begun to stalk him in revenge.[72]

But for every one such narrative, there are many more which do not use History to win remission. Either historical situations are seen as irrelevant to what happened or they are integrated into the story as givens, requiring no comment, rather than being a central ordering device. Jeanne Hennequin's account of a village riot in the Vermandois in 1539 is a fascinating example. Her story opens with tax collectors and sergeants breaking into peasant households and seizing the goods of those who had barred their doors and refused to pay. She recounted how the women armed themselves with pitchforks and pots and threw mud and excrement at them; her excuse for participating in the "assembly" was that she mistook the king's tax collectors for the king's soldiers ("gens de guerre"). New or unjust taxes are not the explanatory context; instead Jeanne's pardon tale builds to a proposition about when and against whom one has the right to defend one's house and one's goods.[73]

Similarly, heretics can be done in in the 1540's without finding it necessary to elaborate on the dangers of innovation; it is enough to say the victim was preventing the priest from carrying the host in a Corpus Christi procession. Witches, too, can be killed in the same decade without explaining (as did a seventeenth-century peasant remission, where we detect the secretary's hand) that "the countryside is today infected with wickedness, enemies jealous of the prosperity of the human race"; it is enough for the supplicant to call the victim a "sorcière" and to describe the illness she has caused.[74]

This relative infrequency of appeal to historical explanation is partly due to the legal requirement of the remission letter. The king can understand fear of soldiers breaking down the door; too much dwelling on historical circumstances about taxes might make legitimate self-defense look like premeditated resistance. But it is also not too different from contemporary habits of storytelling in other forms. Anecdotes recorded in private journals have dates, but usually do not reach for explanatory historical frames. "In this year was a marvelous adventure," wrote the draper Philippe de Vigneulles of Metz in introducing in his *Chronique* the murder of a rich man by his wife and her lover. His unpublished *Cent Nouvelles Nouvelles* of 1505–15 (he gave his manuscript the same name as the much reprinted Burgundian collection of stories) is filled with real names, streets, and episodes from his own day and gives historical settings to about fifteen stories: a plague, a blockade, a war, a campaign and the like. On the whole, they add the flavor of the actual—"this really happened"—to the tales, rather than a reason for why the events happened. Some of his recent history settings are used simply to renew old tales from literary sources. Similar strategies are found in the 1530's in the unpublished *nouvelles* of the saddler Nicolas de Troyes.[75] As for Marguerite de Navarre's *Heptaméron*, it is peopled with historical figures like herself, but the questions her stranded storytellers ask about the intrigue are moral and psychological, not historical. In family histories and autobiographical writing of the first half of the century, unless the subjects are themselves public actors, the time field is usually local and domestic until the Reformation erupts in a life and changes its course.[76]

By contrast, another kind of larger time reference does play an important role in remission narratives, that of ritual and festive time. Thomas Manny killed his lubricious wife on the day of the Magdalene. Maybe it was a coincidence her lover came to the house on July 22—we can't know—but as Manny sorted it out and remembered it afterwards, the Magdalene's feast was the appropriate time to decide not to die for a whore and not to let her live. This way of thinking about connection takes some sustenance from medieval and Renaissance notions of correspondences and analogies between the supernatural and the natural world, and from age-old beliefs about lucky and unlucky days.[77] But it is not quite the same thing. Here we have a dynamic convergence between ritual programs and ceremonial scenarios on the one hand and particular life events on the other, between the prescribed of sacred or sacroprofane time and the unexpected and improvised of experience. The storyteller uses the ritual or festive frame to help excuse and make sense of what has happened. The feast day guides and judges the action; the action exposes some of the dangers and latent conflicts of the feast.[78]

So a number of remission stories open with carnival and end with blood, sometimes the blood of a person known to the supplicant behind his mask, sometimes of a stranger. One such, recorded by a royal secretary's pen, actually began in a royal secretary's house: a young doctor of law at Aix was dancing there with other "people of quality" ("gens de qualité") and ultimately killed a mere Basoche attorney, who thought he could take advantage of Mardi Gras to judge the dances "and undertake grander things than he should."[79] So accounts of homicide during a country dance begin not at the dance itself, but hours before the musicians start up the bagpipes, with the morning mass in honor of the village patron saint or the patron of a local shrine. Gradually the unity of worshippers enjoined by the liturgy founders on the rivalry of young men from different villages:

In the last month of May, the supplicant went with no evil thoughts to the locality of Saint Claire in pilgrimage . . . with others from the village of Rethondes, and he was one of the varlets of the feast and brought minstrels for dancing and rejoicing as was customary each year on that day. . . . And then a man from the village of Berneuil told the minstrels to strike up a branle . . . and the supplicant said to the man, "I didn't hire the minstrels for you."[80]

The brotherhood of a rural confraternity could be rent as well: a winegrower from the Ile-de-France sets his actors in motion at a vespers service in honor of Saint Barbara, and then takes them to their annual banquet, which erupts into drunken truth telling. The poor brother (the supplicant) tells the rich brother he should give to, not take from, the poor, and the rich brother tells the poor brother that he is a thief just like his father. The banquet ends with the rich one with a knife in his stomach, but admitting that he is in the wrong ("J'ay le tort") and the poor one agreeing to pay all the damages. After the victim's death, the king's pardon rounds off the story in peace.[81]

But let me give my best example, a many-layered fiction in the archives recorded from Guillaume Caranda, "only twenty years old," a barber living in 1530 in the town of Senlis:

The day of the Holy Sacrament of the Altar just past, to do honor to God and in record and representation of his holy resurrection, the supplicant put himself in a tomb, playing and representing the figure of Our Lord in his tomb, and with him were some of his neighbors, playing and representing the other personages at the tomb of Our Lord Jesus Christ. And they stayed thus at the tomb while the [Corpus Christi] procession passed by their street.

Now he had never done or said anything wrong to one Claude Caure, a maker of cutting tools living in our town of Senlis, and there had never been any noise or quarrel between them. Nonetheless, on the day of the Holy Sacrament around nine o'clock in the evening, Caure was in front of his house as the supplicant passed by with his neighbors to go amuse themselves at the Saint Rieulle gate, and he said . . . to the supplicant, "I see the god on earth. Did you keep your virile and shameful member stiff in playing God?" [our barber presumably said, "Did you keep your prick stiff?"—the secretary replacing "prick" with "virile and shameful member"], uttering these dishonest words arrogantly and against the honor of Christianity. To which the supplicant responded that "his was neither very hard nor heated up, and that he [Caure] was gelded," and after these words he and his company went on their way . . . to the Saint Rieulle gate and spent the time joyously till it was the hour to go to bed.

Coming back, they again passed Caure's doorway and he was still there. More sharply and arrogantly than before, he repeated the dishonest words, insulting to our Lord Jesus Christ and to the holiness of the day. The supplicant made the same response as before and kept on toward his house to go to sleep. But Caure, a quarrelsome man and often drunk, followed after him and gave him two slaps on his head and face and made his bonnet fall to the ground. With that, to protect himself from danger . . . and in hot anger . . . he drew a little knife he customarily wore and struck at Caure's left eye . . . and wounded him he doesn't know exactly where, and then retired to his house. Soon after he was told that Caure, because he had not taken care of himself or otherwise, had died of his wound. Fearing the rigor of justice the supplicant fled.

A few weeks later, François Ier orders the bailiff of Senlis to extend to Guillaume Caranda his pardon.[82]

From tomb to tomb, from resurrection to erection, from death to life and back again, Caranda's tale wove together the day's events in an interpretive whole. Some of its motifs we can meet in literary settings: in the *Decameron*, when the young hermit Rustico feels rising desire for the beautiful acolyte Alibech, Boccaccio calls it "the resurrection of the flesh" ("la resurrezion della carne"). In Rabelais' *Tiers Livre*, published sixteen years after Caranda got his pardon, Panurge's penis and Christ's passion are juxtaposed. Panurge brags that so powerful is the energy behind his codpiece that his mere entrance into the audience of a Passion Play tempted angels and devils into fornication. And Leo Steinberg has shown how,

31

from the fourteenth through the sixteenth centuries, artists could suggest the erection of the dead Christ as a symbol for the triumph of resurrection.[83]

The archival narrative from Senlis may seem to us stranger than art, but to sixteenth-century judges hearing and verifying it, its ritual frame would have added to its plausibility. Why not be wondering about Christ's organ on Corpus Christi day? And what more natural than two artisans in the cutting trades negotiating the baffling distance between Jesus's humanity and ordinary manliness? Their argument would be all the more convincing because it was inconclusive, Caranda objecting to Caure's speculation about his having an erection in Christ's garb and at the same time taunting Caure for having no balls at all. Further, the ritual setting helped clarify for guilty teller and judging listeners where the day went wrong, the barber killing instead of curing with his knife, the concord around the blood and body of Christ broken by homicide.

The relation between festive time and literary structure has been analyzed to excellent effect, as in *Shakespeare's Festive Comedy* by C. L. Barber, Bakhtin's *Rabelais*, and other important works.[84] In fact this habit of mind and telling was widespread. Group fights between Catholics and Protestants often broke out at the occasion of a religious ritual, the sacrifice of the mass or the message of the Psalms provoking and legitimating the violence—or at least that is how the riots were presented in the apologetic tracts published about them afterward: the unprescribed events were scooped up and ordered around the main lines of the ritual, the violence seeming to continue the rite or expose its lies.[85] Those remission narratives that were linked to a feast day often gave the same cast to individual violence, as we have just seen, though the moral lessons remained either implicit or subservient to the larger teaching of the king's mercy.

So too, in private journals, when disorder or unexpected violence was described in a festive setting, the outcome was judged with special trenchancy. In 1556, a Lyon draper wrote about the dazzling games and masking that the rich Italians were introducing to the local elite for carnival play. That year they began a little early, on January 21, with an orange skirmish held right in the Banking Square:

And the oranges being on the ground, some *gaignedeniers* [poor workers] wanted to pick them up, and one of the players on horseback rushed in to knock over a worker, and his horse giving a kick opened the gaignedenier's

32

head and his brains spilled out all over the ground . . . and two or three others were gravely wounded.[86]

Now this is a classic situation in which a letter of remission would be sought (and undoubtedly was sought) and obtained for unintended homicide during a game. But the draper was not a supplicant and the king and chancellor were not listening, so he went on in his journal, "It was a great villainy and folly, seeing the place where it happened . . . and that judicial officers were there [among the players]; it set a bad example for the poor populace, a scandal for them and for justice."[87]

The *fête* would long be used in France to deepen or complicate the meaning of events.[88] But the historical setting always remained as an option, and religious changes and the Wars of Religion led to its being chosen more often for letters of remission in the 1560's and 1570's, as it had been in earlier periods of upheaval. On the level of perception, we might expect the Calvinists, with their transformation of liturgical time and their reduction of holy days, to prefer historical settings to ritual ones when they had a choice; but I do not have the evidence to evaluate this possibility.[89] On the level of opportunistic practice, "the times" surely offered new excuses for homicide and for other wrongful behavior. A legal satire of 1582 presents a judge who, among his many misdeeds, took bribes from a gentleman "to pass off a premeditated murder ['un assassinat'] under color of the troubles . . . and embellished his remission."[90] Without assuming such duplicity, we find a Lyon merchant insisting on "the troubles" as the context for killing a Protestant soldier at the dinner table; and a Languedoc seigneur, for killing a former tenant who had harassed his parents and burned their chateau. Civic guard duty "because of the times" was the frame for other supplications; indeed, a Beauvais merchant slew a trouble-making fellow guard in 1567 after warning him that "given the necessity of the times everyone must be accommodating and get along amicably."[91]

The most interesting examples of time frame from the 1560's, however, are two that combine the festive and historical modes. They come from officers, one a Protestant, the other a Catholic. Maître Pierre Prugno served as an attorney for the Queen of Navarre in her lower court of Armagnac at Novaro. His supplication of 1567 starts at Mardi Gras with a transvestite carnival being conducted in violation of the decrees of the Parlement of Toulouse. Its leader,

Maître Jean de La Fargue, was regent of the College of Novaro, and, under the festive title of Captain Pellebourse (Shovelpurse), he had commanded the inhabitants to stay out of the streets while he and his troop marched and danced. Prugno's remission letter follows them through town, the women masked and dressed as men, the men masked and armed and dressed as women, beating up and wounding those that dared to be in their way. Prugno details his efforts that day and in the next four weeks either to arrest La Fargue or to get him to surrender, but it was impossible, as Pellebourse, surrounded by armed students, carried on his carnival justice, saying "he would make a ball of the judge's head and ninepins of his feet" and slapping the attorney on the cheek.

On March 22, the movement in the story reverses, with the supplicant, the sergeants, and specially recruited householders chasing La Fargue through town to get him to be "obeissant à Justice." They finally cornered him in a house, from which he continued to shout his own justice: "Rabble, cowards . . . I won't give myself up to you, to the king or queen, nor to all the men of Armagnac." Then it was the attorney's turn: "Kill, kill, get him dead or alive," and while he went up a ladder into the house, someone shot at Pellebourse and hit him in the belly. The next day when the supplicant came to retrieve the body, he was wrongfully arrested without a judicial order, but since he had the keys to the prison, he opened the doors and fled. Prugno now asks pardon, for everything he did was in pursuit of duty. It was granted him provided he stay away from the sénéchaussée of Toulouse for two years.[92]

Prugno's supplication opens with a festive time that is finally toppled by the time of the state. The second supplication, from Bertrand Pulveret, captain of the royal chateau of Pierre Scize at Lyon, opens with the time of the state, but slips in and out of a festive frame. On July 18, 1568, at the command of the governor, Pulveret had arrested two dinner guests at the Castle, Captains Latour and Lacombe, men "who didn't want to obey any command" and from whom he expected resistance. Pulveret fills in the hours after their imprisonment with the signs that made his suspicions grow: soldiers collecting outside, rumors about Latour's brother getting him out before nightfall, boasts from Latour about how many men he had "to put order to our affairs." Since they were "personages to be treated honorably," Pulveret invited them to sup with him, but misgivings about his guests mounted as one warned the other not to drink too much and they seemed to dawdle over their food. After they were escorted back to their rooms, he heard a great noise outside and word of an uprising in town, and fearing a conspiracy to seize the chateau, he allowed his soldiers to kill Latour and Lacombe in their beds. Pulveret adds that all Lyon rejoiced at the death of these two men, who were going to turn the city over to the king's enemies, but he wants the king's pardon just in case. Charles IX not only gives it, but adds that his privy council found the action "well done . . . for the public good."[93]

Readers may have noticed that in appealing to the times, neither Prugno nor Pulveret made precise reference to their religion or to that of their victims. Sixteenth-century listeners and readers would have easily filled that in: at that date, the officers of the Huguenot queen of Navarre would be Protestant, carnival-makers Catholic; the captain of the king's fort Catholic, conspiring captains Protestant. But the gaps suggest how much more there is in remission tales than can be known at first hearing. They must be reread and questioned again to uncover their literary strategies, the assumptions on which they rest and their relations to royal power. The plowman Manny, Sire Charles de Villelume, and the barber Caranda got their pardons in time, but the said and unsaid of their stories also served plots quite different from their own.

TWO

Angry Men and Self-Defense

he world of the letters of remission was one of anger and the unexpected. It was a world where the king, not the Lord, was the pardoner, and, although the prince was God's servant, the sources of action were not always interpreted in a strict Christian mode. Sudden attacks on a supplicant were never providential or merited because of one's sins, but were always wrongful, undeserved, or accidental. And the states of mind that pardon-seekers attributed to themselves might be measured differently by chancellery officer and confessor.

By both divine and civil law, protecting one's life or that of one's neighbor was an allowable exception to the Lord's command not to kill, though the canon law recommended running away if one could. Preachers also quoted Deuteronomy 19 on the God-given order of asylum for him who "killeth his neighbor ignorantly, whom he hated not in time past."[1] But anger was one of the Seven Deadly Sins in Catholic teaching, whether in its slow or sudden form, and vengeance and homicide were its characteristic fruit. For Calvin, "however much the hand gives birth to homicide, the heart conceives it when it is stained with wrath and hatred."[2] The "chaude colle," the sudden hot anger, that in the right circumstances could allow the king to *excuse* a slaying—that is, could make it remissible— was in the religious frame a sin that had to be forgiven. So too with drunkenness, which was sometimes used to establish the unpremeditated character of a crime: it was a branch of gluttony.

36

(Supplicants tried to play down their responsibility by the phrase "surprised by wine"—"surprins de vin.")[3] In sixteenth-century letters of remission, pardon-seekers did not say they were "repentant," though they might be "very sorry and chagrined" ("fort marry et desplaisant") or "full of regret."[4]

This freedom from being judged by the strictest Christian standards gave the supplicant some leeway in characterization, if not the latitude of the *Decameron* or of Marguerite de Navarre's *Heptaméron*. One was supposed to be "of good life and conversation," but one did not have to be a saint. (A young peasant from Berry compared himself to Saint George in defending his gang of New Year's revellers against swordblows, but this is an unusual reference.)[5] Nor did one say that one had been tempted by the Enemy, as was occasionally done in remission requests from the fifteenth century; the devil might be referred to in ordinary speech, but he was evidently a dangerous, or at least unprovable, presence in formal excuse tales of the next hundred years.[6] Though the term "chaude colle," literally hot bile (as contrasted with "sang froid," cold blood), was drawn from the language of the humors,[7] no supplicant wanted to refer to himself as of choleric temperament, for that would suggest one had provoked the violence to begin with. (By mid-century some requests use the simpler "in anger"—"grosse collere," "en collere estant ainsi emu.") One's victim could sometimes be portrayed as an irascible type—"a quarrelsome man, bad-living and with a bad reputation"—but the image was not easily available when the victim had been a regular companion or could not be established by independent testimony to be the angry sort.[8]

Remission narratives were pushed, then, into much "showing" rather than just "telling" what the actors were like and what they were feeling. Or to use Gérard Genette's phrase, their greatest ingenuity was in creating "the illusion of mimesis": of recreating for their readers and hearers a situation where the supplicant became all of a sudden justifiably or understandably heated up and angry and may have feared for his or her life, a situation where everything was supposedly out in the open (no *subreption*, as the judge would say), and nothing concealed.[9] Even an insanity plea was in itself not enough, but needed a story in which, say, a Paris shoemaker, "out of his mind and senses," had to be shown eating and drinking too much with a priest and being pushed into fury by a sergeant who should have known better.[10] Where one was trying to claim a total accident—the supplicant was shooting a dove from a boat on the Saône and by chance hit a journeyman butcher—then the story need not build to "chaude colle," but narrative was still required to give signs of innocence and regret, with Ascension day mass, island dining, and joyous river pastimes.[11]

Not surprisingly in the sixteenth century, these anger plots can vary with social location, especially when they come from the men: certain themes and assumptions about behavior seem to cluster around social types. Though the peasant's tales were diverse, you can certainly distinguish a Peasant from a Gentleman, and the Artisans' stories are often different from both.

A characteristic Peasant Tale centers on young unmarried men and a wedding. The supplicant, a relative of the bride or groom, takes a girl by the hand, tells the minstrels to play and leads the dance. An uninvited guest appears, perhaps from a different village, takes another girl by the hand and tries to displace him. Then the intruder goes up to the supplicant, slaps his face till his hat falls to the ground, maybe pulls his head down by the hair. The supplicant, all *ému* (aroused), *outragé* (deeply offended, violated), takes out a knife and kills him.[12] These recitals of blood wedding are told starkly and simply; they compress within them the rivalry of suitors and the components of what we may call male peasant honor, but which the peasants talked about in terms of hats and hair. Indeed, the hat, doffed before seigneurs, judges, and other notables, seems to have been an important personal symbol among men of the lower orders, peasants and artisans both. (Remember the barber Caranda: the toolmaker "made his bonnet fall to the ground.") Exchanged, demanded, stolen, and especially knocked off, hats triggered trouble in remission stories.[13]

A second type of Peasant Tale centers around inheritance; it involves insiders rather than outsiders, and smoldering grievances that suddenly surface in anger. The story of Antoine Simon, a vine-grower from the Ile-de-France, opens with the celebration of his engagement to a second wife at her family's farmhouse. At the banquet he overhears his sister and brother-in-law wondering whether he has not held on to their share of the patrimony, and though Simon tries to hush them, claiming he has done them no wrong, his two nephews accuse him openly of fraud and slap him before the guests. The sister's family then repair to the supplicant's house, where the nephews break in—"We'll show Uncle good this time." Simon returns with his future in-laws and "in hot anger" hits one of the intruders with a little trowel. The nephews plead for mercy, the sister begs them to stay indoors, but instead they return in stealth to attack the supplicant. A fight ensues, and one nephew loses a hand and the other eventually his life.[14] Other inheritance quarrels have different details[15]—sometimes it is even the claimant rather than the possessor who survives—but they are all chronicled around life-cycle events, and they all rest on the assumption, accepted at every stage of composing a letter of remission, that a peasant's right to a legitimate share in family property is important enough to arouse deadly anger.

A Gentleman's Tale might be more prolix, including more than one episode, if not all the eighteen years of misadventure of the Sire de Villelume. It characteristically casts the supplicant as defending his rights as a seigneur and his honor as a gentleman. For example, a squire from the Berry upbraids a royal sergeant for harassing his sharecropper for nonpayment of taxes and indeed for holding at ransom the whole countryside; when the sergeant calls him "ung mauvais garçon" (not just a "bad boy," but a knave), the supplicant, "aroused" ("ému") by remembering that he is "a gentleman serving in the king's army, 35 or 36 years old and married to a good gentle-woman," starts a fight. He ends up killing not the sergeant, but the sergeant's pregnant daughter. In scene two the squire is trying to collect back rent from a man who claims he is not a tenant at all, "but as much a gentleman as he." The squire tells the would-be gentleman that if it were not a saint's day, he would "make him eat his words." Whereupon the tenant assails him with several "mauvais garçons," and eventually the supplicant has to whack him with a sword. Finally, there is a slapping encounter on horseback with a person who had previously beaten the squire's servants. The supplicant ends up (so he tells it) beating his own servant for hitting the enemy before he did and wounding him too severely. Squire Baraton had composed with the woman's family after the first affair, but after the third one he was arrested. His servants broke down the prison door, he fled, and now in the winter of 1535, he asks for pardon.[16]

I again resist the social historian's temptation to elaborate on how these episodes epitomize the mixed situation of the country nobility in the first half of the sixteenth century—both protecting and pressuring their tenants, both resisting royal officers and serving the king. Here I want to emphasize only the cultural issue: telling King François Ier such a story of humiliating and dishonorable killing was an embarrassment for the squire, a "tres grant desplaisir." What a contrast with accounts of a judicial duel on a point of honor between two gentlemen of the same province of Berry three years later! That duel, growing out of a long quarrel over an accusation of lying, took place with elaborate ritual before the eyes of the king himself, who finally decided both men had been so brave there would be no victor or vanquished.[17]

On the other hand, a remission tale was needed for a fight between unequals or between gentlemen on the spur of the moment* or for an ambush that one wanted to present as unpremeditated. It could cover demeaning cases like that of a Picardy squire who, at a Saint Nicolas fair to buy pigs, was insulted by a "simple laboureur" with a drawn sword; the squire, who had his sword rightfully "as gentlemen are accustomed to wear," smote the peasant in the stomach.[18] And it could stretch to cases of import, as when a seigneur of Anjou, dining with his curé and other priests on the feast of the Annunciation 1547, ended up killing an intruder who denied that one needed to fast at Lent. Though the quarrel here concerned matters of personal honor—Who knew better the eating habits of the court? Was the intruder as much an "homme de bien" as the seigneur?—it moved to the wider question of the honor of the Church and what it was to be a good Christian.[19]

With the tales of artisans and tradesmen, we enter the realm of work, payment, theft, and debt. A baker of Crépy-en-Valois sends away his apprentice for taking three sous—"Thief, I don't want such a servant"—and the master becomes vexed when the apprentice refuses to leave without his clothes and says he hasn't stolen. A young tapestry maker of Châtelleraut berates his journeyman for fooling around so much that they are going to miss their deadline, and becomes furious when the worker goes out in the street and shouts that he is "a Lutheran, a wicked Lutheran."[20]

---

*See the note on p. 57 below on the evolution of the legal status of the duel in the last half of the sixteenth century.

Especially interesting are the Payment Stories, which put to the test Panurge's claim in Rabelais' *Tiers Livre* that creditors always wish their debtors long life.[21] A Touraine carpenter tells how in 1545 he went to a seigneur and asked "graciously" to be paid for extensive work completed on the seigneur's house, for he needed the money to support his wife and children. The seigneur refused to pay the agreed-upon sum—he'd given him twelve sous worth of scrap metal and that was enough—and followed after the supplicant and hit him on the head. "Treated outrageously with no reason for asking for what was due him for his labor," the carpenter struck the seigneur with his workman's dagger, inflicting a mortal wound. Here the pardoning king seems to have agreed the laborer was worthy of his hire.[22]

Meanwhile a young surgeon from the town of La Charité-sur-Loire held his victim responsible not only for his debt but for dying of his wound.[23] He had gone out to the country to collect his fee from a villager whose son he had cured. The father attacked him, the surgeon defended himself, and the debtor expired a month later. The surgeon explained that the victim had died "by lack of good provision, medication and regimen"—thus far he was following a notarial formula used in sixteenth-century remission letters to strengthen the supplicant's case—but added indignantly, "and because he had himself cared for by a village barber of no experience, with whom he had bargained for fifty sous."*

Finally, the tradesmen's stories take them from the workshop into

---

*Some formula—"par faulte de bon appareil, gouvernement, ou aultrement," "par faulte de bon gouvernement, medicaments, ou aultrement"—is used in sixteenth-century letters of remission whenever the victim does not die on the spot or very soon afterward. Every once in a while letters will go beyond the formulas, as did that of the surgeon: a young Lyonnais villager described the butcher he wounded as banqueting and drinking with his cronies in the eleven days before he died (ADR, BP441, sentence of June 15, 1551); an advocate of Aix said of the attorney he felled with a single sword blow that he did not bother to take care of himself or obey the physicians, but "obstinately wanted to live at his own pleasure," and then died seven months later (AN, JJ262, 196ʳ–197ᵛ). Such descriptions with elaborate detail (foods eaten by and sexual activities of the wounded person, etc.) seem to play a more important role in fourteenth-century letters of remission (Jules Viard, ed., *Documents parisiens du règne de Philippe VI de Valois [1328–1350] extraits des registres de la Chancellerie de France*, 2 vols. [Paris, 1900], vol. 2, #291, #380, #395). The sixteenth-century remission narrative concentrates on the excusability of the supplicant's action; the fourteenth-century narrative attenuates the supplicant's responsibility, suggesting how much can intervene between wound and death.

the tavern, where the artisan's sense of honor comes to the fore. A Lyon metal refiner says his blood began to boil when another metal-worker maintained obstinately and drunkenly his opinion about the weight of a gold crown.[24] A Paris butcher recounts how he and fellow journeymen played tennis for money on a fast day and then at dinner afterward he proposed that he and the other winners pay the losers' bill. A loser rose up swearing "God's body . . . he didn't want to be beholden to the winners," and the dishes began to fly.[25] A Lyon messenger named Farfannchy reports in 1549 that the customary group drinking to celebrate a fellow courier's assignment to an Italian voyage went agreeably enough. But as the group left the tavern to go out in the street, a messenger named Laffaney, jealous of the man who got the job, began to ride him, "saying he wouldn't do it well."

Irritated at this, the supplicant said to Laffaney, "You wouldn't dare carry a package to Pisa." Whereupon words and quarrels led to their giving the lie direct to each other ["jusques à desmentyr l'ung l'aultre"], and the supplicant gave Laffaney a slap.[26]

Perhaps it was the royal secretary who put in "démentir," currently so important in the scenario in the gentlemen's duel;[27] perhaps the word was simply a part of the vocabulary of world-traveling messengers. Whatever the case, these recitals show that artisans presented themselves to notary, king, and judge as having a strong sense of pride, and that notary, king, and judge acknowledged it was pardonable for them to get angry when so offended.

It is important to stress here that these stories I have clumped around their tellers' social position by no means exhaust all remission requests made by male peasants, artisans, and gentlemen, nor are these motifs strictly confined to one social niche. Uninvited wedding guests could disturb an artisan's wedding dance as well as a peasant's, while a Gascon lawyer had to kill a man who was just trying to get his name on the guest list.[28] Peasants could get angry about being asked to pay a debt, especially when they thought a gift in order; a seigneur could turn a loan quarrel with another seigneur into homicide, especially when he thought he would look "pusillanimous" if he did not strike a man who had insulted him.[29] Fights about inheritance or adultery could be related at every social rank. From novelties like Protestantism could emerge individual accounts that fracture older types—like that of the Picardy gardener who killed a priest not at a country dance, but in arguing with him at a tavern about whether there was one God or three.[30]

Nonetheless, out of the total corpus of remission narratives, certain of them depend so critically on the supplicant's consciousness of his estate that it is not just a twentieth-century artifice to refer to them as Peasants' Tales or Gentlemen's Tales or Barbers' Tales. Chaucer entitled his stories by the calling of the teller (the Miller's Tale, the Knight's Tale, the Merchant's Tale, and the like), and this has been well described as a transformation and concretization of the older Estates satire.[31] Philippe de Vigneulles distinguished his *Nouvelles* one from the other by detailed observation on the social class of the actors; literary specialists have related this to a "new realism," savored alike by writer and by early sixteenth-century reader.[32] A few decades later the lawyer Noël du Fail tried to evoke a peasant universe in his *Propos Rustiques* (literally Rustic Talk), while Bonaventure Des Periers suited the manner of speaking of each character in his *Joyeux Devis* (literally Joyful Conversation) to his or her condition.[33] What implications do these tales and the letters of remission have for each other? On the one hand, they attest to a widespread habit of storytelling in which estate gave coherence to the action. On the other hand, they show that such narrative need not originate only in satirical, comic, or ethnographic intentions. To save one's life, to account for oneself, one could draw upon the same distinctive understandings intrinsic to one's estate.

Let us now look more finely at the narrative construction of remission tales. Some of them—a minority—open with a personal quarrel or feud. "About a year ago the supplicant's brother married the . . . stepdaughter of Jacques Menguet of Montmartre . . . who had previously refused her in marriage to a man named Galan. . . . On the day of the wedding, Galan's cousin and . . . other kin came to the house armed with swords and daggers and . . . tried to seize the girl by force, and failing that, set fire to the house, and the rings and several other jewels were burned."[34] The desire for revenge of the rejected peasant suitor sets the stage for predictable struggle with the supplicant. Whatever the literary merits of this beginning—and many great tales have opened with a quarrel—it has a distinct disadvantage for someone seeking a pardon. It suggests that the supplicant was not taken by surprise or sudden hot anger when he killed his victim; it puts in jeopardy the claim of unpremeditated homicide. A Gascon peasant starts off with the grievance of his victim against him and his father (the man he slew had married the supplicant's cousin without consent, and she had been denied her share of the patrimony), his victim's "mortal hatred," and past court cases and violent threats. Thus when they meet after ten o'clock at night near the barn, the reader wonders—despite all the details suggesting coincidence—whether they did not have a rendezvous for a village duel.[35]

Many more of the remission tales begin with the supplicant going about daily business or festive pleasure in a peaceable way and build to a climax from which a tragic or bloody outcome is inevitable: an insult ("you have sold your blood and would eat it and drink it," said by a Béarnais peasant to his friend on a wooded country road after holy-day drinking);[36] an outburst about money (from one's share of the bill to one's share of the inheritance); a sudden revelation ("he went upstairs and found [the Parisian] on top of his wife");[37] and the like. The ending comes more or less quickly, sometimes delayed by the intercession of bystanders, or even, in an unusual case, by a reported appeal from the victim ("Uncle, I cry mercy"); more often by the efforts of the supplicant to make peace ("Mon amy, je ne vous demande rien"—"My friend, I'm not asking you for anything," a sixteenth-century phrase of appeasement that could be said even to someone one barely knew, rather like our "Take it easy, my friend, I'm not looking for trouble").[38] But, of course, the trouble persists, and the last scene is the movement of flight or pursuit, weapons, and blows.

When well realized, this format allowed supplicants to achieve several goals important for winning pardon. First, the innocence, unintentionality, or legitimacy of their actions grew out of the events themselves, the words exchanged, the objects and images used. Roland Barthes' narrative mainspring—"the confusion of consecution and consequence"—is just what the supplicant needs.[39] Such devices could also serve to compensate for embarrassing gaps or silences in a story, as when a young Parisian stonecutter tells how he went at a friend's behest to get some herbal medicine from his old mother and found her being beaten by a strange man. His description of the crowd gathered in front of her house, their shouts ("See, her son is arriving"), and her various wounds made it easier for him not to explain that his mother was undoubtedly known as a magical healer and witch and that the mysterious assailant was trying to force her to lift a spell.[40] At least he could slip the story by the chancellor's office, if not by the investigating judge.

Further, this format gave scope to the supplicant to tell a story true enough so that at least some other persons would corroborate it during the judicial inquiry, and, in the frequent absence of witnesses, with enough verisimilitude that it would be believed. The mention of precise persons, places, movements, and gestures was intended partly to generate supporting witnesses, but also to give concreteness and credibility to the story, what Barthes would call the "reality effect," details that guarantee that the event really happened.[41] It was sometimes possible to obtain a special royal letter that ordered judges to accept the truth of a remission account on the basis of the supplicant's oath alone since there were no living witnesses to the homicide.[42] A persuasive story in the first place could certainly help this along.

Here is an example from Jean Faurier, a small-town notary and seigneurial judge in Gascony in 1547. He begins the account of his homicide by narrating his movements to specific villages where he ordinarily held court or received instruments on Wednesdays, adding that he took his sword with him because he was going on foot "by the fields." Then on his way home to Mirande,

on the road behind Monclar, he stopped to piss in a ditch at the crossroad, and as he was urinating with his codpiece all detached, up came Me Jean Espes the apothecary on his horse, and threatened to kill him, as he had often done before, in hatred arising from a suit for fraud that the supplicant was bringing against his brother. Espes rode right at him with his sword bared ["espée nue"] while he was pissing [the near pun on the apothecary's name would hardly have been lost on the sixteenth-century reader] and suddenly struck a blow which hit the supplicant's right hand and made it bleed heavily. The supplicant, who had not been thinking of any evil and who could not run away, reached for his sword, and in defending himself gave the apothecary a blow across the body . . . from which he died not long after.[43]

In this story, Faurier established witnesses for his irreproachable Wednesday activities, made the apothecary's grudge a mere aside to his stopping to piss, and created an image of that unobserved event as sure to win him pardon as Pantagruel's urinary drowning of the Dipsodes was to win him victory.[44]

The second example is the tale of a journeyman butcher of Paris, Louis Paisant, aged 36, responsible for a wife and three little children. Listen to the way his innocent butchering slips into the chance of homicide. He begins with his going to mass one Sunday in November 1525, the weekly mass founded by the butchers of the Saint Jean cemetery. Then back to the butcher's shop at the cemetery, where he split the carcasses of six bulls for several masters and their servants, whom he names. Then with other journeymen to eat midday dinner and drink at the nearby tavern of Our Lady, where he paid the bill for himself and one of his friends. Then to the skinning shop, where he carved and dressed more beef, delivered it to the butchery, stopped for a drink with two fellow journeymen, and finished his day's work at the skinnery at four o'clock.

Back to the tavern of Our Lady with Philippe Boniface, Jean Geoffroy, and others from his shop; the butchers had supper and peaceably paid their bill, and five or six of them started to play dice. Boniface played till he lost all his money. Louis gave him five sous, a percentage of "some cash they had between them," but Boniface, "who was said to have killed two or three men" (only now we learn this), began to swear and insist that Paisant give him his cloak. Louis said he couldn't, he had it on security for a loan. They exchanged words and accused each other of lying; Boniface asked one of the other butchers for his knife. Whereupon fearing that Boniface, who was quick to strike, would kill him, "he drew one of the knives he wore in his belt for the work of his craft and in hot anger gave Boniface a blow," from which he died. Made a prisoner, Louis was pardoned a few weeks later provided he pay sixty sous for prayers to be said for Boniface's soul.[45]

Some remission tales are given coherence and enhanced meaning, as we saw in the last chapter, by their festive and ritual setting, which guides and is commented upon by the events. In Louis Paisant's story, the mass at the cemetery sets the stage for later death, but it can not be used to interpret the journeyman's day, since butchering was one of the trades allowed to continue on the Sabbath unless it was a period of fast.[46] Instead of the mass, it is the meat carving and the butcher's knife that move the disparate action along: a changing motif, creating mood in shop and tavern; a synecdoche,

46

reminding journeyman, secretary, and judge of the narrow edge between work gone right and work gone wrong.

Other supplications use a similar device. For a poor Orléanais woodman, Jean Charbonnier dit Nain (Dwarf), with a wife and hungry children in 1524, it is his tools that shape the tale of his mounting desperation and anger: the ax with which he starts his work day for a seigneur, and the billhook which he has pawned to help out his brother Robin, but which he needs if he is to fagot the wood on the morrow. He turns down the invitation of his brother Thomas to go to their uncle's wedding because he has no money— Robin has made him spend it all—and because he must get his billhook back. When the lender's wife refuses to return it with only the ax as security, Jean goes, much afflicted ("tout desconfortè"), to look for Robin. He accuses his brother of taking him to taverns for his pleasure; they exchange insults, Robin punches him, and the supplicant strikes him with the ax, cutting his head in two.[47]

Elsewhere the moving motif is a payment, as in a plowman's tale from the Ile-de-France. Payment surfaces early in a promised gift for a comrade's wedding banquet, then in the "denier à dieu" (the token money of assent to an engagement) returned by the disgruntled mother to the would-be groom, then in the bill—the "escot"—that the disappointed suitor refuses to pay, and finally in the plowman's money bag, which the suitor tries to seize.[48] Sometimes the motif is a simple word, as in a student's tale from Orléans, which starts with his passing a "fille de joye," to whom he says in "paroles joyeuses" (playful, joyful words) to give him her handkerchief, from whom he seizes the handkerchief "joyeusement" and wipes his face with it, and on till he hits her in chaude colle.[49]

These various examples show how remission stories succeeded in creating a sense of the real, a narrative that satisfied the requirements of the pardonable and also had a kind of literary unity. At the same time, their primary authors were people with a corpse to explain, and their texts had "wounds" in them, open cuts or gaps in the argument (What *was* that strange money arrangement between butcher Paisant and butcher Boniface?) and/or hidden ones (Why couldn't the woodman say no to his brother Robin?), a rupture between what was said and what happened. But these were recitals written to be debated before they were ratified. At their best, through a ritual or historical frame, through their ordering and choice of detail or dynamic motif, they raised questions about themselves, called attention to their own partiality and moral uncertainties, and prompted reflection on the nature of the fortuitous.[50]

Why are we hearing only about good stories, readers may be asking impatiently? Aren't there bad stories, mediocre supplications? Why should the world of archives be any better than the world of ordinary authors? The answer is yes, there are stories where the telling is routine, a heavy dose of notarial formulae around a few sheep strayed into a neighboring pasture (either the young shepherd was inarticulate or the secretary indifferent or both); or aimless, as in a fratricidal fight so abrupt and unmotivated that there is almost no plot (the royal notary may have meant it when he called the supplicant "a poor simple man").[51]

But some poorly told stories raise interesting questions about the pardoning process. For instance, here is a brief, unpleasant tale from a person in the suite of the court of François Ier as it was passing through Cluny in 1541. His humble supplication immediately names two important noblemen, one who had just presented him with a handsome sword and the other to whom he was showing it off in the street. A boy came by on a horse leading a mule, the horse stepped on the supplicant's foot, leaving him all soiled with mud, which put him "in a hot anger." He hit at the boy with the flat of the new sword; the point somehow went into his stomach; the boy fell off his horse and died. The supplicant quotes himself as saying "God help me" and claims to the king it was an accident. He never did find out who the boy was. His remission was signed by master of requests Lazare de Baïf, whose name had already appeared on the title page of several important humanist editions.[52]

The success of such a letter of remission makes one wonder if it made any difference whether the story one told were true and/or well-constructed so long as one had powerful connections to the court. Let us pause over this issue and see where it leads in the understanding of the "fictional," the creative crafting in remission tales. In the private journals of well-informed Parisian observers in the reign of François Ier, the report is a mixed one: the king's pardon was sometimes perceived as a mere matter of favor, sometimes not. On the one hand, the journal of the so-called Burgher of Paris remarked about the grace given to a rich and ennobled Lyonnais in 1528 for the "murder" of a relative of the chancellor, "And this was because he had married the sister of the viceroy of Naples, and so his life was saved."[53] On the other hand, the "facts" carried the day in the case of the master of the king's mint in Paris: he invited his brother-in-law to his house for the feast of the Annunciation and then, "by treachery," "killed him after they had dined together." He managed to get a letter of remission sealed, but it was dismissed and he was beheaded: "no matter what money he offered, he couldn't have his grace."[54] Looking back at the reign of François Ier from the troubled 1570's, the jurist Papon recalled it as a golden age of just remission, the king refusing his grace in 1546 to one of his favorites because his homicide of another seigneur was in fact an ambush.[55]

By the time of the Estates-General of 1560, both the Clergy and the Third Estate were worried about remissions "too easily granted"; at the Estates of 1576, the Third Estate made no bones about it: "there is no crime however great or odious for which, by the passage of time and the intervention of the right people, a letter of remission can not be obtained." They begged the king that pardons be accorded only for remissible cases.[56] The way it looked to chancellery officer Pierre de L'Estoile, barbed commentator on the foibles of Henri III, favor played a major role, whether the pardon was granted or not. An Italian arriviste, raised to high financial office by Catherine de Médicis, had ambushed an enemy in 1581, "expecting," wrote L'Estoile in his journal, "immediately to have the king's grace because his Majesty often went to dine at his house." The king kept him dangling because he had recently failed to pay for some expensive pearls, but then when the wounded man recovered (so bungled was the brave attack by twelve armed men), the queen mother's favor got him off, despite "all the laws of this kingdom," with a payment to the victim and a payment to the poor. A Protestant nobleman killed an enemy in cold blood, "counting on the favor of M. le Duc [the king's brother]," who indeed intervened to ask for grace. L'Estoile quoted the king's refusal: "La Primaudaye is judged and must die today. . . . Beyond the fact that his act is evil and irremissible, I loved [the man he killed], and if he hadn't been a Huguenot, would have made him great."[57]

In such accounts of important persons, L'Estoile gives an "inside story"—the events as he knew them and the vagaries of royal favoritism—to place next to the contents of the letter of remission. Does this mean that the remission tale itself was irrelevant to the outcome of a request for pardon? Only in some few cases exceptionally close to the king were the merits of the letter immaterial. What these "inside stories" do is, first, show us the field of doubt that could spread around a remission story and, second, remind us that favor was continually at work in French society, affecting how the remission would be heard. We see it at the village level far from court: in 1561 a local priest stopped by the Cotentin manor house of the Sire de Gouberville to ask him to say a word to his cousin, the king's lawyer in Valognes, about the ratification of his brother's remission.[58]

Even if Gouberville obliged (his diary does not say), the brother's story still had to remain the center of the quest for pardon. It was the text around which all the battles were fought. It had to satisfy two audiences attuned to "the laws of the land" in regard to what constituted remissible crime, namely the chancellery officials and the ratifying judges. It had to survive the challenges of the members of the victim's family; it had to win the assent of witnesses. Some supplicants, rather than trust in their story, tried to bribe or browbeat judges in the lower jurisdictions to ratify their letters; others took their letters as far as possible from the place of the crime so that it would be difficult for the judges to get testimony from the victim's kin or witnesses; still others waited illegally three or four years to seek ratification in hopes that the interested parties would all be dead.[59] But if the judges in question did their duty or the victim's kin appealed to the Parlement, the burden would again be on the story.

And the claims and counterclaims before the judges could be sharp. A Lyon carter said that his victim suddenly dragged him along by his collar, hitting him with a dagger while he shouted "Mercy, mercy, what have I done?" but witnesses claimed he was chasing the victim up the street with his sword unsheathed.[60] Etienne Dolet published a poetic account of his remission tale, describing his New Year's Eve stroll through the Lyon streets, suddenly interrupted by a murderous painter and his armed band, with Dolet then killing the painter in self-defense. A literary opponent published a counter-story a few years later, in which Dolet was pictured as arranging a false reconciliation with the painter and then hitting him repeatedly with his dagger as he lay bleeding on the ground.[61] True or false, assisted by favor or not, the remission tale could not be shelved in the struggle for grace.

What about the overall success rate of the quest for pardon, that is, the percentage of the king's letters which were ratified? And does it reflect at all the initial qualities of the story? For this project I have not undertaken to draw up a full balance sheet, since the most readily available corpus of chancellery documents (the copies made for the chancellery's own archive, the Trésor des Chartes) do not consistently tell what the ultimate disposition of the pardon was.[62] We can get a rough idea of the ratio, however, from the records of the Paris Conciergerie, where the fate of prisoners is reported along with the date of their incarceration. Of all the people who were in that prison awaiting judicial review of their letters from 1564, when the register begins, to 1580, only 6.5 percent were deprived of the king's grace.[63] Now these are the years when the Third Estate and Jean Papon were complaining about how easy it was to get letters of remission sealed and approved, so this success rate is undoubtedly on the high side, but a sample of Sentences of the Parlement of Paris and the Sénéchaussée of Lyon from earlier years shows many more remissions ratified than dismissed.[64]

This high rate of letters approved must mean in the first place that the stories of the supplicants and their claim to previous good life got significant local support and that the judges were satisfied that, where appropriate,[65] the victim's kin had been or would be compensated enough to keep the peace. When we find detailed evidence about a dismissed letter of grace, as with a Lyon printer's journeyman who had seriously wounded a proofreader in 1559, the letter is vague—the journeyman never says what made him so angry—and there is unrelenting opposition from the proofreader and the master printer. They established through witnesses that the supplicant had omitted some of his misdeeds in the shop, and they alleged he had once killed a printer and had taken part in illegal workers' assemblies. The judges agreed that at least he was a troublemaker, and allowed his five-year banishment and fine to be put into effect.[66] A true story could help win support; a plausible, well-told story could help persuade the judges; but the judicial goals of local stability and pacification could shape a ratification on their own.

The high rate of ratification suggests in the second place that the king's name on the salutation of the letter—François, Henri, Charles by the grace of God, King of France—and his orders to his officers at its close to pardon and remit were not pro forma. The first finding of the king's chancellery came to the verifying judges as more than a mere hypothesis; the royal frame to the supplication predisposed the judges to read it with some respect, or as the Lyon judge put it in the course of a hearing, "having regard for the letters of grace, pardon, and remission obtained."[67] In borderline cases they could remit as the king commanded, then require the supplicant to make a larger peace settlement with the kin of the deceased and to stay away from the scene of the crime for a year or two.

Furthermore, the judges knew that in any situation of conflict where the king wanted to bother, he could force the ratification of his letters, just the way François Ier did in 1518 in regard to his Concordat with the pope. This is what happened in a scandalous adultery case involving members of the Paris legal world in the years 1521–22. "Through personages with credit at court," the guilty wife—spouse of a local judge and daughter of a royal attorney—got a letter abolishing her penalty of life-long enclosure in a nunnery, and "after repeated command of the king" the Parlement ratified it.[68] And this is what happened with Etienne Dolet's dubious remission for killing the painter. The Sénéchaussée of Lyon refused to ratify it, releasing him from prison with the order to pay a large sum to the painter's heir. Six years later Dolet still had protectors who had the king's ear, and François compelled Parlement to ratify a new pardon for heresy and the old pardon for homicide.[69]

Thus the success rate of remission letters goes beyond the strength of the story, as the supplicant was integrated into the larger drama of the build-up of monarchical power. By the end of the fifteenth century the king had largely established his monopoly over the right to pardon for homicide or for any other capital crime. Dukes were not to pardon as they once had done, nor was any holder of seigneurial justice; parlementary courts and other royal judges could recommend that an accused seek a letter of remission, as we have seen, but were not themselves to pardon; archaic holdovers, like the privilege of the Church of Rouen to pardon anyone in Normandy on the day before the feast of Saint Romain, were restricted as the sixteenth century wore on.[70] From the Ordinance of Blois of 1499 through the *Republic* of Jean Bodin, pardon was celebrated as one of the "fairest marks of sovereignty." "Kings have always glorified themselves through their clemency," said the Dauphiné lawyer Claude Expilly in his plea for the ratification of a mountaineer's remission letter, and went on to quote Ronsard's poem for Charles IX comparing royal mercy to divine mercy:

> Or, Sire, imitez Dieu, lequel vous a donné
> Le Sceptre & vous a fait un grand Roy couronné,
> Faites misericorde à celuy qui supplie.
>
> [Now, Sire, imitate God, who has given you
> The Scepter and made of you a great crowned King,
> Give mercy to him who supplicates you.][71]

The king's special pardons when he entered a town for the first time after his coronation were as important as his touching for scrofula.[72]

As the public execution displayed the king's justice, so the semi-public ratification of the pardon displayed his mercy (see illustrations 3 and 4), with every supplicant, whether shepherd or seigneur, required to be present, humbly kneeling before the court with head bared. (Indeed, the letter of remission and the rites of pardon should clearly be added to the "political anatomy" of Old Regime confession and execution, analyzed by Michel Foucault in *Discipline and Punish*.)[73] Once in a while, the two rituals happened together, as with the Sire de Saint-Vallier, condemned to die for treason in 1524, but pardoned at the last moment at the prayers of his son-in-law, the sénéchal of Normandy, who had served the king well. An observer drew the incident in his notebook (see illustration 5) and the Burgher of Paris recorded it in his journal:

[Saint-Vallier] was on the scaffold, head bare and hands tied . . . praying God and awaiting the hour of his death, when arrived on horseback a servant of the chancellor shouting "Holla, holla, stop, stop, here is the king's remission." Whereupon one of the clerks of the criminal court . . . mounted the scaffold and read the letter of remission, sealed with green wax, word for word.[74]

The pardon was greeted "with great joy by the people of Paris," a lawyer reported, "for it was commonly said that in making him die, one would do him wrong."[75]

The system of royal pardon clearly held many benefits for suddenly angry men in sixteenth-century France. If the Third Estate feared, and with some reason, the extent to which wrongly granted remissions allowed the duels, démentis, and disorders of gentlemen

3. A supplicant humbly requests the Parlement to ratify his letter of remission in the presence of the widow and child of the deceased. From Jean Milles de Souvigny, *Praxis Criminis Persequendi* (Paris, 1541).

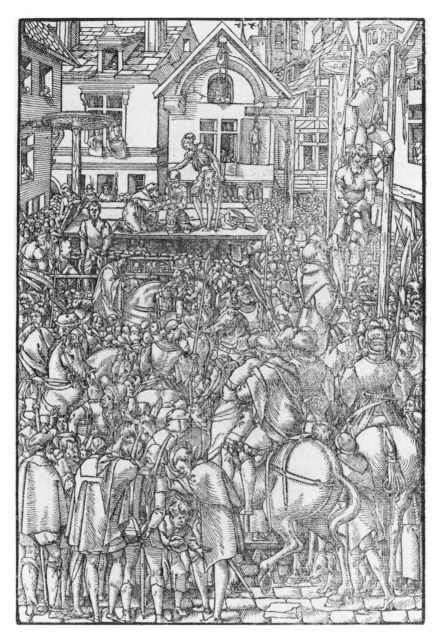

4. A composite portrait of public executions. From Jean Milles de Souvigny, *Praxis Criminis Persequendi* (Paris, 1541).

5. Pardon arrives for the Sire de Saint-Vallier, 1524. From a contemporary Paris journal, Bibliothèque Nationale, Ms. fr. 17527, 54ᵣ.

and soldiers to go unpunished,* it is still true that the interests of commoners were much served. How else could a carpenter who had killed a seigneur have ever been forgiven? Everyone knew, as one pamphlet complained, what influence gentlemen could have over local prosecution, especially in the countryside.[76] At every social niche, the pardon could change the tragic situation of unpremeditated killing and expected execution into the tragi-comedy of reprieve and peaceful reconciliation.

But this transformation required playing by the king's rules: the actor must become a supplicant, a notary's third person, and not recount his adventures as though he were a hero in a folktale showing his strength. No strutting around to the king the way journeyman Galiot Thibout was heard to do in a Lyon printing shop, showing his sword and saying "it had lots of teeth, and he had made it eat more than a thousand crowns of flesh." No cocky tone to the king as men sometimes assumed in writing about violence in a *Life* for their children.[77] Certainly not the tone of "proud virtue" without supplication, which Montaigne so appreciated in Socrates's speech to the judges deciding his fate. And if the duel was a way to bypass the king's justice in favor of noble courage and God's mysterious intervention, a gentleman who sought a remission afterward had to reset the Lie Direct, change the righteous anger of revenge into sudden hot bile, and beg for mercy like everyone else.[78] The habit of language insisted upon in the letters of remission and the roles in which supplicants were required to present themselves were among the civilizing mechanisms of the early modern French state, reminding people subjectively of the locus of power, even while never

---

*As François Billacois has shown in his splendid book *Le duel*, the duel of Jarnac in 1547, where the king's champion was killed, marked the end of the publicly sanctioned judicial duel on a point of honor. Over the next decades, royal legislation inched toward prohibiting duels, especially an ordinance of 1579 aimed at stopping the violence of "all the subjects," including gentlemen. But it was not till the edict of Henri IV in 1602 that the duel was declared illegal by name. (François Billacois, *Le duel dans la société française des XVIe–XVIIe siècles. Essai de psychologie historique* [Paris, 1986], pp. 92–93, 146–48). Duels continued and multiplied after 1547, and, even though they were not specifically a criminal offense, the survivor might be liable to prosecution under more general edicts and at the urging of the slain man's heirs. When this happened, a remission was usually won (ibid., p. 133). The Third Estate asked the king in 1560 to forbid duels to persons of any quality whatsoever "and to take away any hope of remission for them" (C. Lalourcé, ed., *Recueil des Cahiers Généraux des Trois Ordres aux Etats-Généraux*, 4 vols. [Paris, 1789], vol. 1: Etats d'Orléans, 1560, Third Estate, articles 101–2, pp. 324–25).

silencing competing modes in which they dramatized their actions or mishaps.*

Similarly, there was a connection between the gaps in remission tales, that uncertain relation between the *vraisemblable* and the *vrai*, and the gaps in the king's remissions, that uncertain relation between actual royal pardons and what was pardonable by divine and human law. The king might promise his Estates that his uses of mercy would always be "for just occasion and according to law" (that is, pardoning truly unpremeditated homicide or legitimate self-defense), but in fact the strengthening of sovereignty involved the king's will pushing beyond the law.[79] In the field between the true and the plausible, royal grace and power could grow, and supplicants could harvest restored life and good name.

This complicity between sovereign and subject accounts in part for the double reputation of letters of remission in the sixteenth century. They were simultaneously believed in as a needed mechanism for social peace and reintegration, and scoffed at as a sham. Within a few years of each other, Marguerite de Navarre and Bonaventure Des Periers wrote stories expressing this range of view.

For the king's sister, who was herself Queen of Navarre, pardons are sometimes rightly granted, sometimes not. Two *Heptaméron* nouvelles lead up to requests for royal mercy. In one (nouvelle 23) a gentleman gives to the king's court the true story of a homicide committed through misunderstanding (that is, the story that Marguerite has just written) and gets a Good Friday pardon with the support of a virtuous master of requests. In the other (nouvelle 1), drawn from actual events in the 1520's, an attorney of Alençon,

---

*I am constructing the argument about the uses of mercy somewhat differently from Douglas Hay and John Langbein in their divergent analyses of the relation of social class to criminal justice and to pardon in eighteenth-century England (Douglas Hay, "Property, Authority, and the Criminal Law," in Douglas Hay et al., *Albion's Fatal Tree: Crime and Society in Eighteenth-Century England* [New York, 1975], especially pp. 40–48; John H. Langbein, "*Albion's* Fatal Flaw," *Past and Present*, 98 [Feb. 1983]: 96–120). There are many differences between the two settings: socio-political ones, such as the different relation of the nobility to the institutions of royal justice; and legal ones, such as the greater discretionary power of local judges and the application of pardon to a wider range of cases in eighteenth-century England than in sixteenth-century France. In sixteenth-century France, favor cut through the system to the advantage of the powerful, but it was by no means the only factor operating. Pardon often brought peace among equals and sometimes assisted the poor against the rich. The most consistent winner was probably monarchical authority, but in a way that did not erase the subjects' understanding of how pardons were crafted.

named Sainct-Aignan, does everything possible to conceal the fact of a premeditated murder (compromising a witness, burning the body, hastening the accomplice out of the kingdom) and sends to the chancellor for grace with a false story about a night intruder, whom he slew outside his wife's chamber "more in anger than in reason." But the false story does not make its way, because the father of the victim appeals to the Duke and Duchess of Alençon (that is, to Marguerite herself, once married to the duke), and they warn the chancellor not to issue the letter of remission. Sainct-Aignan and his wife flee to England and in their absence are condemned to death and to heavy fines; but the attorney ingratiates himself so by his services to Henry VIII that the English king intercedes with François Ier for a remission. Back in Alençon, Sainct-Aignan pursues his evil ways, turning to magic "to seek his good grace" with the king and chancellor and to get revenge against his enemies, including the Duchess. He is discovered and condemned to death with the king's approval, but Marguerite intervenes and has his penalty commuted to life in the galleys.[80]

Things turn out all right in the end from the Queen's point of view, but her tale shows nostalgia for the days in which dukes and duchesses had the full privileges of granting or withholding pardon in their dominions. And, though the *Heptaméron* version of what happened would eventually spread to many readers of the printed book, Sainct-Aignan's version remains inscribed in the chancellery registers, a testimony to the terms on which pardon was won.*

*The letter of remission for Michel de Sainct-Aignen (*sic*), dated July 1526, gives a vivid and curious account of the homicide (AN, JJ239, 48ᵛ–49ʳ; published, with incorrect call number, in Marguerite de Navarre, *L'Heptaméron des Nouvelles*, ed. A. J. V. Le Roux de Lincy and Anatole de Montaiglon, 4 vols. [Paris, 1880], vol. 4, pp. 214–17). Sainct-Aignen portrays his victim, the solicitor Jacques Dumesnil, as maliciously betraying his hospitality, turning his wife against him, getting a chambermaid to let him into her bedroom so he can sleep with her, and plotting his murder by poison and other means (Marguerite portrays young Dumesnil as an honorable lover, disappointed in the wife and with no ill intention toward her husband). Sainct-Aignen portrays his high-born wife as mostly resisting the liaison with Dumesnil and as unaware of anything connected with the death of her former lover (we'll see in Chapter 3 how Marguerite depicts the lady). In the supplicant's tale, Dumesnil comes to his house masked and in wild disguise, hides in a wardrobe, and is discovered by Sainct-Aignen's servant when he goes to get his master's night clothes (Marguerite has the murderers hiding in the wardrobe, waiting to attack the unwitting Dumesnil). Dumesnil comes out, sword bared, and in the fight that ensues, Sainct-Aignen finally recognizes who he is and "de chaude colle" gives him two or three blows. Before he expires, Dumesnil asks the supplicant's pardon for his wickedness.

The attack of Bonaventure Des Periers is much more straightforward. In his *Joyeux Devis*, he tells of a clever thief of Issoudun who, condemned to death for his crimes and on his way to the gallows, saw a seigneur in the vicinity, "by whose means he obtained his grace from the king for having spat out some words in roasted Latin, which, though they weren't understood, made people believe he was some man of service." His penalty remitted, he was sent off to Newfoundland by the king and returned as much a robber as he went.[81] The flowering of real remission stories depended on a society that could live with all of these fictions.

Not surprisingly, this laxity was unsatisfactory to some Calvinist observers. During the Wars of Religion, they mounted a critique of pardons that started with the supplicant's soul and ended with the practice of the state. The argument appeared in a news account of a parricide in Châtillon-sur-Loing in 1565, published by a Reformed printer of Orléans.[82] It tells about the hatter's son Jean Guy, whom we met in the last chapter. He slew his father with a sword when the latter came to beat him, his father pardoned him before he died, and Jean said when arrested that he had not intended to kill him, "that his father's anger alone had been the cause." Jean was promptly condemned to death by the court at Châtillon, specifically, to be executed in a fashion suitable to the atrocious crime of parricide: to have his right hand cut off, to be branded on the chest, and then to be hanged from his feet and strangled by a heavy stone attached to his neck. Encouraged by another prisoner, Jean decided to appeal, and we can see from the story that he had formulated—his father had precipitated himself upon his sword—that he was moving toward a remission request, unlikely though it was to be granted where a father had died at a son's hands. While awaiting removal to Paris, he was kept in the tower of the castle of Admiral de Coligny, the great leader of France's Reformed cause. Visited by the daughter and the wife of the Admiral, the household tutor, and the local pastor, Jean was persuaded to repent truly for his parricide, to confess his fault to God and ask His pardon.

What was to be the outward sign of his conversion to the Reformed religion? That he not appeal his case, not seek royal mercy, but recognize that he deserved a death even more painful than that to which he had been condemned. The pamphlet ends with his execution, singing Psalms and urging the spectators to attend to the

Word of God. He said he needed no blindfold for his eyes, though the executioner insisted on it because it was part of the law; he put his right hand out to be cut off as simply "as if he had been at the barber's" and remained tranquil of face throughout his torment. Jean Guy's constancy was God's work, the writer concluded, a sign that He had answered his prayers.

The concern here was first with Guy's salvation. For him to seek human remission would mean telling a false or dubious story and benefiting from a this-worldly indulgence that fed sin. This was of a piece with the deceptions of Catholic confession and the priest's absolution. (As Calvin had said in his *Institutes*, confession was a hypocritical business that concealed the abyss of internal sinfulness, while providing incidents that priests could enjoy swapping with one another, "like telling pleasant stories"—"comme de faire plaisans comptes.")[83] The Christian man like Guy must accept full responsibility for his wrongful actions before the world and let God pardon him. The implication is that human sovereigns, rather than imitating the merciful God, should be wary lest they encroach on His providential pardon.

This was in fact what the Venerable Company of Pastors of Geneva was saying to the government of that republic in the last part of the century. In Geneva one did not write formal letters of remission; appeals from the decisions of the judges on the Small Council went to the Council of Two Hundred, which had the right to pardon, and sometimes the Small Council decided on grace as well.[84] The government was not lavish in its mercy: one refugee "meriting whipping or even death for his blasphemies . . . and excesses" was given his grace in 1563 only on condition that he become the city executioner.[85] But the Councils went too far for the pastors in wishing to pardon banished adulterers and to give grace to a man who had committed a murder before coming to Geneva, though he had served the republic loyally since. "Had not God granted the magistrate the power to give grace without exception?" the Councils asked. "No," the pastors answered, "that is reserved to Him alone." The Councils could rightfully pardon in specific cases not touched by divine and universal law, but never in violation of such law.*

---

*In sermons on Deut. 19, given in 1555, Calvin defined what kind of homicide was designated in the Lord's command to allow sanctuary to "Whoso killeth his

Murder with premeditation was a capital crime; did Messieurs think they were "sovereigns above God and the laws He has granted?" They could best serve the public interest by working within the frame of justice, making punishments more or less moderate and forms of execution more or less severe as the case deserved.[86]

In the Protestant city-state, Pastor Beza warned against pardon tales and wanted the criminal's mercy to come mostly from the Lord. Instead of plausible stories and royal grace, he hoped for honest Christians, and just and sometimes clement magistrates. Calvin had set out the guidelines for such a position decades before.[87]

The pastors' view reflects an important strand in Reformed sensibility, not a fully realized program. In France, Huguenots still sought letters of remission; in Geneva, the Council of Two Hundred accorded grace to the one-time murderer and then banished him.[88] Nonetheless, the Protestant end of Jean Guy makes an interesting comparison with an old and popular Catholic belief about miracles at executions. When the condemned person survived the execution, everyone took this as a sign of God's pardon for the crime or of God's revelation of the accused's innocence, either directly given or won through the intercession of the saints. The model was well known through the much circulated *Golden Legend*, in which Saint Jacques sustained a young Compostella pilgrim on the gibbet for 36 days after he had been falsely convicted of theft and hanged in Toulouse.[89] In the sixteenth century such miracles found their way into journals, like the one about a young Angevin in Paris in 1528, who claimed he had buried a man without knowing he had been killed by his wife and her lover. Condemned to death as a murderer, the Angevin came down from the gallows still breathing, and, when the executioner tried to cut his throat, the spectators attacked the hangman as a traitor and bore the saved man to the Carmelite church. It turned out he had prayed to the Carmelite's statue of Our Lady

---

neighbor ignorantly, whom he hated not in time past." This right was limited to the person who has killed involuntarily, "in what is called an accident" ("de cas d'aventure, qu'on appelle"—in fact, nothing is fortuitous, he went on; all is guided by God). This did not include homicide in hot anger: "a murder committed in chaude cholere, as it's called, is not excusable, and the earth remains polluted until it is punished." (Jean Calvin, *Sermons sur le Deutéronome*, in *Opera Omnia*, ed. G. Baum, E. Cunitz, and E. Reuss [Corpus Reformatorum, 55; Brunswick, 1884], vol. 27, sermon 112, p. 541; sermon 113, p. 563.)

and she had kept him alive. Because of the Virgin's action, the king then gave him a remission.[90]

The account of Marguerite Pascal, a chambermaid in a town of Lorraine in the opening years of the seventeenth century, was published in a pamphlet, and who knows whether its author really witnessed what he wrote in his *Discours veritable*. Out of revenge for being thwarted in seduction and rape, a gentleman had killed a little girl in Marguerite's charge and then accused her of the act. On the ladder to the gallows, she spoke of her innocence and, in good Counter-Reformation fashion, prayed directly to God: "'By all your power, let the people here assembled know the truth.' The minute she was thrown [from the ladder], the rope unwound till she was on the ground with no harm done." The gentleman was tried and beheaded, and Marguerite became a nun.[91]

The miracles of the young Angevin and Marguerite Pascal were kinder than the Lord's assistance to Jean Guy, and they fitted more comfortably with royal pardons. They generated narratives the Protestants would have found superstitious. Yet in a curious way they responded to the same tensions that underlay the conversion account of the young hatter who killed his father: in all three cases the Lord's decision stood above the king's, and it was assumed that when God was the listener, He could know that the tales He heard were true.

Sixteenth-century French readers, writers, and listeners clearly had an appetite for stories about crime quite apart from situations where they had to talk about their own offenses or misadventures. I want to conclude this chapter by asking to what extent remission tales or their motifs fed the wider literature of pamphlet and published nouvelle or story. Did it make a difference that the literary tale was told by someone not in principle engaged in self-defense? Was attention called to the nature of truth-telling and/or the ambiguities of royal pardon? Certainly Renaissance rhetorical theory would have expected a different product, contrasting, as had Aristotle, what could be put in and left out of speech depending on whether it was intended to influence a judge or to interpret an event. Thus Montaigne said about a book of *Memoirs* on the reign of François Ier, it is rather a "plaidoyer," a plea, than an "histoire."[92]

The details about remission events were not hard to come by. Told to secretary and clerk, master of requests and chancellor, to king and privy council, judge and jailer; repeated and challenged and restated in different jurisdictions; circulated and evaluated in the milieus of supplicant and victim—remission stories were part of a storehouse from which people could draw, if they wished, for a village scolding, a sermon, a moral lesson, or a literary tale. Curiously enough, apart from the accounts of miraculous survivals at the gallows, pardon tales as such figure very little in the numerous crime pamphlets of sixteenth-century France, which range in subject from documentable crimes to archetypical slayings.[93] Rather than end in mercy, these pamphlets end on the scaffold where the author can stress how the Lord intervenes in the world to punish murder or miraculously to stay an assassin's knife (as in 1594, when Pierre Barrière found himself unable to kill Henri IV at mass at Saint Denis). If the murderer is still alive on the last pages, it is because he or she has escaped for the moment, but "God will make the stones speak to reveal them." The crimes are planned, their cruelty spelled out; they allow the writer to warn of the dangers of the Evil Spirit or of the Jesuits or of a misspent youth. They have irony but little humor in them, though we do find the remark about a Franche-Comté werewolf murderer that he ate the flesh of one of his victims "even though it was Friday." In the cases where there is repentance before execution, it underscores the perils of vicious parents or of the temptations of the flesh or of gambling.[94] Now we might argue that a good remission tale published as a *fait divers* could also attest to the bad consequences of gambling, but its force would depend on the sorrows of the fortuitous or the deep regrets at killing a friend. Sixteenth-century pamphlet writers wanted something clear-cut, with exemplary punishment and the privileged last words of the condemned. A grateful supplicant and a merciful king were not persuasive enough as a finish.

Yet there are a few interesting ways in which pardon tales and crime pamphlets overlap. They were both somewhat one-sided in characterization; self-defense and moral defense could lead to similar craft. The pamphlet ordinarily constructed a narrative about the crime and the criminal and used concrete details and sometimes even excerpts from the legal records (if such there were) to convince the reader that the events really happened.[95] Like the remission tale, the *fait divers* operated within a double field of belief and doubt.

Let us look at two examples, one close in style to a remission letter, the other not. In 1576, Martial Deschamps, a physician of Bordeaux, published an *Histoire tragique et miraculeuse*, telling how he was robbed and left for dead in a pond in Berry three years earlier by a faithless priest and two hired assassins. A first-person narrative addressed by Deschamps to the king, it is like a ghost's answer to a wrongly granted remission—and, indeed, Deschamps may have feared his enemies were going to seek one. The body of the story begins with a quarrel over property between two widowed relatives of Deschamps and the violent Gaspard Foucault, Sieur de Beaupré. Suspicious that the women are being betrayed to Foucault by their own attorney, Deschamps begins his own legal sleuthing, interviewing tenants and the like. Foucault conspires to have him ambushed and his papers seized after he and his party leave a country inn one November day. Even in this mercenary aggression, anger is seen as a fuel: "all enflamed . . . [the assassins] began to air their anger and fury . . . 'We'll teach you to sue gentlemen.'" But rather than killing Deschamps, they leave him in a pond in the dark of night tied to his companion. Praying to God, the two shivering men cut the ropes with their teeth, make their way out of the woods, and are saved by poor peasants, who warm them in straw and ticking. They finally arrive in peasant garb in Châteauroux, and a couple of days later the news of their survival interrupts the celebrations of Foucault.

Deschamps' account is full of suspense and nice touches (the list of the learned books in his stolen trunk, the deaf peasant woman who chases them away as thieves when they first come out of the woods). It is very much part of the world of storytelling, of verifiable or plausible fact, that we have met in the letters of remission. But as an "histoire miraculeuse" as well as "tragique," it is given a frame different from the king's mercy: it was God's providence that saved Deschamps on that cold November night.[96]

Our second example, the *Histoire merveilleuse et veritable Des homicides, voleries, et assassinats infinis et detestables, commis par le Capitaine la Noye*, appeared at Lyon during the reign of Henri IV and is close to a moral tale or folktale. The only contextual facts offered in it are the place of the action, a village near the seemingly invented Géant-sur-Loire, and the date of the execution, March 3, 1608. Except for

Captain La Noye, no one else in the *Histoire* has a name. La Noye is a hotelkeeper, who out of avarice convinces his wife, children, and servant to help him rob and kill the travelers who stay the night at their lodging. The account opens evoking another such violation of hospitality in the long-distant "time of Louis VII." La Noye's undoing is his murder of the young cattle merchant who has come to woo his daughter. When the lad's parents try to find out what has happened to him, his fellow merchants reveal where he went after the fair. Other evidence mounts—the bread baked on the fire in which the suitor's body was burned starts to bleed when purchased and cut—and the whole family is finally arrested, condemned, and burned alive.[97]

The *Histoire merveilleuse et veritable* is brief and quite absorbing, with some attention to the conflicting feelings of the daughter, but it is an exemplary tale without roots in time or place. Not surprisingly, it was retold two years later as a *True Discourse*, a *Discours au vray*, about one Captain La Noue, who now kept his hotel on the road between Bayonne and Bordeaux and was burned with his family June 7, 1610.[98] Pardon tales, scrutinized by the chancellery and fought over before judges, could not be so easily transported from one supplicant to another. Stories in self-defense needed "reality effects" that moral tales could do without.

Let us now leave the world of mostly anonymous news pamphlets and see how remission themes fare in the story collections of known authors and in the more expansive "faicts et dicts" of Rabelais' giants. To begin with, we find two scenes of the prince pardoning, both funny. "Here's a story for our evening talk," wrote the Poitevin merchant Guillaume Bouchet in the late sixteenth century in his *Serée* on the witty last remarks of "The Beheaded and the Hanged." In the days of Louis XI, a poor offender was being led to the gallows and, spying the king, asked him for a gift:

"I know what you're going to ask," said the king, "that I save your life."
"No, Sire, not that, but if I tell you, do you promise on your soul to carry out what I ask?" The king swore he would, provided he not beg for a pardon.
"I pray you only, Sire, to kiss my ass after I'm dead."

He got his grace.[99]

Bouchet's Louis is a good king of the fifteenth-century past, who keeps his promise even to an irreverent subject. Rabelais' Pantagruel

66

is an ideal prince of his own day, who recommends pardon within the limits of the law and with a sense of humility about how difficult it is for any man to make just decisions. He is called upon by the Parlement of Myrelingues to give sentence on Judge Bridoye, who has been deciding cases for 40 years by a throw of the dice. All of them have turned out well except the last case, but Bridoye explains this is only because his eyes have got so bad he misread the dice. Pantagruel says pardon is in order on the grounds of old age, simplicity, and the good sentences he has given over the years, all excuses "granted in our laws." Afterwards he and his companions talk about the perplexities facing a good judge—contradictory laws, lawyers who turn black into white—and conclude that a throw of the dice by a simple and sincere man allows God to manifest his will.[100] The fortuitous is not just excusable; it is welcome.

Both Bouchet and Rabelais explode the conventions of the letter of remission in these portrayals of the prince. This is not the way the king would tell it, and it is not even certain the king would laugh if he heard these tales.

But what about the supplicant's view of the matter? It turns out that though letters of remission and nouvelles use the same narrative devices, there are not many literary stories that replicate the supplicant's exact predicament: an unexpected situation to which a good man responds with angry and/or legitimate defense and for which he must make amends and ask pardon. Certain moments in the pardon tale are echoed often—specifically, the unpredictable eruption of angry violence against an innocent party—but they lead to other outcomes. For example, in the *Grand Parangon des Nouvelles Nouvelles* by the saddler-storyteller Nicolas de Troyes, a page, garrisoned with the soldiers in Chalon-sur-Saône, slays a dog that barks at his horse, then gets into a quarrel with the dog's master, a beloved painter, who protests indignantly at what the page has done. At this point the story might have forked into a pardon tale, with the painter in hot anger killing the page, his neighbors defending him when arrested (garrisoned soldiers were not popular), and his being granted remission. But what kind of a humble ending would that have been for this excellent painter and where would it have brought sufficient intrigue? Instead, the page runs his sword through the painter, is denounced by the neighbors, and is condemned by the judge to be hanged. The tale ends as a story of a good judge, who calls all the citizens to arms to prevent the garrison from seizing their comrade from the executioner's hands.[101]

The pardon plot may have presented the same problem to Renaissance authors as it did to supplicants: it left the hero on his knees.* Better to use a revenge plot put into motion by long and grandiose anger; either the hero gets away with the revenge or, as on the tragic stage, dies after the action.[102] Marguerite de Navarre was among the few who gave a pardon ending to a revenge story: in the twenty-third nouvelle of her *Heptaméron*, a Périgord gentleman kills his brother-in-law in sudden angry sorrow, wrongly believing that he is avenging his sister's death, and then, as we saw a few pages back, is granted a Good Friday remission. But the nouvelle centers on the sister and her husband; it is their actions and the Franciscan who tricked them that are debated by the listeners after the story is told, not whether the brother behaved in the right way. The interesting problem is why the sister could not forgive herself (we'll come back to her in the next chapter), not why the brother got his remission, which the Queen of Navarre assumes is properly given.[103] One of the things that can happen to a pardon tale when it is written by an author rather than a supplicant is that the latter is displaced as subject.

There are, however, two treatments of angry men that allow us to

---

*One great story from the past that was circulating in sixteenth-century France did not leave a pardoned hero in such a stance, but it came from a very different polity and religious culture: Sophocles's *Oedipus the King* and *Oedipus at Colonus*, available to those few who could read Greek and, by mid-century, to those who could read Latin (Latin editions of Sophocles's *Tragedies*: Venice, 1543, Paris, 1557). Oedipus's account to Jocasta of how in sudden anger he slew a man who outraged him at the crossroads reads like a perfect remission tale. And at Colonus, in asking for sanctuary on holy ground, he stresses his innocence in killing his father, Laius. But Oedipus is not a humble supplicant to Theseus; he is an exile with a "desire" for Theseus to fulfill, a man "endowed with grace," who offers Theseus and Athens the gift of himself (*Oedipus at Colonus*, trans. Robert Fitzgerald, in Sophocles, *Three Tragedies* [Chicago, 1954], ll. 574–77, 287). Given sanctuary, hospitality, and protection, Oedipus dies borne off to the realm of the gods; his bones will bring safety and benefit to Athens in the future. The sixteenth-century commentator on the play, Joachim Camerarius, interpreted the reception of Oedipus in terms of the "humanity" of Theseus and the Greek institutions of hospitality (Sophocles, *Tragoediae Septem* [in Greek] [Geneva: Henri Estienne, 1568], "Commentatio," pp. 194–95). This way of constructing a supplication and the destiny of a pardoned person would not come readily to a sixteenth-century teller of nouvelles. In the 1550's, the young Joseph Scaliger wrote a now-lost "Tragedy of Oedipus" (*Autobiography*, trans. G. W. Robinson [Cambridge, Mass., 1927], p. 30); it would have been interesting to see how he handled the themes of angry men, self-defense, and pardon.

see more fully how circulating recitals of fight and pardon were taken up and reinterpreted by writers. The first is a comic episode from the *Propos Rustiques* of Noël du Fail, published in 1547, when he had just finished his legal studies and was about to begin his long career as lawyer, then judge in the Parlement of Rennes.[104] The tale concerns a New Year's quarrel in which a clever peasant named Mistoudin revenges himself against a pugnacious band from another village led by Maistre Pierre Baguette.

Let us hear first, for comparison, a New Year's fight in the Berry, recounted for his letter of remission some ten years earlier by a young peasant named Benoît Dorgnat. (Du Fail himself may well have heard this story in some form, since the letter was sent for ratification to Bourges, where he became a law student.)[105] Benoît and his friends were joyfully collecting the *aguilanneuf* (literally, the mistletoe), by which term was meant the customary New Year's serenading of neighbors with songs and bagpipes in return for gifts of chicken, ham, and other food.[106] They were equipped with staffs and pitchforks only to protect themselves from dogs and to cross streams on a dark night. Meanwhile a group of rowdies—"quarrelsome types . . . with a bad reputation"—led by Gros Jean Pornyn had been taunting them and, despite gracious answers from the revelers, suddenly attacked with swords and other weapons. Benoît and his comrades responded in kind—it was here that he compared himself to Saint George with a duty to self-defense—and he gave Pornyn two blows with his pitchfork, from which he died not long after. Fearing the rigor of justice, Benoît fled the region, etc.[107]

In du Fail's story, mixing as always made-up names and places with real ones from his Breton countryside,[108] it is the aguilanneuf collectors who are asking for trouble, even when they say they are not. (And indeed New Year's collecting often did have more of a threatening air than Benoît Dorgnat cared to admit.) They are armed with pitchforks and a few old rusty swords, and, in between playing the fife and tambourine and amassing sausage and ham, Maistre Pierre shows off his blade—"there's a blow for which a remission won't be given" or "[with this one] be sure to say 'Je ne vous demande rien.'" When they meet Mistoudin on the road, he says he has nothing on him for aguilanneuf, but invites them please to come to his house for gifts and a drink. Maistre Pierre snaps, "Do you want to send us a league away for a lump of lard?" and hits at him with a knife. Mistoudin flees swearing revenge; tearfully tells everything to his wife who makes light of it; and "en cholere," "outragé," plots an ambush with his brother. They wait by a pond they know the band must pass; the brother raises the plank once Maistre Pierre and his men are over, and Mistoudin, dressed in a shroud with his scythe in hand, arises in the mist like the dead. Terrified at the ghost, the band fall into the water trying to escape, and Mistoudin and his brother depart—laughing—with all their aguilanneuf. And the outcome? One new village song at the expense of Maistre Pierre's band, and two new lawsuits (one for theft, the other for battery) brought by either side and likely to be settled by the next session of Parlement.[109]

Du Fail's comic pen exposes some of the illusions in remission stories, even though Mistoudin's revenge is a ghostly one, scaring Maistre Pierre to death rather than killing him. Remission is talked of as a game of allowed and disallowed blows and a mere show of appeasement. Mistoudin, though a sympathetic character, is caught exaggerating to his brother: "he added and subtracted, as a man recounts a quarrel, giving more color where he's most favored, making the case better." Maistre Pierre's bragging is found to be a sham; Mistoudin's anger makes his wife laugh. Du Fail's narrative of the village quarrels shows the gap between what happened and what people say happened. There is one thing that may be submerged, however, in the lawyer's comedy: the laughter—the wife's, du Fail's, the reader's—makes it hard to hear the serious claims for peasant honor that we know did exist from their own actions and reporting.[110]

Our second example is tragic: the tale of Romeo and Juliet. Whether told in its Italian originals or in its French and English redoings, it displayed fortune's works in love and anger both, elders crossing the young through marriage and through feud. Readers will quickly see the possibility of remission motifs in the story of "fortune's fool," even though the pardon is hoped for and/or expected rather than received. (Indeed, if Romeo had received it, the tragedy would have been nipped in the bud.) Of the two accounts we will look at, one expresses no doubts about the possibility of a truthful remission tale and a merciful but clear-eyed prince; the other cuts deep into the questions of anger, homicide, pardon-seeking, and the state.

The story of Romeo and Juliet became known to French readers in 1559, when Pierre Boaistuau included it in his translation of six of Bandello's novellas, giving them the fresh new title of *Histoires Tragiques*, Tragic Histories.[111] Like Bandello, he assured his readers the events recounted really happened—an "histoire tres-veritable"— but he also embellished the Italian text. Lawyer that he was, Boaistuau made some changes in the feud-homicide-pardon axis of the story, but they do not add to the troubles of his characters. Against a background of recent legislation punishing clandestine marriage in France, he used disobedience to parents rather than chaude colle to complicate the plot.[112]

The story opens with the Capellets-Montesches feud in a temporary lull; the fight between Rhomeo and Julliette's cousin Thibault breaks out a month or two after the young couple has been secretly married, that is, "at Eastertide, for bloodthirsty men are accustomed to do their wicked works on feast days." Rhomeo walks into the street battle and tries to make peace—"My friends, it's time our quarrels stopped." He responds with indignant violence to Thibault only after the latter has insulted him furiously and almost cut off his head. Once Thibault is slain, Rhomeo takes refuge with Friar Laurens; a trial is held with witnesses and claims from both sides; and the lord of Verona and his council decide that "because Rhomeo had killed another in self-defense, he would be banished from Verona forever." When the agonized Julliette begs to accompany Rhomeo into exile, dressed as a male servant if necessary, he dissuades her by saying that her father will track them down and he will be punished as an abductor and she as a disobedient daughter. He reassures her that he can get his banishment revoked in a short time. Up to this point, Boaistuau's tale could serve as a remission request for Rhomeo; French readers, familiar as they were with pardon practice, would expect it to be granted.[113]

At the end of the tragic history, the tale of the young lovers is told again before a public court of magistrates and citizens by Friar Laurens, who must explain why he was found with their corpses in the Capellets' vault. With his account "verified" by witnesses and by Rhomeo's letter to his father, there follow the sentences recommended by the lord of Verona or by the court: banishment for Julliette's nurse, because she had concealed the clandestine marriage, "which if she had revealed it in season would have brought a great good"; hanging for the apothecary who had sold Rhomeo the poison; and no prosecution or infamy for Friar Laurens in recognition of his past good life and service to the republic. It is only after all the legal questions have been tidied up that Boaistuau tells of the tears of the Capellets and Montesches, which melt their anger into reconciliation.[114]

There are several things that might explain Boaistuau's untroubled handling of remission themes in his "History . . . of the Two Lovers." Perhaps it was due to his intention to make this, in the words of one critic, "the clearest example of the tragedy of Fortune"; there should be no muddying of the waters with possible responsibility, uncertain stories, or imperfect sentencing. Perhaps it was a larger and prudent commitment to a way of portraying law and sovereignty: Boaistuau had studied law with an important philosopher of sovereignty, Jean de Coras, and was soon to present his *Histoires Tragiques* to the Queen of England.[115] But whatever the case, he was accepting the world of remission, royal justice, and mercy as a fixed, understandable frame for the story.

Across the channel, in Shakespeare's grander tragedy, our archival plots receive their most complex treatment.[116] The legal application of pardon in Elizabeth's England was not quite the same as in France, as we shall see, but the narrative and moral issues were alike. Shakespeare's *Romeo and Juliet* draws on the world of homicides and pardon pleas, but gives it multiple frames by which to be understood.

Shakespeare's prologue states the ancient and still glowing grudge between the Capulets and Montagues, and the play opens with the Capulet servants Sampson and Gregory not going about their business innocently, but talking about anger—"I mean, an we be in choler, we'll draw"—and siding with their masters against the Montagues and their men. When the latter enter, Sampson and Gregory pick a fight, while trying to trim their language to the law ("No, sir, I do not bite my thumb at you, sir. But I bite my thumb, sir"). They clash with their swords, Romeo's friend Benvolio enters and tries to stop them, the Capulet nephew Tybalt rushes in expressing his hate, and a street melee ensues. Citizens finally end the fray, and the prince of Verona denounces the "pernicious rage" of the fighters

72

and the "canker'd hate" of old Capulet and Montague, threatening the fathers, "If ever you disturb our streets again, / Your lives shall pay the forfeit of the peace."[117]

The next encounter is at the Capulets' feast, where Romeo and Benvolio decide to go in mask as uninvited guests. Though Romeo enters the feast with premonition and Benvolio with some irreverence, it is the comparison of beauties they intend, not a fight. We remission readers know, however, that uninvited guests are a harbinger of trouble: Tybalt recognizes Romeo's voice, wants to kill him on the spot, and is prevented from doing so only by very strong language from his uncle. Tybalt makes his plans—"Patience perforce with wilful choler meeting / Makes my flesh tremble"— and sends Romeo a letter of challenge the next morning.[118]

The great fight scene of Act III begins, as in Act I, with talk about anger and quarrels. Benvolio tells Mercutio they should go in because the Capulets are abroad ("for now, these hot days, is the mad blood stirring"), whereupon they banter about which is the less quarrelsome. Mercutio's teasing is a succession of parodic remission tales: "thou hast quarrelled with a man for coughing in the street, because he has wakened thy dog . . . and yet thou wilt tutor me from quarrelling." Tybalt arrives, and he and Mercutio exchange taunts, while Benvolio begs that they retire. Romeo arrives and is insulted by Tybalt as a "villain," "a boy." When Romeo remains pacifying, speaking of a mysterious reason for his love, Mercutio draws his sword, shocked at such "dishonorable submission." Tybalt then draws, and, as Romeo tries to stop the fight, reminding them of the prince's order, Tybalt gives Mercutio a fatal blow under Romeo's arm.

It is only then that Romeo gets angry. Suddenly it seems to him his love for Juliet has made him "effeminate" and "lenient." "Fire-eyed fury be my conduct now," he says, returns Tybalt's challenge and slays him in a fight. At Benvolio's urging—"Romeo, away, be gone! . . . The Prince will doom thee death / if thou art taken"—he flees.

The scene closes with a judgment. The prince asks Benvolio, "Who began this bloody fray?" and the answer constitutes a supplication for Romeo. "Tybalt," says Benvolio, and exaggerating Romeo's efforts to appease (Benvolio pictures him with "knees humbly bowed" before Tybalt), he also neglects to mention that

Mercutio had drawn first. "He is kinsman to the Montague," Lady Capulet objects, "Affection makes him false. . . . Romeo slew Tybalt, Romeo must not live." The prince decides to fine the fathers heavily and to exile Romeo. He wants no tears or prayers: "Mercy but murders, pardoning those that kill." Friar Lawrence later points out to the weeping, railing Romeo that banishment is in fact mercy in this situation ("thy fault our law calls death"), and that someday he can beg pardon of the prince and be allowed to return.[119]

Shakespeare's scenes of young men's quarrels reproduce the main lines of the French quarrels we have been hearing about, with similar settings, words, motifs, and denouements. If the servants' fight is portrayed with comic caricature rather than with the earnestness that we can get in servants' tales in the archives,[120] still Shakespeare can suggest that these outbursts are of a piece, whether the actors are high-born or low. Anger is, of course, the essential fuel to keep the feud going, both Tybalt's constant fire and the "mad blood," the chaude colle, of the supplication texts.[121]

But "hot anger" does not serve as a sufficient excuse for pardoning, neither for the prince of Verona nor, for that matter, for the English law, which was narrower in its definition of excusable homicide than the French. Since the thirteenth century, English pardons had been granted in two forms: "pardons of grace," given at the king's discretion and usually for a payment or in consideration of past or future military service (Parliament tried to insist that these not be given for a premeditated murder or ambush); and "pardons of course," given at the request of an individual and at the recommendation of a jury when the homicide was legally excusable—that is, committed in self-defense or accidentally. Self-defense was interpreted *strictly*: the slayer must have tried first to do everything possible to escape, must have had his back against the wall. The result, as Thomas A. Green has shown so well, was much crafting of pardon tales over the centuries, in which homicides described as hot quarrels in the coroners' rolls turn out as self-defense stories or accidents in the juries' enrollments. Adulterers are not slain in the act; they get out of bed and strike the husband first.[122]

At the time Shakespeare wrote *Romeo and Juliet*, the definition of excusable (pardonable) homicide remained as narrow as ever, but two changes had occurred in England that help us understand how pardon and pardon tales were viewed in the play and by its audience, even though the tragedy is set in Italy. First, the Tudor monarchs were showing themselves agreeable to legislation that prohibited the discretionary "pardon of grace" in extreme cases like homicide with malice aforethought. In practice, as Lawrence Stone has told us, Elizabeth gave such pardons to aristocratic murderers except when their crimes verged on treason or were outrageous public scandals; but the late sixteenth century was nonetheless a period when great magnates were slowly learning that some violence was inexcusable.[123]

Second, a new legal category had just been created between excusable and capital homicide, namely, manslaughter, which could cover a first-offense homicide committed "suddenly" and (though this was controversial) "in hot blood." Here one had to establish not outward actions of flight, but inner states of mind. A man who had done such a deed and was able to read a "neck-verse" from the Psalms could then "plead clergy"; if his story held up, the punishment would be branding with an M on the thumb and, at the judge's discretion, imprisonment for up to a year. The rate of "pardons of course" for homicide, with their self-defense claim, went down; the manslaughter verdicts went up. The accounts given of homicides changed accordingly.[124]

For the moment in England, the field of mercy and pardon was contracting in regard to homicide, that of law and discriminating punishment expanding.[125] It is in this setting that Shakespeare stages homicides where the wounds and gaps are in the open. The actions of the duellist Tybalt, the hot-blood Mercutio, and the self-defending Romeo, which suppliants and judges would struggle to distinguish, here frankly overlap, Tybalt's animosity contaminating Romeo's innocence. The tales of violence and the fortuitous vary in their truth status not only with the teller, but with the occasion. Benvolio's reliability is at its lowest when he pleads for Romeo's mercy; Friar Lawrence's at its highest at the end of the play when he offers to take responsibility:

> If aught in this
> Miscarried by my fault, let my old life
> Be sacrificed, some hour before his time,
> Unto the rigor of severest law.[126]

Even the prince, who has the final word, is perplexed to know where mercy lies or where the right line is between punishment and pardon. His threat to execute Capulet and Montague in the event of further violence he does not carry out, but he worries at his "winking at [their] discords." His banishment of Romeo is a kind of mercy that he represents as rigor. At the end we are left in doubt with his "Some shall be pardoned, and some punished." [127] Spectator and reader may have to judge for themselves.

THREE

Bloodshed and the Woman's Voice

Let us begin once again with an archival text: François, by the grace of God king of France, let it be known to all those present and to come that we have received a humble supplication from the relatives of Marguerite Vallée, widow of the late Jacquemin Valenton, living in Villers-le-Sec in Perthois [a village in Champagne], aged about 34, prisoner in the prisons of Vitry in Perthois, Saying that about thirteen or fourteen years ago, she was taken in marriage by the said Valenton, and had always conducted herself honestly in his regard, with no reproach or bad repute to her person, and had devoted herself to taking care of her husband, her children, and her household as best she could, without giving any displeasure to her husband or disobeying him. And from the marriage she had had six children, including six or seven months ago, two girls, twins from the same belly. Nonetheless her husband had always treated her very badly, beating her and outraging her often on different parts of her body with sticks and other things and leaving her terribly bruised and hurt. This beating and wounding went on all the time, every day, so that she often became disturbed, bewildered, and distracted. Many times over the years she, and others for her, went to make an offering and say a novena before Madame Saint Bertha at the Abbey of Aulnoy far distant from Villers and her house, because it was much recommended for persons who were going out of their mind and understanding. But the beating and mistreatment made her fall into despair and often wish she were dead. . . .

Then toward evening on a Saturday, last October 21 [1536], which was about eight days after Marguerite had got up from the birth of her daughters, without her having done or said anything wrong, the late Valenton threw a clay goblet at her and then a clay pitcher which hurt her badly on the arm, and then took a piece of wood and a heavy vessel used for measuring grain and hit her with these and with his fists so that her body, arms, and legs were all bruised . . . and especially her face was black with blood.

To escape danger and peril to her person, already so battered, she fled to the neighbors and showing them her wounds and weeping like a desperate woman, said she wished she were dead. Her neighbors consoled and comforted her as best they could, and taking pity on her two children, tried to talk her into going back to her house. She refused several times saying that she'd rather die than return and that she was just fading away there, desiring her death and her end, and that her husband would kill her with an ax and he'd already threatened her with it.

But out of great pity for her twin daughters whom she was nursing and who were only about three weeks old, they persuaded her to go back with them to her husband's house. There they found him, a man subject to wine and to swearing and blaspheming the name of God; he was lying on a little bed near the fire, the bed on which Marguerite had had her confinement. He began to insult and threaten Marguerite and swear and curse that she had not slept with him for a month. Marguerite, desperate and out of her mind from the beating and violence, said to her husband Valenton, "There's the ax you threatened me with so often. Kill me. Don't make me suffer any more. My life disgusts me. I don't know how to live any more in this state."

After the neighbors had left and Marguerite was alone with her late husband, he went from bad to worse and suddenly got up from the little bed in fury, picked up the ax, and, swearing more than ever, said to Marguerite that he'd keep her from going out of the house and talking. And saying this, he approached her and hit at her with the ax. She turned away his blow as best she could and started to flee. He hurled the ax after her, and it just missed her head. And seeing her husband's rage and that he was running to get the ax and hit her, Marguerite, sick at heart and a desperate woman, turned around and suddenly picked up the ax and, repelling his violence and defending herself, gave Valenton two or three blows. She doesn't know rightly where, for she was so upset by his beating that she didn't know what she was doing. And to escape from her husband's fury, she left the room and, very shaken and not thinking he was badly wounded, went to a neighbor's house to rest.

The next day she heard that people had been to their house and found the door to the room barred from within by pieces of wood and her husband dead inside. And because of this, Marguerite left the scene and wandered through fields and villages in despair, mourning, and displeasure, both because of what people said about her husband being dead and because of her poor children left all alone and especially her little twins who were so young; and she wanted to drown herself, but the people she was walking with kept her from it. And then remembering her children and filled with marvelous regret at leaving them, she decided to go back to see them and take care of them, though along the road she several times tried to throw herself into the water and drown but was always prevented from it.

Then being near Bettancourt, which is next to Villers, she was made prisoner by the officers of the seigneury for the Lord or Lady of Bettan-court and was questioned and confronted with witnesses and her trial was begun before the prévôt of Vitry. Out of fear of Justice, she denied having struck or touched the deceased and made several different denials and con-fessions. . . . Fearing that rigorous prosecution will be made against Mar-guerite Vallée if our grace and mercy are not imparted to her, the suppli-cants, Marguerite and her relatives, [humbly ask for pardon].

In February 1537, François Ier, out of compassion for the children of Marguerite Vallée, especially her little twins, and considering that she had been acting in self-defense against her husband and had always governed herself well in the past, ordered the prévôt of Vitry that she be given royal grace.[1]

The wordy supplication of Marguerite Vallée and her relatives suggests the lengths to which a sixteenth-century woman might have to go, even with the prompting of a royal secretary, to justify or excuse her violence. Whether she will kill herself or her husband is the question throughout. In the many repetitions about Mar-guerite's despair and Valenton's mistreatment (and I have even ex-cised a few so as not to tire the twentieth-century reader), she is never described as angry.[2] In contrast, when a Lyonnais rustic sought pardon for killing his husband-beating wife, he got quickly to the day in May on which she threw a wine bottle, a loaf of bread, and a tureen at him, and reported how he stuck a bread knife in her stom-ach, "in anger, upset and furious."[3]

Not that it was doubted in the sixteenth century that women were susceptible to that deadly sin. "There is no wrath above the wrath of a woman," Ecclesiasticus had said, providing a convenient proof-text for witch-hunting manuals like the *Malleus Maleficarum*. Or one could find the same point made more calmly in Seneca, as Cal-vin did, explaining in his commentary on *De Clementia*, "Where the strength to cause harm is lacking, there blind madness, without self-control, rages and howls."[4] The riotous wife surfaced in prov-erb, story, and ballad, while sixteenth-century woodcuts of wrath (see illustration 6) included women slaughtering in anger as well as men.[5] On a more down-to-earth note, the experienced midwife Louise Bourgeois observed that anger was the source of many of her patients' complaints; they had too much choleric blood in their wombs and it led to infertility or abortion.[6]

79

6. The sin of wrath and its fruits, from Léon Davent, *Les sept péchés capitaux*, after Luca Penni, ca. 1545. Bibliothèque Nationale, Cabinet des Estampes, Da. 67 fol.

The trouble was that women's anger seemed to have few acceptable uses. By the traditional humoral theory, men were hot and dry, and could be led by fiery yellow bile into both angry killing and the quick passion of courageous battle.[7] Women were cold and wet, their anger thickened by phlegm and compromised by melancholy. Their *chole* might not be spent in the heat of the moment, but could last like Medea's fury or like the obstinacy of Montaigne's Gascon women, who "would sooner . . . bite into hot iron than let go their bite of an opinion they had conceived in anger."[8] If a woman's anger erupted into violence, it could be approved in the exceptional case of defending her children or her religion, as in a grain riot or a religious uprising, or her people, as with Judith and Joan of Arc, but most rightful bloodshed was better left to men.[9]

The literary Christine de Pizan, in a fifteenth-century text few of our supplicants would or could have read, tried to make the best of women's problematic relation to violence:

But as for boldness and physical strength, God and Nature have done a great deal for women by giving them such weakness, because at least, thanks to this agreeable defect, they are excused from committing the horrible cruelties, the murders, and the terrible and serious crimes which have been perpetrated through force. . . . Thus women will never receive the punishment which such cases demand, and it . . . would have been better, for the souls of several of the strongest men, if they had spent their pilgrimage in this world in weak feminine bodies.

She did go on to talk about the brave Amazons like Thamaris, who "out of anger over the death of one of her beloved sons," took a cruel though appropriate revenge on the Persian Cyrus.[10] But she did not urge them as models for her own time.

Homicide in genuine self-defense was, of course, permissible to either sex, and sixteenth-century canonists acknowledged that it was not sinful for a woman to kill a man who raped her if she had no other means to escape or defend herself.[11] Still the killing of a husband was particularly hard to justify. It was not petty treason in France the way it was in England, and the jurist Papon commented with just symmetry that no killing was more inhuman and detestable than that between husband and wife.[12] On the other hand, in the hierarchical nature of things, wives were to obey their husbands in patience, and husbands were to correct and govern their wives, moderate beating being permissible. This meant that wives might

have to search more widely to find a language to legitimate a grievance. Husbands could talk about the wife's disobedience fueling
their chaude colle, and wives could talk about their fear—but what
to do about their anger?

The female supplicants of the sixteenth century, whether on the
advice of a royal notary or from their own sense of things, used different strategies to describe their state of mind as they committed
sudden homicide, without ever presenting themselves as unpardonable avenging furies—but also without resorting to the nineteenth-century polarization between the "good" woman and the
angry woman up in the attic.[13] Rather they placed themselves on a
spectrum of affect.* Some reported no trigger of feeling and let
events speak for themselves. Some were like Marguerite Vallée, "so
upset ['troublée,' 'esmeue'], [they] didn't know what they were
doing."[14] Some were "heated up" ("reschauffée," "eschauffée"),
while a woman who killed her grown son over an inheritance quarrel with his brother, acted "in anger ['en collere'] intending only

---

*There is much interesting publication on the expression of women's anger and
aggression in their writing in the nineteenth and early twentieth centuries, especially
in England (see note 13 to this chapter for titles). Anger is either repressed by the
heroines in these texts (or by the authors, when the texts are autobiographical) or is
"indirect and deflected" or "disguised"; or is limited in "sensationalist" novels,
where women almost kill their husbands, but are punished and repentant in the end;
or, as in the case of Jane Eyre, is attributed to a double who lives in the attic, the mad
wife Blanche, who tries to burn her husband Rochester in his bed when Jane re-
presses her anger at him. The sixteenth-century supplicants show a similar discomfort in presenting their anger to notary, king, and judge, but they are less likely to
efface their passions. The difference might be explained by immediate context (hot
anger was in principle a legal excuse for both sexes) or by the social origin of the
supplicants. But there may also be some effect from changing cultural assumptions.
Women were told in the sixteenth century that they were uncontrollably angry, as
they were also uncontrollably libidinous. Even in countering this negative view (as
we will see with Marguerite de Navarre), it was hard to exorcise anger. As the image
of strong and disorderly female desire was being redrawn by the end of the eighteenth century as a diminished sexual appetite that the woman could turn on and off,
so the female's overwhelming wrath was being redrawn as an emotion that the large
middle class of good women could and should control. By the first part of the twentieth century, the relinquishing of aggression was not merely a moral prescription,
but, to the Freud-trained analyst, an ordinary part of growing up for every little girl.
A different trajectory from the sixteenth century is suggested by the cases of two
middle-class women in France toward the end of the nineteenth century: both confessed to "crimes de passion," one killing a man who she claimed tried to rape her ("I
saw red") and the other killing her husband's lover, her former best friend ("I was
strangled with emotion"). Both were acquitted. (Mary Hartman, *Victorian Murderesses* [New York, 1977], chaps. 4, 6.)

to correct him." [15] A peasant wife threw stones at her husband's lover "de chaulde colle," but also "by force of jealousy" ("par force de la Jallosie"), thereby mentioning an emotion that men did not admit in slaying their adulterous wives or their wives' lovers. A husband merely said, as did a merchant apothecary of Tours, that he "had previously forbidden his wife the company of the said Estienne." Honor and obedience were at stake for him, not demeaning jealousy. What self-respecting man would want to present himself like the ridiculous husbands of Rabelais' *Tiers Livre*, eaten by jealousy? [16]

Finally, two women amplified on their anger in ways that show that when women used the formula before king and judge, it was not for them an easy excuse. In Picardy, widow Jeanne de Francastel told how she punished a fourteen-year-old girl, who, to keep herself warm while guarding a clothesline for the washerwomen one January day, had set a fire inside Jeanne's oak tree: her son held the girl's bare legs over the fire while Jeanne said "Va, va, chauffe"— "Go on, go on, warm yourself." Jeanne and her son composed with the girl's father, but then the girl died of her burns. Jeanne explained she had been "incensed, sorry," "mal meue et de chaulde colle" when she saw what was happening to her ancient oak tree. The heat of feeling and action merge in a shameful scene. [17]

In Touraine, Jeanne Mayct's victim was her son-in-law, a man she described as beating her daughter, abusing both her and her husband, and drinking up at the tavern the income from the family fulling mill. One day "in great anger and affliction," she told her servant to kill him and he could have her daughter as his wife. "Right after she'd spoken the words, she returned to her senses. She was over her anger and distressed at what she'd said." She went immediately to her priest to confess and was absolved. Jeanne Mayet presents herself as apologizing for her anger, not acting on it. But, of course, the servant did not forget and ultimately, egged on by the father, threw the son-in-law into the Indre River. [18]

Jeanne Mayet was a widow when she made her supplication to François Ier. In the last sentence of her narrative, she told why: Etienne Mayet had been executed for murder and on the scaffold had absolved her of any responsibility. Here we come to an interesting characteristic of women's pardon tales, or at least of the ones discovered for this study. The women do not ordinarily plead their special "imbécillité" (to use the legal term), the female weakness of mind and will that in judicial proceedings might win acquittal or lighter sentences for certain crimes.* In pardon tales, everyone is a supplicant, and there are "poor simple men" as well as "poor simple women." Nor do the wives fall back on direction from their husbands to kill someone else, though this too could be part of judicial defense in some cases.[19] To win mercy, they account for their behavior without accusing their spouses of capital crimes. Indeed, there are petitions from husband and wife together where their actions are entangled. An Orléans miller and his wife both confess to false testimony about an intruder, given because of threats and bribes and their "simplicity and youth." A poor farming couple living near Châteaudun tell how a neighbor had undone their work in their vineyard and begun to throw stones at the husband; the wife came out of the house at the noise and they gave him blows with staffs and stones.[20] Perhaps the husbands hoped that the presence of the wife would add to the "pity," but the wives did not exploit the presence of the husband to add to their irresponsibility.

Reluctant to use the simple anger formula and likewise reluctant (except when the husband was the one killed) to use the subject-wife formula, the women were thus impelled to be more inventive in crafting their story, to offer more detail to fit the constraints of mercy.

Not that very many French women had occasion to make supplications for pardon. Christine de Pizan was right in her observation: in the medieval period, in the Old Regime, and today, women constitute a much smaller segment of those prosecuted for violent crimes than men. Quantitative studies of indictments or appeals in homicide cases in France and England at various times during the thirteenth through eighteenth centuries show that cases involving

---

*The difficulties caused to women by their wombs were not referred to in either criminal procedure or in remission requests. In any case, the "suffocation of the mother," as hysteria was called, led to paralysis or loss of speech, not violence to others, while premenstrual tension was not described and perhaps not experienced as a serious problem (see Patricia Crawford, "Attitudes Toward Menstruation in Seventeenth-Century England," *Past and Present,* 91 [May 1981]: 47–73). Marguerite Vallée's use of the state of her body—recently up from childbirth and nursing twins—was intended to arouse compassion for her and disapproval of her husband's beating rather than provide an excuse for her behavior.

women range from 7.3 to 11.7 percent of the total.[21] But in six-teenth-century France, they are an even smaller fraction of those getting letters of pardon for their wrongdoing. To give readers a rough idea, out of some four thousand remissions searched espe-cially for this purpose, about 1 percent were sealed for women. Out of a hundred people waiting in the Paris Conciergerie to have their letters ratified from 1564 to 1580, three were women.[22]

There are several conceivable reasons for this low figure,[23] but the most interesting for our present purposes is that the two capital crimes most associated with women—witchcraft and infanticide—were not pardonable. In the case of witchcraft, appellants to the Parlement of Paris got fairer justice (by sixteenth-century stan-dards) than has been traditionally thought: Alfred Soman's new re-search is showing that a significant number were found not to be sorcerers, many of them undergoing torture without confessing, and were released.[24] But seeking mercy meant avowing one's of-fense, as we know, and one could not excuse making a pact with the devil by *chaude colle* or by self-defense (whatever happened in folk tales), while poisoning someone by black magic was hardly un-premeditated. Killing a witch might be remissible,[25] being a witch was not.

In the case of infanticide, defined here as the killing of a newly born,[26] women (and even an occasional man) had been pardoned for it in the fourteenth and fifteenth centuries. The women's tales opened with abandonment to love or seduction and climaxed in an infant's death. An eighteen-year-old said that she had "fainted from the great pain . . . and, coming to, found a male child . . . which had no life"; a nineteen-year-old, that her new husband, discovering her pregnant by her former master, had beat her till she had a stillbirth. But supplicants were not always passive in the death: as one of them said in 1393, "desperate, fearing the vituperation of the world and the blame of her friends . . . [she] tied her garters around the child's throat and stopped its mouth," and another in 1474 said, "fearing the shame of the world and the correction of her parents . . . [she] struck the child's head upon the ground and hid it in the straw." The king was assured that the infants had been baptized by the mother first and that the supplicants were sorrowful and—here the word was used—"repentant."[27]

During the sixteenth century, sentiment hardened against infanticide. From 1495 to 1515 in Metz, Philippe de Vigneulles records cases in his Journal: there the exemplary tale of a young woman made pregnant by a foreign merchant or a priest ends not with her being pardoned, but with her being executed. The little corpses are found in cisterns and wells, the mothers are discovered and burned; one has "une belle repentance" before she dies, her charred body being laid in the street next to an infant carved from wood and a painting of the killing.[28] In the mid-1530's, Nicolas de Troyes writes a nouvelle, not drawn from an earlier story collection, but originating with him, in which a peasant prevents an infanticide in a nearby field and, with the help of the local countess, tracks the fleeing mother down to a Benedictine monastery. The baby is saved, the mother is burned, and the monks are whipped.[29]

In February 1557, Henri II issued a decree on infanticide whose force was to last through the whole Ancien Régime: any infant death following a concealed pregnancy or clandestine childbirth, and with no formal baptism or burial, was presumed to be homicide and punishable by death.[30] Long before that date, however, infanticide was being treated with the rigor of the law. (I have found no letters of remission for this offense in any sixteenth-century register examined. If they exist, they are few and far between.)[31] A royal notary was unlikely to record a tale of infanticide for a pardon letter; a chancellery officer was unlikely to order it or sign and seal it, let alone allow it to be heard for ratification. As for the judges, they were impatient with these cases in any setting: the women were claiming stillbirth and would not change their story even when tortured, and there were rarely witnesses. The Parlement of Paris or Rouen might reduce a death sentence in an infanticide case to whipping and banishment—say, when a confession was not forthcoming—but suggesting or hearing royal letters of remission was another matter.[32]

What might account for this denial of the pardon path, this new reluctance to allow women's shame and desperation to excuse infanticide no matter how free of stain their past reputation? The tightening sexual values characteristic of both religious reform and family strategy in France surely played their role. Contemporary pronouncements on infanticide had more to say about sexual appetite than about the soul of an innocent child. The crime originated in female lubriciousness, they claimed, and then the woman's shame at being found out as a paillarde did the rest. Sixteenth- and early seventeenth-century news pamphlets put such words into the mother's mouth, as in a repentance speech on the gallows in which she accused each part of her body of betraying her into sexual sin and then into killing the fruit of her womb.[33]

In addition, the drama of royal grandeur was not going to be played out in the sixteenth century in extending mercy to infanticide. The unwed mother, widow, or cheating wife who had killed her newborn was both too weak and too wicked for the king's pardon. Family morality and royal majesty were better served by giving her the justice she deserved.

***

Whatever they said in their own circles, the band of women supplicants had to tell other stories to the king in the sixteenth century. As a group, they have somewhat different characteristics from the male supplicants. They are more evenly distributed in age: there is no clustering around a fiery period of youth, especially with the cases of infanticide gone. A young servant who accidentally killed a six-year-old girl in a snowball fight is less typical of the female supplicants than the Parisian linenmaker, married to a mason and with a house full of little children, who accidentally killed her apprentice with a fireplace tool.[34] On the other hand, in regard to status, they are less widely distributed than the men, almost all of them from artisan and village families. Jeanne de Francastel, who burned the girl at her oak tree, was clearly from a prosperous rural household, but there is no equivalent among the women to the numerous country gentlemen who begged the king for pardon. Marie Quatrelivres, the adulterous wife who won abolition of her lifetime imprisonment in a nunnery,[35] was from a prestigious legal family, but there is a gap between her and the wives of sergeants and millers among the supplicants, not to mention the dairymaids and cowherds.

Interestingly enough, the women's supplications do not cohere as often as do the men's around a scenario of occupation or estate. There are Washerwomen's Tales, as we will hear; there are Mistresses' Tales (a Vermandois widow bawls out her farmhand on the manure pile as lazy, costing her more than he's worth, and when he answers back, strikes him with a barnyard tool), and there are Servants' Tales (a priest's servant in Champagne flies to her master as he cries "murder" in the bean garden, and hits his assailant with a stick).[36] But especially there are Wives' Tales and Widows' Tales, where gender rather than social rank sets the stage. Or rather a gender role constitutes the woman's estate, and her account sweeps the facts of work and place into a narrative carried by themes of family, sexual honor, and inheritance.[37]

Whether city dwellers or peasants, the women were surely used to storytelling situations. At the veillées, they were at least as important as the men: the spinning women offering prescriptions and advice "during the long evenings from Christmas to Candlemas" in the *Evangiles des Quenouilles* (The Gospels of the Distaffs) were not just a literary conceit.[38] Indeed, women were represented as turning every meeting into an occasion for swapping tales: at the mill, the washing stream, the fountain; at the baker's, the bathhouse, the back of the church, and around the new mother's bed (see illustration 7). They also gave accounts of the family past to their children and, when they were literate, might even write a family history.[39]

Of course, one may wonder whether they did not watch their tongues in the presence of an attorney or a royal secretary. Were they "modest" in recounting their experience, as theologian Benedicti warned confessors they might be? Or did they speak forthrightly even on intimate matters, as did the peasant Bertrande de Rols in the trial of her impostor husband "Martin Guerre" and the Parisian model Catherine in her criminal case against Benvenuto Cellini "for using her in the Italian fashion"?[40] The situation must have varied from woman to woman, but the resulting supplications show considerable storytelling skill quite apart from the formulas and advice of the secretary and his clerks.

An example of that skill is the supplication of Françoise Pounet, a 35-year-old widow in field service to a peasant family in the Maine: she created a plausible narrative of killing a village youth in a closed pasture, where the only witness was her master's cow. She starts off affirming her honesty and good conduct. The cause of the trouble was one Ambrose Bauldry; he was hanging out with the local soldiers, who frightened her so with their pillaging and raping that she "didn't know what she was doing or saying." One July day, spinning alone in the pasture, she heard the village women in the road calling Ambrose the soldiers' pimp and whoremonger ("macquereau," "houllier"), and she shouted to him from her hedge,

"What wrong have I done you that you want to send me to the soldiers? After the favors ['les plaisirs'] that I've done for you . . . why
bring me dishonor?" A while later he crept into her pasture "all
heated up" and armed with a sword. "With no one there to save her
or to testify to his violence," she supplies the details of her self-
defense with the same vividness as our urinating Gascon notary: his
slaps, her stupefaction, and finally her fatal blows with distaff and
bread knife. Imprisoned and condemned to death, Widow Françoise
pleaded for pardon. Her story has the gaps we have come to expect—What were those past "plaisirs" she had provided him?—but
its verisimilitude, together with support from her master, surely
won her a ratification.[41]

Françoise Pounet's pastoral killing had taken place on an ordinary
summer workday. On the whole, the women's accounts make less
explicit use of ritual and festive contexts than the men's. This can
not be due to any gender-specific preference in all sixteenth-century
storytelling. Rather these are tales of homicide in which wifeliness
and/or woman's sexual honor are at stake, and it is easier to order
and excuse what happened in the setting of her everyday life.

The exception that proves the rule is the Mardi Gras homicide
committed in 1529 by Claudine (her last name is not given), the
eighteen-year-old wife of a villager living near Sens. She begins her
supplication ominously with her husband and his "varlet" Michau
killing one of her chickens for the supper feast, which displeased
her somewhat because she often cooked its eggs. But supper was
full of good cheer, with guests, including a certain Etiennette; and
then everyone but Claudine's husband went to a neighbor's "to finish carnival joyously." In the midst of their games, the varlet Michau
took Etiennette into the alley; Claudine heard her call for help, ran
out, and saw them on the ground. A fight ensued between mistress
and varlet, which ended with him bleeding heavily from the eye.
Claudine finishes her supplication telling how she tried to take care
of him and of her "sadness" at his death.[42]

In this tale, Carnival points the day so that Claudine's killing
seems as much motivated by jealousy as by desire to protect Etiennette. The festive inversion takes the woman out of her house and
into the street, with the potential that she will end up with her legs
spread apart with the wrong man. Mardi Gras is the setting for
adultery, as in one of Philippe de Vigneulles' novellas: the wife hopes

LE CAQVET DES FEMMES

7. Women's conversations in many settings. From *Le Caquet des Femmes*, ca. 1560, Bibliothèque Nationale, Cabinet des Estampes, Tf. 2, fol. 49.

that in the license of masking, she can finally get to her lover.[43] When carnival or festive ritual goes too far for the men into social scandal, the supplicant can reach for a way to excuse himself, as we saw in the tale of the winegrower at the Saint Barbara's day banquet and other cases in Chapter 1. When it holds sexual scandal in store for the woman, there is the chance she will look wrong no matter what she says.

Similarly, the women's pardon tales rarely drew upon the remissible excuse of unexpected drunkenness, of being "surprinse de vin," whether or not their homicides were committed in such a state. Christine de Pizan had long ago claimed that "women by nature be sober," and popular poems of the mid-sixteenth century portrayed wives as rejoicing when Henri II forbade their husbands to drink at the taverns. Of course, the women did drink on their own, and this was sometimes the subject of innocent merriment. But when linked with a crime story, drinking was "against her nature," the beginning of a bad end. A news pamphlet on an incest case described the girl's initial entrapment by "too much wine" and concluded with her being hanged before her father was burned.[44]

In contrast with the difficulties posed to a female supplicant by a festive or vinous setting is a remarkable Wife's Tale by Bonne Goberde. It occurred on Sunday, but the Sabbath made no difference, for it was a fight about preparing supper, which she did every day of the week. It turns out that making meals was a major arena for obedience struggles in sixteenth-century marriage. Two male supplicants killed their wives after such a refusal. One was a Lyon silk weaver, who, returning home to his wife from a Saint Catherine's day feast in the country, asked her to make some carp he'd bought for him and his friends. "To his shame and great dishonor before those who were with him, she would not obey her husband," saying he and his friends could go and eat wherever they wanted. After finally persuading a hotelkeeper to cook the carp, he came back to the house, got angry at his wife when he suspected her of allowing a widow's sexual mischief in an upstairs room, and even angrier when "there returned to his memory her obstinate refusal to prepare the carp." He hit her several blows with the dagger he had taken with him for his Saint Catherine's day revels. When she died, he fled and now seeks remission.[45]

Bonne Goberde's recital is a different matter. Aged 36, she was the wife of one Toussaint Savary, alias Baron, a man not of noble status, but who hobnobbed with seigneurs and captains around his Burgundian village of Arnay-sous-Vitteaux. She builds her defense through a leitmotif of language, gesture, and color, and obedient kitchen work slips into a strange passive homicide:

On Sunday, last May 22 [1540], the deceased Savary invited to sup with him Jean de Lynot, seigneur de Molins, and Thomas de Heriot, seigneur de Cousy, and others from the garrison of Vitteaux and Arnay. He told the supplicant, his wife, that she should prepare the supper for them, and that he'd go about his affairs. Around three o'clock in the afternoon he came back to the house and found Michel Savary, their eighteen-year-old son, lighting the fire for supper and the supplicant cutting the throats of the chickens, which she was going to prepare with other things for supper. Right away he began to get agitated and irate, as was his custom, and said to his son, "You worthless paillard, why haven't you got the supper fixed?" The supplicant spoke up to excuse their son, saying "Baron, my friend, the hour for supper has not yet come" ["Baron, mon amy, l'heure de soupper n'est pas encore venue"]. At her words, the deceased gave his son a big kick on his side, swearing and blaspheming the name, flesh, and mother of Our Lord, and growling that he'd scare him out of his wits. Whereupon Michel ran from his father's presence.

As for the supplicant, she hurried to finish cutting the chickens' throats. The deceased then addressed his wife with harsh and threatening words, to which she responded once again, "Baron, mon amy, don't get so angry. L'heure de soupper n'est pas encore venue. Everything will be ready on time. You were wrong to have beaten our son for no cause."

Without saying a word, the said Toussaint slapped her twice so hard that she fell to the floor. As she got up, the chickens tumbled down, and she had the knife all bloody in her hand, and she said once again that he did ill to beat her when she had done no wrong [note that she concedes in this phrase his right to beat her if she had done wrong]. And then, though she did or said nothing else to displease him, in great fury he took a wooden stake . . . called a "chamberiere," used to hold up the roasting log, and hit her on the side so that she fell stupefied on both her knees and on one hand, the other hand curved above her head still holding the knife. And she said to the deceased that he was wicked to strike her so without cause. He returned to hit her once again, and approaching with force, he met the knife ["rencontra ledit cousteau"], which the supplicant still held above her head, and it pierced his chest just below the heart. And though it was a big pointed kitchen knife, still the wound was marvelously small. . . .

Not thinking her husband hurt, the supplicant got herself up, enormously injured though she was, and believing she was doing the right thing, went into their garden to pick some currants to appease him. Hear-

93

ing noise from the house, she came right back, saw her husband on the ground, and someone said he was dead. Overcome with terror, she fled the country, to which she fears to return, or to any place else in the kingdom.

François Ier accorded her his mercy.[46]

Bonne Goberde said she killed her husband on her knees, a very different posture from that taken by our Lyon silk worker when he did in his wife. But Bonne told a more frightening tale—more frightening even than that of butcher Louis Paisant—with her kitchen knife and bleeding chickens creating mood, a changing motif reminding her, the royal secretary, the chancellery men, and her judges of the danger in the hands of even the best of wives. She also achieved this with an economy missing from Marguerite Vallée's account of slaying her husband Valenton. Remember that opening a pardon tale with a feud or a supplicant's grievance was hazardous, for it could suggest premeditation. But what was a battered wife to do? There had to be both an explanatory background and a sudden homicide in self-defense "without knowing what she was doing." Bonne Goberde found a way out by building Baron's habitual fury into the kitchen drama and her own innocence into her reported words and gestures.

Wives were not always so defensive in seeking mercy for killing their husbands. One last example can serve to introduce a set of pardon tales in which women's action and anger seem as readily justifiable to themselves and to their listeners as men's: those in defense of rightful property claims and inheritance. Jeanne Regnart had lived "peacefully" with her second husband Jean Foucart for many years in their Picard village, until (as she told it) about seven years before, when he began to drink at the taverns and make bad bargains, dissipating their goods, and specifically the goods and property she had brought into the marriage. Her account of the day of his death starts with him drinking at a tavern while she paid their vinegrower, and ends with a fight at their fireplace, in which she rebuked him for his false and silly bargains ("ses faulx marchez et ses sotz marchez") and his expenses, which were driving them to poverty. They came to blows in front of their son and a neighbor (who, of course, could serve as witnesses), he hitting her with a knife and she in "chaulde colle" striking him near the eye with an iron fork. He died and she fled. Jeanne Regnart was a humble supplicant to the king for his pardon, but she was not apologetic to the ghost of Jean Foucart.[47]

If Jeanne Regnart can assume such a tone in connection with killing her husband, all the more understandable are the women striking blows, sometimes at their husband's side, against men seizing their widowed mother's inheritance, their peasant holdings, or their husband's shirts.[48] Here women's indignation did not threaten hierarchy, but supported family property values, deeply held in society at large; and their homicides could be defended with the same kind of story their spouses would use.

When we leave the question of patrimonial property for that of sexual property and sexual honor, male and female pardon tales diverge once again, contrasting both in content and presentation. For husbands the issue was adultery, and they sought royal remission for killing wives found in the act, and even for wives killed while merely being accused of or chastised for adultery.* Their accounts might begin with a craft errand or other good-husbandly business, a supper party or a Twelfth-Night feast, but they often indicate that they had prior knowledge of the wife's behavior.[49] Confident of sympathetic readers, the supplicants were not worried that their homicide might appear premeditated. So barber-surgeon Simon Guy of Lyon told in 1537 how he heard that his wife was being

---

*The reader will recall that one of the two cases where homicide was "excusable" in the sixteenth century was "to avenge the adultery of a wife or daughter, because of the intolerable anguish ["desplaisir"] to him offended" (Jean Papon, *Trias Iudiciel du Second Notaire* [Lyon: Jean de Tournes, 1575], p. 465). When a husband kills a wife and/or her lover caught in the act, "he obtains his grace easily" (Jean Papon, *Recueil d'arrests notables des cours souveraines de France* [Cologny: Mathieu Berjon, 1616], book 22, title 9, p. 1265; Daniel Jousse, *Traité de la Justice criminelle de France*, 4 vols. [Paris, 1771], vol. 3, part IV, title 21, pp. 491–92). Jousse adds, with a citation from the late sixteenth-century Italian lawyer Prospero Farinacci, "it does not appear that the wife who kills her husband surprised in adultery should enjoy the same privilege and it seems she cannot avoid the death penalty." Friar Benedicti reminded the readers of his *Somme des Pechez* that though killing a wife found in the act "is not punished by civil laws, still it is condemned by divine law and in the forum of the conscience." The husband should instead prosecute the wife in the courts (Jean Benedicti, *La Somme des Pechez et le Remede d'iceux* [Paris: Denis Binet, 1595], book 2, chap. 4, p. 111). In Geneva, the greater reserve in granting pardons and the intensive use of the Consistory to investigate and punish adultery presumably cut down on this form of "excusable" homicide. See Appendix B and note 88 to Chapter 2 on the Consistory's reaction to the homicide by Claude Dater of his adulterous wife, which had been pardoned in France.

"carnally enjoyed" by a Luccan banking agent, who frequented their house "under cover of being godparent to their child." Simon took his wife to the grain attic one morning and whipped her with the laces from his hosen (these are the laces, or "aiguillettes," that sorceresses tied to make a man impotent). She cried so loud the neighbors came, but it was too late; she was already "broken in parts of her body." Before she died, so Simon declared to the king, she admitted her fault and made a will in which her husband was her universal heir.[50]

When royal favor was involved, the husband might get pardoned even when there was no ambiguity about premeditation. These were the kinds of remission "against the law of the land" that the chancellery official Pierre de L'Estoile found so hard to take during the reign of Henri III. Of a royal favorite, who had intercepted a compromising letter from his wife and then knifed her at her toilette, he said in his journal: "the ease with which Villequier obtained grace and remission led one to believe that [the murder] was done at the secret command or with the tacit consent of the king, who hated the lady (even though he had long taken advantage of her by the intermediary of her pimp husband) because . . . she had spoken badly of His Majesty in public." But they didn't all get away with it, and L'Estoile drew a vivid portrait of a Huguenot seigneur of Poitou beheaded in 1579 for a planned murder of both his wife and the man who he had heard reliably was her lover. When sentenced, he told his judges that they were all cuckolds, if they looked closely enough, and he had killed so as not to be one. When executed, he refused to be blindfold, joked with the beheader about the sharpness of his sword, and died praying aloud, "in the mode of those of his religion."[51] A responsible Protestant ending even though Pastor Beza would not have approved of the ambush.

For women the more frequent issue was protecting their houses[52] and especially their bodies and persons from the taint of illicit sexuality. Their tales of killing in such defense open with their housewifely activities, far removed from sexual invitation, and then introduce an insult hurled at them from the street, which was interpreted and probably intended as the first step toward sexual intercourse or sexual attack.[53] The supplication of Agnès Fauresse begins with her selling her bread respectably in the town market of La Rochefoucauld "to provide for her household and little children," while her

husband was away at his wage work. Then a verbal attack from Antoine Ferron—"villaine putain, moynesse, prestresse" (dirty whore,
monk's woman, priest's woman)—and she goes on to describe his
violent efforts to get her back to her house and force himself on her
until she hit him with a stick. That night he got drunk and went to
the town square and bragged that he'd surprise her yet. But instead
he died, and she fled and got her grace.[54]

Not surprisingly, the rare case where the story of male sexual
honor has a form similar to that of the women is one in which the
homoerotic issue is raised. It takes place among priests and their
hangers-on, a milieu especially targeted for sodomitic denuncia-
tion.[55] When a priest had a woman, it was she who was insulted
("prestresse"), "concubinaire" (a priest with a concubine) being a
word for ecclesiastical reform proclamations rather than a jibe likely
to raise a man's hackles. But in the sixteenth century, when a priest
was accused of sex with a man, he was as vulnerable as a woman,
and as much in need as she of a story establishing his innocence in a
persuasive drama of words.

Jean Le Bon, a priest and religious of the order of Fontevrault,
began a March day in 1546 with a mass for the dead, sung at the
little Picard church of Bézu-le-Guéry. Then with a fellow priest,
Messire Guillaume Haultin, and a few other men, he went to various taverns and to a priest's house in another village "to taste some
wine." At a last tavern, the male sodality exploded. The supplicant
asked Haultin to lend him money to pay his bill, whereupon Ezan
Garnier said, "Leave the bugger there" ("Laisse là ce bougre";
the word had a much more focused and literal meaning in the sixteenth century than today or even than it would have in the mid-
seventeenth century).[56] Le Bon answered that "that was a wicked
word, and that he was not such, and had enough other vices without that one." Haultin tried to smooth it over, saying that Garnier
was joking and would ask his pardon, but Le Bon was not satisfied
and warned that he would seek reparation before the courts. "Take it
as you wish," said Garnier (always in Le Bon's account); "take it,
and don't pardon me if that's what you want," and advanced to attack him. Whereupon, to avoid Garnier's fury—Garnier was, it
turns out, a "mauvais garçon" who beat up clerics—Le Bon said
"good-night, messieurs" and left. Garnier followed him with stones
under his mantle, and, in the fight that followed, Le Bon wounded

him with a knife blow to the eye. He died two weeks later, and Le Bon now seeks pardon for the homicide of the man who wounded him with an unpardonable word.[57]

Sexual honor was not just a source of contention between men and women and among men, but also within the circles of women themselves. This brings us to the whole question of how women told about their own quarrels, ordinarily the subject of great merriment in images and literary texts of the time.* (Amazons used their dignity and might only against men, not against women.)[58] A late sixteenth-century picture of women of different estates fighting for a phallic eel was supposed to make viewers laugh at least as hard as the traditional husband-wife fight for the breeches. They were silly, these feminine fights with bare hands, a chance to show a bare bottom if the woman's skirt slipped up (see illustrations 8 and 9). In his *Propos Rustiques*, Noël du Fail drew the women into a quarrel between the same Breton villages we have already met at the Aguilanneuf caper. Hearing the noise of a fight among their husbands one May day, they arrive on the scene and begin to throw stones and pebbles at each other. A good fellow nearby tells them that with every toss they are showing their thighs, so they begin to punch each other in the nose, scratch, bite, tear off each other's hats, and pull each other's hair. By evening, their dresses are all torn, their ears almost pulled off, their hair every which way, and they begin to shout indignities at each other: "Putain, Vesse, Prestresse, Bordeliere... Vieille Edentée... Larronnesse... Sorciere... Macquerelle... Truye" (whore, slutbag, priest's woman, brothel madam, old toothless, thief, witch, procuress, sow), and on to 38 epithets these "Goddesses" screamed. The fight was inconclusive for women and men both.[59]

Lawyer du Fail made fun of both sexes in his peasant book, but

---

*Or if not merriment, which was the usual response, then great bafflement. Pierre de L'Estoile recounted in his journal in Sept. 1584 the murder by Thiennette Petit, one of the White Sisters at the Hôtel-Dieu of Paris, of another nun. She cut the throat of Sister Jeanne La Noire with a knife, tried to kill a second nun, and then jumped from a high window into the Seine. Unhurt, she was tried, condemned, and hanged with her homicide knife. "Strange it was that a young maiden of 25 years of age, raised for ten years at the Hôtel-Dieu in the habit of a religious, should have the recklessness and assurance to want to kill in premeditated cold blood two of her sister religious to avenge a light offense that they had given her three months before." (*Journal de L'Estoile pour le règne de Henri III, 1574–1589*, ed. Louis-Raymond Lefèvre [Paris, 1943], pp. 362–63.)

8. Women fighting. Detail from *Le Caquet des Femmes,* ca. 1560, Bibliothèque Nationale, Cabinet des Estampes.

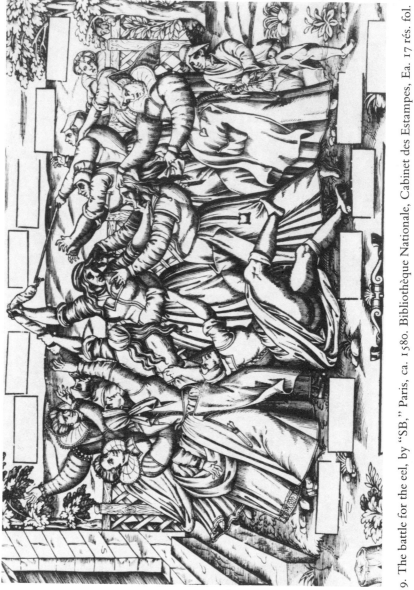

9. The battle for the eel, by "SB," Paris, ca. 1580. Bibliothèque Nationale, Cabinet des Estampes, Ea. 17 rés. fol.

his women have no cause of their own and are especially ridiculous in the way they fight and the way they look afterward. Not even a chance of heroism here.

When the women pardon-seekers tell about women's conflicts, they do shout sexual insults at each other—"vesse, putain, excommuniée" was how a village woman outraged a carpenter's wife in the Saintonge in 1534—and they do pull each other's hair and use distinctive instruments of assault, such as manure and milking stools.[60] But they are serious. What seems to be lacking in these supplications is a dependable set of narrative techniques to give drama or intensity to the all-female quarrels. They do not build to tragic outbursts between companions as in the Butcher's Tale. They do not create a terrifying counterpoint between husbandly violence, suicidal despair, and the infant pull of milk in one's breasts, as in the tale of Marguerite Vallée. They do not mount through repeated tests, as does Bonne Goberde's kitchen tale. They stay matter-of-fact, commonplace.

To give an example, a certain Robinette, a middle-aged widow and domestic servant in Normandy, tells Henri II about a sheet-washing quarrel she had at the village fountain-washtub several years before. When she and her companion Magdeleine came up to the tub, a local wife named Katherine had been there for a long time washing her sheets. They asked her to wring them out and give them room, but she said she wouldn't do it. A fight took place in which Katherine threw a pounding-stick (see the washerwomen in illustration 8), and they pulled each other's hair, but there is no lingering in the story over the dishonor or scandal—indeed, sexual scandal—of uncoiffing. (The women's hats do not play the same symbolic or narrative role as hats do in the men's tales, even though it must have been something of an operation to pull off that headgear.) Finally, Robinette felled Katherine with a stone. "Leave her there," said Magdeleine. "Let's go wash our sheets." ("Laissez là. Allons laver nos drappeaulx.") Katherine died five or six days later, as did the child with which she was pregnant.[61]

What might be the reasons for the seeming flatness in this account and in some of the other recitals of quarrels among women? Is it just my own eyes, so adjusted to the sixteenth-century public notions that male talk is politics and female talk is gossip (cackle, caquet), that male fights are usually serious and female fights funny, that I cannot read the women's stories with the right private understandings? Is it the hand of the royal secretaries and their clerks, usually facilitating the supplicants' tales, but not able to pay attention to the squabbles of women even when they ended in death? Is it something related to the character of women's sociability in the sixteenth century, their patterns of friendship and enmity outside of the family? Or perhaps a desire to keep "the secrets of women," the real strength of their quarrels, from public eyes?

I am not sure of the answer, but I have one suggestion that does not necessarily exclude the social possibilities just listed: the general storytelling, Biblical, and folktale tradition was ill-supplied with accounts of how women fought seriously among themselves by means other than magic, poisoning, or stealth (Sarah's rough treatment of her servant Hagar [Gen. 16:6] is a rare exception); and this made it difficult for female supplicants to find an adventuresome or tragic mode in which to ask for mercy in situations where they fought physically and overtly. At the same time, the existing storytelling tradition gave significant expression to only one particular kind of female strife, that which pitted a young woman against a stepmother or surrogate mother, but provided little guidance for how to craft accounts of other quarrels.[62]

Support for these speculations comes from the fact that the best-shaped stories of female fights are precisely those with themes of witchcraft and mother-figure / daughter conflict. One of the former was told in 1544 by Jeanne Pasquellet, a furrier's wife of Lyon and mother of five children. She explained to the king that while she was a woman of honor who had always governed her household well, a lascivious woman named Benoîte had conceived a mortal hatred for her out of "jealousy" about her lover, a moneychanger who lived near the supplicant. Benoîte had addressed herself to one Ysabeau Malefine, "long suspected of being a witch," who through poison, so the doctors said, had caused the supplicant to become grievously ill. Jeanne had tried and failed to have Benoîte and Ysabeau condemned to death for poisoning, and then, in despair at her long sickness, got a porter to entice Ysabeau to her house on the pretext of needing his wash done. Jeanne asked Ysabeau in vain to lift her spell; after Ysabeau had insulted her and pushed her to the floor, "outraged in her own house," the supplicant struck the witch on the head with a staff and she dropped dead. "Fearing her husband and the rigor of Justice," Jeanne had her buried in the church cemetery behind her house (evidently she stopped worrying about Ysabeau's witch connections when she had her interred in holy ground) and fled. She was granted remission provided she give 100 sous for charitable alms.[63]

Jeanne Pasquellet's story did raise women's quarrels above the everyday, and conceived of "mortal hatred" between members of the sex, but it did so by working within a current belief system about women and sorcery, and traced the enmity back to sexual jealousy. Marguerite Panete's tale about killing her mother-in-law drew upon a traditional literary structuring of family conflict and helped her win remission for an act which might well have been punished as unforgivable parricide. She lived in a Bourbonnais village where, at age 25, she was the second wife of Mathieu de La Faye.[64] Her supplication begins on Saint Anthony's eve 1524 when, out of concern for her husband's son by his first wife, she asked her mother-in-law Denise, "Where is Laurent?" Denise responded that he was enjoying himself in town (the feast is a setting for Laurent's activity, not for the supplicant's), and, when Marguerite noted that it was nine or ten at night, too late for him to go wandering about, her mother-in-law said it was not up to her to punish Laurent, who was not her son—"Va, villaine putain, paillarde, pourceau" ("Get out of here, dirty whore, paillarde, pig"). Marguerite said her mother-in-law was lying, she was not a whore. The fight moved to slaps and blows, Denise throwing a fire brand and Marguerite an iron pot, which hit the older woman on the head. Tried and condemned to banishment from the kingdom, Marguerite was granted pardon so long as she made satisfaction to the civil party (her father-in-law?). Mathieu de La Faye, who had not been present at the homicide, must have accepted Marguerite's version; suggested by the story is a second marriage much appreciated by the husband and resented by the mother-in-law.

What can we conclude about women's voices in the corpus of the letters of remission? Though they are not heard very often, their pardon tales could be set off from the men's by a distinctive complexity and texture. Somewhat removed by cultural assumptions and/or by their own choices from the acceptable legal excuses of impulse (hot anger, drunkenness), women were either silent about their feelings or many-tongued, bringing jealousy, despair, and

103

guilt to the action, along with anger. Less able to depend on ritual or festive settings to give workable coherence to their remission narratives, they created atmosphere by building up dialogue or prosey detail alone. Like thrifty housewives, they wove their fictions from materials ready at hand.

We saw in the last chapter how the storytelling skills of the men seeking mercy were channeled away from the heroism of the folktale or romance to the tragi-comedy of the supplication to the king. For the women, their supplications may have required less change in their modes of self-presentation. Within the narrative of the letter, they had to cast themselves more like the patient Griselda than like the trickster wife of the comic nouvelle, but they could also show initiative in getting out of tight spots, like the young woman nick-named Peau d'Ane (Donkey Skin), whose adventures were recounted at the sixteenth-century veillée.[65] Especially, being on their knees in humble supplication was of less moment for women. Wives were used to assuming the language and posture of humility and subjection, even when they played a central role in running the household and family. They did not have a tradition of manly courage to defend at all costs, nor need they worry about the Lie Direct when they positioned a chicken knife on their heads. In fact, the familiarity of women as supplicants may be one of the reasons they played so peripheral a role in the theater of royal mercy.

What would be interesting to know was whether the happy ending of the remission letter—pardon and a good name—was as easy for a woman to enjoy as for a man when she got back to her village or city street. We can follow the careers of a number of men after their letters were ratified, such as the barber-surgeon Simon Guy who "broke" his adulterous wife in a beating in 1537. He made a very good second marriage not long afterward, was a leader of the surgeon's gild in 1540, was recipient of a dedication—"au tresfidel et excellent Chirurgien M. Maistre Simon Guy"—from the Lyon humanist Barthélemy Aneau, and was a pillar of the Reformed community in that city in the 1560's.[66] That Bonne Goberde and Marguerite Vallée had a line of suitors at their door is unlikely.

How did women's pardon tales fare in texts beyond those of the king's chancellery and courts? Observers reported them rather little in their journals, not only because there were so few of them, but also because a letter of remission for a woman rarely aroused political scandal (the abolition of Marie Quatrelivres' adultery penalty was an exception). Philippe de Vigneulles described a female pardon in his chronicle of Metz, but it had a very unusual twist to it and a good moral. A teenager spent the night with her godmother and tried to murder her in her sleep because (so Vigneulles said) the older woman was a prostitute who was leading the girl's mother astray. In the morning, the godmother, thinking she had been assaulted in the dark by thieves, was showing the weapon to her neighbors in the street, when the girl's father happened by and said innocently the billhook was his. Thus revealed, the daughter was arrested and was about to be drowned when the prayers of the neighbors, comparing her good repute with the godmother's ill repute, won her pardon.[67]

In the printed crime literature, women's pardon stories had no more presence than the men's and for the same reason—the lesson they taught was not sharp enough. On the other hand, women's homicides that ended in execution were, if anything, over-represented in the pamphlets. Marguerite Haldeboys of Cahors, who killed her two children and her husband because he had gambled away all the money for food, was a perfect exemplary figure in her voluntary confession and scaffold remonstrance: "O you men whom God has made in his image . . . and established to govern your wives, refrain, I beg you, from dice and cards." The 1584 story was still good enough fifty years later to be reprinted with a fresh date of execution.[68] Marguerite Vallée's tale could not compete with this one, and even less with reports of husband-killers who conspired with a lover to rid them of their spouse. Vallée's self-defense against Valenton might seem too strong a rebuke to husbandly government, while the schemes of an adulterous wife could be blamed on female concupiscence and so were a favorite motif in pamphlets and sermons.[69]

Much more fruitful for understanding the possibilities of the woman's voice is, of course, the *Heptaméron* of Marguerite de Navarre. Freed from the constraints of an actual mercy plea, how does the Queen of Navarre construct women's violence and the feelings behind it? And with her inventive and complex format—the nouvelles first told and then discussed by the gentlemen and gentlewomen stranded in their Pyrenean abbey of Sarrance—how does she present the narrators on such topics? In the sexual adventures that are the subject of many a tale, Marguerite treats men and women with symmetry, cutting through the topoi of insatiable female appetite and modesty. Both sexes can be chaste, resisting unwanted sexual overtures; both sexes initiate love affairs and deceive their mates. Is there a like symmetry in regard to bloodshed, especially since the demoiselle Ennasuitte introduces a homicide story, "I will spare neither man nor woman, to make everything equal"?[70]

As far as plots go, Marguerite's tales say less than the letters of remission. The men lay violent hands on and do away with wives, wives' lovers, women they want to rape, men who have threatened honor and chastity, and servants who stand in their wicked way. In only two stories do women directly kill anyone, and it is themselves: a lady of Cremona out of immense sorrow when her lover suddenly dies in her arms (nouvelle 50), and a gentlewoman of Périgord out of despair because she has been tricked into sexual intercourse by a Franciscan just after getting up from childbirth (nouvelle 23). "Forgetting all humanity and a woman's nature" (the phrase is that of Oisille, the old widow telling the latter tale), the lady of Périgord begs her husband on her knees to avenge her shame, and while he is gone, "cut off from God and herself, like a woman enraged and in fury," she strangles herself, unknowingly killing her baby in the process. The violence snowballs, as her brother mistakenly avenges her death on her husband, ultimately being pardoned for the act, as we saw in Chapter 2.

In a few stories, recounted by men and women both, the women's anger is directed outward, as their passion is spurned by young men and in wrath they devise revenge through their husbands. The highborn wife of the first nouvelle lies to her spouse about Dumesnil's attempts on her honor once the lover has withdrawn because of her promiscuity. Whereas Saint-Aignen's real-life letter of remission casts himself and his servants as the (excusable) killers of Dumesnil, as noted in Chapter 2, Marguerite's Sainct-Aignan is governed by his wife, "more beautiful than virtuous." In nouvelle 70, the Duchess of Burgundy lies and wheedles till her husband extracts the love secret of the gentleman who has rebuffed her. She uses it to dishonor the youth and his mistress, whereupon the lady dies of shame and regret and the gentleman commits suicide. After the bloodshed, things go badly for Marguerite's angry and jealous women:

Sainct-Aignan's wife dies miserably in sin while her husband pays the penalty in the galleys, and the Duchess of Burgundy is knifed by the duke after he discovers her treachery. In a third comic tale (nouvelle 35), a lady of Navarre, "enraged and out of her senses" as she believes herself scorned and even threatened by a handsome ascetic preacher, shouts insults at him and scratches his face. Scratches, kicks, and bites are also used to dissuade men from forcing their favors (nouvelles 4, 46).

Now these are all interesting and intricate nouvelles, told (as the Prologue prescribes) as events "seen" by the narrators "or else heard from a person worthy of faith."[71] But among the many "histoires" that surface in Marguerite's storytelling field above the Gave d'Aspe, the woman physically taking another's life, even for pardonable reasons, is not one. Such women are prosecuted in her courts,[72] but not in her nouvelles. Can we imagine the Queen's gentle party wanting to hear and discuss the remission tale of Vidalle Bayonne, the Gascon villager who killed her husband's lover on Saint Martin's day, 1523? Vidalle is vulgar, without the "honesty" and "virtues" of Marguerite's bourgeoise of Tours (nouvelle 38), the patient wife who won her husband back from his sharecropper's arms by her affectionate concern for his health. Vidalle says her husband's lover Catherine was "a woman of bad life," but admits she herself received visits from a priest and his woman, and was susceptible to taunts from Catherine that "she was going to tell her husband she was keeping a brothel in his house." On top of this, Vidalle has epilepsy, which tormented her all the worse because of Catherine and her husband's ill-treatment. In the slaying scene, Vidalle heard Catherine's voice from the street chatting of neighborhood gossip, went outside and "by force of jealousy . . . and chaulde colle" picked up stones and hurled them at Catherine's head.[73]

If Longarine can remark in the *Heptaméron* that the good wife of Tours was all the more admirable because "city women are usually not raised so virtuously," then she might simply dismiss Vidalle Bayonne's resort to violence—violence against another woman—as what one would expect from the upbringing of a peasant.[74] In real life, would the Duchess of Alençon (as Marguerite still was in 1523) have intervened for a pardon for a case like Vidalle's?

As far as feelings and critical interpretation go, Marguerite's *Heptaméron* says much more than the letters of remission and indeed than most sixteenth-century discussion of anger and violence between men and women. If she creates no plots of pardonable bloodshed for women—the anger they act on always leads them astray—she nonetheless portrays a range of pardonable violent sentiment for them. At the same time, she has her storytellers debate how and whether men should act on their anger, and in so doing, shows the limits of both high Senecan teaching and popular marital wisdom on that subject.

Two stories (36, 37), told and argued about back-to-back on the Fourth Day, provide our strongest evidence. In the first, recounted by Ennasuitte, an elderly President in the Parlement of Grenoble finds his wife in the sexual act with a young law clerk and feigns to forgive them. In the next weeks he gives banquets and balls as signs to everyone of his attachment to his wife, even letting the clerk dance with her before sending him away forever; he patiently waits some months and then poisons his wife's salad. His mourning is so marked that no one suspects him of her death.

As any judge and the Queen of Navarre well knew, poisoning was a murder of stealth and premeditation (and characteristically female in style), even if it was "to save the honor of his house." The listeners break into dispute. The young wife Parlamente thinks the wife got what she deserved, the husband's revenge prudent and wise. The young widow Longarine thinks it cruel and full of malice: "I would rather he had killed her in anger, for the doctors say that such a sin is more remissible, its first impulse not being in man's power to control." Better yet, once his full anger has passed, he should have lived with her in peace, for she would have changed her ways. The men chime in to defend revenge for "the greatest injury a woman can do to a man," Saffradent insisting that anger lasts till it is acted upon and that he is happy to say that theologians easily pardon such sins. Parlamente snorts at this—but, as usual with Marguerite's tales, there is no agreement, and the interpretation is left in doubt.[75] (Even the truth status of the *histoire* is unsure: how did Ennasuitte hear about it if the judge had dissimulated and covered his tracks so well?) *

---

*The freshness of this discussion is evident when one compares it with two tales of revenge on adulterous wives from the Burgundian *Cent Nouvelles Nouvelles* of the mid-fifteenth century, which lack such a frame. In one a President in the courts of Provence feigns unawareness of his wife's adultery and then kills her by the stratagem

The possible meanings are deepened by the next nouvelle, told by the gentleman Dagoucin to the honor of virtuous women, that is, women patient like the President but not seeking such revenge. A highborn lady is suddenly abandoned at night by her husband, who goes off to sleep with someone else. After a first reaction of "great jealousy" and withdrawal, she resumes the ordering of her household and children and uses guilt inducement on her husband, rising out of bed when he returns, kissing him and giving him a basin of water to wash away the dirt of his activities. After a year with still no results, she (finally!) goes through their great house looking for him and discovers him fast asleep in a back wardrobe with the dirtiest, ugliest chambermaid in their service. To teach him a lesson, she sets fire to some straw; when the smoke threatens to kill him, she shouts "Fire!" and tells her husband off. She has tried gentle patience and water for a year; now she is trying fire. "Monsieur, if this doesn't reform you, I don't know whether the second time I'll pull you out of danger." Mortified, he promises to cease tormenting her, sends the chambermaid away, and they live henceforth in great contentment.

Again there is no agreement on how to evaluate the episode, especially among the women. Old Oisille thinks the wife exemplary. Parlamente thinks there is a limit to patience; suffering insult such a long time will destroy affection. Ennasuitte points to some of the hard realities of the wife's situation: an impatient wife might meet a furious husband, who would beat her, put her in the straw, and move the chambermaid up to the marriage bed. Longarine thinks the wife's only mistake was waking her spouse up, the ashes of such husbands make good laundry soap. Oisille asks her what she would have done if her late husband, with whom she had lived in such devotion, had treated her so. Longarine answers, "I loved him so

---

of sending her to a wedding on a very thirsty mule. She drowns when the mule rushes to the Rhône to drink; the judge gives her an appropriate funeral and decides henceforth to avoid the dangers of marriage. In the other a gentleman of Auvergne sets a trap for his wife and her priestly lover—a literal trap into which a wolf, the curé, the servant go-between, and the wife all fall and are then burned to death by the husband. The nouvelle ends, "After this, he left the area and sent to the king to seek his remission, which he obtained easily. Some said the king should say that the only damage was to the poor wolf who was burned" (*Cent Nouvelles Nouvelles*, ed. Pierre Champion [Paris, 1928], nouvelle 47, pp. 146–48, nouvelle 56, pp. 166–68). Marguerite's nouvelles 36 and 37 are in part a rewriting of and response to these recitals.

much that I think I would have killed him and then killed myself afterwards, for to die after such a vengeance would have been better than to live loyally with a disloyal husband." "I see," says one of the men, "that you love your husbands only for yourselves."

In the realm of test, threat, and fantasy, the Queen–author allows her ladies a wider range of feeling than women allow themselves in letters of remission, and also pardons them for it. If the plots of the *Heptaméron* are of a piece with a world in which women's bloodshed and anger are troublesome for them to face and report, its narrative form imagines a world in which men and women forgive each other after anger and women can live with their desires for vengeance. (Longarine even makes a distinction between feeling and action for the men: "as long as you don't come to swords," she tells two of the company, "your anger will just redouble our laughter.")[76] The mercy in the Queen's book is in the many chances she extends to her characters to interpret and be interpreted, and no one has to beg for it; "at play," says the husband Hircan as they start the stories, "we are all equals."

Conclusion

y storytelling field has now
yielded its harvest. What further fruits can I claim for my readers?
First, I hope they have seen how the letter of remission, collective
effort though it was among formula-providing notary, advice-giving
attorney (sometimes), and supplicant, can be used as an approxi-
mate source for the narrative ability and styles of sixteenth-century
people. The pardon tale was, of course, limited only to those plots
that were remissible, but it does show narrative skills at work in realistic and self-interested persuasion.

Some of the "simple women" and the "poor plowmen" turn out
to have more rhetorical craft than was assumed by the Renaissance
commonplace about the value of naive or natural recital over that of
the learned. Marguerite said one must be wary of the art of lettered
people, "lest the beauty of the rhetoric harm the truth of the story."[1]
And in Montaigne's "Of Cannibals," he spoke approvingly of the
recital of his traveler returned from Brazil:

a simple, crude fellow—a character fit to bear true witness; for clever
people observe more things and more curiously, but they interpret them;
and to lend weight and conviction to their interpretation, they cannot help
altering history a little. They never show you things the way they are ["ils
ne vous representent jamais les choses pures"]. . . . We need a man either
very honest, or so simple that he has not the stuff to build up false inven-
tions and give them plausibility.[2]

The remission tales show that the "stuff of invention" was widely
distributed throughout society,[3] though formal rhetorical training

like that of Etienne Dolet might lead to a different kind of telling from that acquired by a peasant at the veillée. (In other moods, Montaigne himself would agree: as he said in writing about "the vanity of words," "metonymy, metaphor . . . and other such names in grammar" apply not only to fancy language but "to the babble of your chambermaid.")[4] As for being close to "choses pures," I have not privileged any one group, neither woodsmen nor gentlemen, though I have speculated that the situation of female supplicants prompted a more complex handling of mood and state of mind.

The movement of the pardon tale has also shown us how information, values, and language habits could flow across lines of class and culture. These stories were circulated and debated by people who knew the principals, and were further heard and spread by notaries, clerks, chancellery officials, attorneys, judges, courtroom sergeants, and sometimes by the king himself and his council. The remission encounter was also a way—through the secretary's pen or the lawyer's advice—for literary constructions and royal wording to influence people who could not read. We have here not an impermeable "official culture" imposing its criteria on "popular culture," but cultural exchange, conducted under the king's rules. The stakes were different for supplicants, listeners, and pardoners, but they were all implicated in a common discourse about violence and its pacification.

While comparing the tales of supplicants with stories by sixteenth-century authors, I have suggested how the latter might expose the gaps in self-interested pleading: Mistoudin's "adding and subtracting," Benvolio's exaggeration, the outright lies of the attorney of Alençon. Does the process work the other way? Is there any sense in which pardon tales help us expose the gap in Renaissance nouvelles—that is, the alluring tension between the claim that the events recounted really happened and the actual source of the tale? Authors and readers evidently agreed that nouvelles must be presented as "news," as recently happened events, if they were to give full value as entertainment and as "society's account of itself." Though this claim predated the printing press, the publishers' practice of mixing all kinds of news reports together as "true" may well have helped perpetuate the literary practice, as Lennard Davis has suggested. By the middle of the sixteenth century, good moral reasons had been adduced for *vraisemblance*: the more probable a story, the more instructive it was, in contrast with the fantasies of the chivalric romance.[5]

Now the letter of remission can suggest new sources for this playful tolerance of ambiguity. The world of legal and royal documents had in it stories that were claimed to be true, had been ratified as true, and had been used as a basis for social reconciliation. Yet we have seen them often surrounded by doubt and challenge. That authors and readers found piquancy in uncertainty about truth in literary works was perhaps fed by the inescapable uncertainty about truth in documents relied on for order in a monarchical state.

Was there any other convergence between the remission tale and the literary creation? Were the authors' hands ever placed in the supplicating gesture of pardon-seekers? Book dedications often have humble petition and apology in them, but this was the polite language of gift-giving, of presenting one's work to the dedicatee and the reader. It is certain conclusions and epilogues that give pause. Rabelais ended his *Pantagruel* with a foretaste of his next volume, soon to be on sale, "full of a thousand jolly things, all true," and a request that his readers pardon him: "Pardonnante my—and don't think so much about my faults that you don't give good heed to your own." After the Paris Faculty of Theology had censured the book, he elaborated in a second edition. If his readers said to him that he wasn't very wise to write such idle chat ("balivernes et plaisantes mocquettes"), then he'd answer that they weren't much wiser to enjoy themselves reading it. But he and they were all more worthy of pardon for their merriment in writing and reading than the hypocritical monks who were trying to deceive the world.[6]

Over in England, several of Shakespeare's plays end with an actor before the audience asking for its pardon. "If we shadows have offended," says Puck, "Think but this, and all is mended, / That you have but slumber'd here / . . . Gentles, do not reprehend / If you pardon, we will mend." The offense is in the play, the pardon in the applause. In *The Tempest*, Prospero makes explicit the analogy of the playwright's magic and a crime. His charms now gone and having pardoned his usurping brother in the play, he begs the audience to clap their hands.

> Gentle breath of yours my sails
> Must fill, or else my project fails,
> Which was to please . . .

Conclusion

As you from crimes would pardoned be,
Let your indulgence set me free.[7]

So authors could imagine themselves producing works that
wounded readers and listeners, from whom they had to supplicate
mercy.[8] Royal censorship and ecclesiastical prohibition could make
of a text a literal crime, of course, but the ordinary dependency of
author (and publisher) on the favor of readers and buyers might
make one worry about offending them as well. Rabelais' writing
was in fact full of premeditated targets: his pardon claim was not
self-defense, but that he was only playing, and besides there were
much worse offenses one could commit. In a richly argued book,
Thomas M. Greene has described the "vulnerabilities" of the Renaissance literary text; my evidence would extend that vulnerability
to the audience, the author's plea for pardon a recognition that their
works could both harm and be a source of new power.[9]

In writing this book, I have often wondered whether I should ask
pardon of my long-dead subjects. In retelling their accounts of
bloodshed, which may often have left sorrow, terror, and regret in
their wake, I found I was sometimes laughing—laughing at Thomas
Manny's trials and his Magdalen-day revenge, at Charles de Villelume's tilting with peasants and priests, and the open codpiece of
Jean Faurier as he faced the sword of Jean Espes, at Guillaume Caranda's defense of his playing the Resurrection, and Bonne
Goberde's husband "meeting" her chicken knife and her thought to
please him with currants. If my readers are like my listeners, they
may have laughed as well. What makes them funny? The short
form? The fact that they are in the third person, someone else's
story? The delight in surprise or in subterfuge? In any case, the
mixture of laughter and horror was hardly foreign to the sixteenth
century. Rabelais could expect laughter at Panurge's revenge against
the boring merchant Dindenault, who drowns with all his sheep;
Montaigne wrote of "how we cry and laugh at the same thing";
priests were accused by Calvin of making "pleasant tales" of their
penitents' confessions, and even Friar Benedicti worried about their
"taking pleasure in them."[10] But perhaps there is something deeper
here than the listener relishing a story of what happened to someone
else. Remember that Benedicti said people were confessing their
sins "as if they were telling a story." Turning a terrible action into a
story is a way to distance oneself from it, at worst a form of self-
deception, at best a way to pardon the self.

Appendixes

Transcriptions of Letters of Remission

Seven letters of remission have been selected to give readers a sense of the French behind the translations, paraphrases, and summaries of letters of remission presented in this book. The original sixteenth-century orthography has been kept, as has the use of "etc." in these chancellery copies, but modern capitalization has been used, and punctuation, paragraphing, and some accents have been added to facilitate understanding. Where a word was illegible, this has been indicated by an ellipsis or by a tentative reading followed by a question mark.

1. Letter of remission for Thomas Manny (AN, JJ245B, 149ʳ–150ᵛ; see pp. 1–2 above)

Françoys, etc. Savoir faisons à tous presens et advenir, Nous avons recue l'humble supplicacion de Thomas Manny, pouvre homme de labour, aagé de trante-six ans ou environ, demourant à Sens, Contenant que ledit suppliant auroit esté conjoinct par mariage avec une nommée Claudine Guyart de laquelle il a ung enffant. Et combien que ledit suppliant l'ayt tousiours bien et honnestement traictée et gouvernée et fut de bonne vie, renommée, et honneste conversacion, neantmoins sadicte femme mal conseillée se seroit lubricquement et meschamment conduicte et gouvernée, et tellement que au moyen de sondit gouvernement elle en auroit gaignée la maladie qu'on appelle la grosse verolle, de laquelle ledit suppliant fort desplaisant l'auroit faicte panser et guerir. Et elle ainsi guerie s'en seroit allée avec une chambriere qui l'auroit pensée durant sadite maladie au desceu dudit suppliant en la maison de Jehan Baston, tavernier demourant hors la porte Sainct Anthoine, où elle auroit esté l'espace de deux jours et jusques à ce que ledit suppliant fut adverty par une nommée Symonnette, fille des estuves appellées Chez Noblet, que sadite femme estoit en ladite maison. En laquelle ledit suppliant, accompagné de Thomas Geneteau, maçon, et Pierre Numbiliers, sergent royal à Sens, se seroient transportez et l'auroient trouvée chachée en la cave de ladite maison. Laquelle lesdits suppliant et dessusdits auroient trouvé moyen ramener en la maison d'icelluy suppliant moyennant la promesse faicte par icelluy suppliant de ne la batre et oultrager, ce qu'il n'auroit faict.

Et apres ce qu'elle auroit esté l'espace de cinq ou six jours en ladite maison, promectant tousiours audit suppliant soy bien gouverner et en contrevenant à sadite promesse, trouva moyen pillier et desrobber en ladite maison tout ce que bon luy sembla et s'en seroit allée au desceu dudit suppliant en la maison d'un nommé Graffiquart, mareschal demourant à ladite Porte Sainct Anthoine. En laquelle elle auroit esté l'espace de huit jours ou environ et iusques à ce que une nommée Jaquette, fille de joye, trouva ledit suppliant devant sadite maison, laquelle luy dit que s'il vouloit payer pinte, elle luy enseigneroit où estoit sadite femme, ce qu'il luy promist faire.

Et tost apres icelluy suppliant, accompaigné de Jehan Collart et Pierre Hofflart, sergens royaulx à Sens, et autres, se transporterent à ung dimanche au matin environ le mois de juin cinq cens vingt-neuf en ladite maison dudit Graffiquart, en laquelle luy fut faict commandement de par nous ouvrir la porte de ladite maison, ce qu'il feist en obtemperant à Justice. Et incontinant s'entrerent en icelle maison où ilz trouverent ladite femme couchée en une couchete avec quelque quidem, qui trouva moyen s'en fouyr tout nud et gaigner l'huy de derriere. Et alors lesdits suppliant et sergent ramenerent l'autre, femme d'icelluy suppliant, en sa maison en laquelle ledit suppliant fist à sadite femme plusieurs remonstrances et print ung balay estant en sadite maison, duquel il fist des verges, desquelles il chatya et donna à sadite femme, qui se tint trois jours apres en sadite maison. Lesquelz trois jours passez, se seroit derechef partye et absentée par l'espace de trois sepmaines ou environ, pendant lesquelles ledit suppliant fut adverty que sadite femme estoit en la maison d'ung nommé Edmé Choppin, où il se seroit transporté pour cuider avoir sadite femme. Mais une nommée Katherine, seur de ladite femme, en lieu de ce faire donna ung grant coup de pierre audit suppliant sur la teste, duquel yssut grant effusion de sang.

Et depuis, ledit suppliant au moys de juillet audict an cinq cens vingt-neuf se seroit transporté en certains prez près de notre ville de Sens, où il trouva sadite femme avec plusieurs autres besoignans ausdits prez, entre lesquelz estoit le paillart de sadite femme, à laquelle ledit suppliant remonstroit sesdites faultes, mais les gens illec presens se mocquoient dudit suppliant. Au moyen de quoy et de la honte qu'il en avoit, print une fourche de bois, de laquelle il bailla sur les espaulles de sadite femme, luy disant qu'elle estoit bien meschante d'estre avec son paillart devant ung chacun, et la ramena en sadite maison. Et le jour mesmes environ neuf heures de soir, ledit paillart, acompaigné de deux autres personnes, se seroit transporté devant la maison dudit suppliant en jurant et blasphemant le nom de notre seigneur et gectant grosses pierres contre les fenestres d'icelle, disant qu'il emmeneroit sadite femme, l'appellant "coupaulx," qui equipole à ung que on appelle "quoqu" ou "genyn," et disant plusieurs grosses injures contre ledit suppliant.

Et le jour de la Magdalaine, qui fut quinze jours apres ou environ, ledit paillard se seroit transporté, acompaigné de deux autres, devant la maison dudit suppliant, où il estoit, en jurant et blasphemant le nom de dieu, dist audit suppliant, en luy donnant trois ou quatre grans souffletz sur le visaige, qu'il le tueroit. Et ainsi qu'il secondoit revencher, ung desdits compaignons tira une petite hache qu'il avoit dessoubz sa robbe, de laquelle il s'efforca donner ung coup sur la teste dudit suppliant, mais pour icelluy entremist ledit suppliant son bras audevant, où il fut actaint. Et pour s'en saulver s'en fuyt à une maison d'ung sien voisin, de laquelle incontinant apres et tout esmeu et effrayé de l'otraige qui luy avoit esté faict, ledit suppliant sortyst pour soy s'en aller en sadite maison tenant une pierre en sa main, et en s'en allant, apperceut ledit paillart avec ung de ses compaignons, qui le suyvoient. Au moyen de quoy, plus effrayé que devant, se hasta d'aller en sadite maison, devant laquelle il recontra sadite femme, à laquelle à chaulde colle en jurant le nom de dieu, il dist, "Fault-il que je meure pour une putain?" Et en ce disant, luy bailla ung coup de ladite pierre sur la teste. Et si luy donna, ainsi que ladite femme s'en fuyoit devant luy, deux ou trois coups d'un couteau, qu'il avoit accoustumé porter et dont il se aidoit à table, en d'aucuns endroitz de corps de sadite femme, ne scet en quelle partie.

Au moyen de quoy se seroit lors absenté craignant rigueur de Justice. Et depuis a oy dire que pour raison desdits coups et par faulte d'appareil, pensement, et bon gouvernement, icelle femme seroit allée de vie à trespas. Pour raison dudit cas a esté ledit suppliant constitué prisonnier en noz prisons de Sens, esquelles il est encores de present detenu en grande captivité et mesmes de son corps et danger d'y fynir miserablement ses jours. En nous humblement requerant par ledit suppliant que, actendu ce que dit est mesmement que ledit cas est advenu par chaulde colle et que icelluy suppliant a tousjours esté par cy-devant de bonne vie, renommée, et honneste conversation, sans jamais avoir esté actaint ne convaincu d'aucun villain cas, blasme, ou reproche, Nous luy veullons, etc. Pourquoy, etc. Si donnons en mandement par ces mesmes presentes à notre bailly de Sens ou à son lieutenant, etc. Donne à Paris au moys d'aoust l'an de grace mil cinq cens trente et de notre regne le seiziesme, ainsi signée par le conseil, de La Mare visa, contentor Berthelemy, registrata.

2. Letter of remission for Charles de Villelume (AN, JJ249B, 51^r–52^v; see pp. 25–26 above)

François, etc. Savoir faisons, etc. Nous avons recue l'humble supplication de Charles de Villelume seigneur de [blank], aagé de xxxv ans ou environ et prisonnier en noz prisons de Molins, Contenant que l'an v^c xviii, luy estant jeune en l'age de xviii ans ou environ, acompaigné de Jehan Dechault, religieulx, et de troys ou quatre autres personnaiges du nom desquelz et du jour n'est recordz, et luy estant à Villeneufve, où il faict sa continuelle residence, allerent ung soir pour passetemps au villaige de distant d'une lieue ou envyron en la maison d'un nommé Anthoine Delaage et Marguerite sa femme. Et apres avoir salué ladite Marguerite, qui faisoit la lessive, et par maniere de jeu luy auroit mis la main sur le collet, icelle Marguerite, en regardant que c'estoit et tenant un pot plain de sadite laiscive, en laissa tumber partie sur les gembes dudit suppliant. Au moyen de quoy et qu'elle estoit reputée paillarde publique, luy dist qu'elle en seroit chevaulchée. A quoy elle feit responce que ce ne seroit pas de luy, disant qu'elle aymeroit myeulx que ce fust Dechaulx religieulx estant avec luy. Ce faict, sort ledit suppliant hors ladite maison et y demeura ledit Dechault.

Aussi certain temps apres, dont il n'est recordz, vint ung homme à luy incongneu que l'on dit qu'il avoit esté pourveu du prieuré de Jaruage. Et pource qu'il n'avoit puissance de conserver son droict luy auroit prié luy ayder. A quoy ledit suppliant, qui estoit jeune gentilhomme desirant faire service à ung chacun et par bon zelle, s'accorda. Ce faict, s'en allerent par devers le lieutenant dudit Jarouaige le requerir voulloir mectre ledit personnaige en possession dudit prieuré. Et pource qu'il en auroit esté reffusant, luy auroit ledit suppliant faict response que luy-mesmes luy mectroit bien sans luy. Et de faict se transporterent en l'eglise dudit lieu, où en signe de possession baisa et feit baiser auxdits personnaiges les reliques [et] feit sonner les cloches. Et ce faict luy furent baillées les clefz des greniers où il y avoit quantité de blé, desquelz ne fut riens prins ne enlevé. Et pource que pendant ledit temps ung serviteur estant avec ledit suppliant print debat ou question avec ung cordonnier dudit lieu pour le billaige d'une paire de houzeaulx et que les habitants firent sonner les cloches pour emouvoir le peuple, seroit ledit suppliant sorty dudit prieuré et remonstré aux habitants dudit lieu de Jaruaige, ainsi esmeuz, que si aucun leur auroient faict exces, qu'il mectroit peine de le faire reparer. Et voyant que lesdits habitans permuetoient en grosse clameur par le moyen de quoy se povoit ensuyvre gros scandalle, et pour à ce obvier, rentra ledit suppliant dans ledit prieuré. Et pource que lors et depuys il congneut que lesdits habitans de Jaruaige auroyent faict et faisoient plusieurs assemblées pour le oultraiger, mesmes ung jour que la foire estoit à Chastellez, se retira pour eviter leur fureur et entendit que l'on voulloit faire et conspirer contre luy. Et luy estant près la garenne de Sr de Chaz sur le chemyn prochain dudit Jaruaige, et luy estant audit lieu, survint à luy ung prebstre, qui luy tint quelques propos fascheux et rigoreux. Au moyen de quoy luy bailla ung coup d'un petit baston de bois qu'il tenoit, en disant ces motz, "Tuez, tuez." Aussi auroit donné quelque autre coup de baston à ung nommé Pierre Vincent et à deux ou troys autres habitans ou voisins dudit Jaruaige affin de leur donner terreur et craincte pour empescher qu'ilz ne permuetassent à leur entreprise et intencion.

Et quelque temps apres, luy estant en la parroisse de Teillier, où

121

l'on cellebroit une confrairie le mardy de la Panthecouste, y trouva le seigneur de Boust acompaigné de deux prebstres. Et pour ce que lesdits de Boust et prebstres s'efforcent à dancer à ladite confrairie avec des femmes, qui estoit contre la coustume dudit lieu, de tout temps et d'ancienneté garder, par laquelle est deffendu à tous habitans dancer ledit jour avec femmes, se seroit esmeu gros debat et question entre les confraires de ladite confrairie et lesdicts de Boust et prebstres, comme il fust rapporté audit suppliant estant en logis où il souppoit. Auquel lieu il fut prié et requis par lesdits confraires se transporter à ladite dance pour faire cesser lesdites dicditions [*sic*; for seditions?], disant par lesdits confraires que l'on les voulloit tuer. A quoy ledit suppliant, liberallement et sans penser à aucun mal, s'accorda. Et luy estant au lieu trouva que les confraires tenoient encloz en une maison lesditz prebstres et Duboust. Et voyant par ledit suppliant aucuns desdits confraires estre montez par le dessus de ladite maison, qui tenoient l'un desdits prebstres pour le tuer, pour ce empescher et eviter plus gros scandalle et mal, les prya de ne le point tuer, mais si bon leur sembloit, le pourroient faire depoiller et battre de verges, ce qu'ilz ferent, et en le faisant passer quelque foys entre eulx luy bailloient aucuns coups de verges.

Aussi envyron ce temps Pierre Dars, religieux, prevost de Chambon, oncle dudit suppliant, luy auroit donné une mestaire, appellée La Montenelle, qui luy estoit escheue et advenue par le deces et trespas d'un son subiect de mainmorte. Se seroit icelluy suppliant transporté en ladite mestaire, où il auroit trouvé ung nommé Le Maignan, qui se disoit avoir droict en ladite mestaire. Et pour leur different prindrent compromis. Et pour ce que pendant icelluy, ledit Le Maignan par surprinse auroit emmené le bestail de ladite mestairie pour en cuydre frustrer ledit suppliant, icelluy suppliant, de ce adverty, acompaigné de cinq ou six de ses serviteurs, embastonnez sans propos de mal faire, mais pour garder sa possession, s'addressa à ung laboureur, dont il ne sçait le nom, lequel luy monstra le bestail ainsi emmené par ledit Le Maignen. Et ce faict, print ledit suppliant avec sesdits serviteurs ledit bestail et icelluy emmené en sa maison. Et pource que depuys, en hayne de ce, ledit Le Maignen envyron les moissons s'efforcoit de le deposseder et prandre les bledz provenuz ès terres de ladite mestairie, et que le seigneur des Portes y estoit avec grosse assemblée pour icelluy Le Maignen, ledit suppliant se transporta avec aucuns de ses gens et mercenaires jus-

ques au nombre de quinze, embastonnez pour leur deffances seullement et garder sa possession. Et luy estant sur le lieu pource qu'il
apperçoit ung quidam estant de la part dudit Le Maignan, qui tenoit
une hacquebutte de laquelle ledit suppliant pensoit qu'il voulsist
tirer, dist à ung de ses gens tenant une arbaleste qu'il se gardast
dudit personnaige. Et apres avoir remonstré audit Maignen qu'il ne
devoit ainsi facher ne oultraiger, emmena ledit suppliant sondit blé
sans aucune viollence ne exces.

Et aussi au moyen de ce que ledit Dars prevost, sondit oncle dudit
suppliant, luy auroit par plusieurs foys dit que s'il avoit affaire de
blé, qu'il s'adressast à ses senseurs pour en avoir et que s'ilz en faisoient reffuz qu'il en print, se seroit transporté en la maison de
Mathieu Mardon prebstre accenseur audit Dars son oncle, où il
print en son grenier, apres avoir rompu l'huys pour l'absence dudit
Mardon, la quantité de douze septiers de bled ou envyron, dont
depuys sondit oncle luy bailla acquict sur ce qu'il luy devoit. Et
aussi quelque temps apres, luy estant à la chasse, rencontra deux
charettes chargées de bled et apres avoir esté adverty qu'elles appar-
tenoient à sondit oncle et suyvant ce qu'il luy avoit dit, en print une
qu'il feist mener en sa maison, aussi luy acompanigné de deux ou
troys personnes ayant affaire de bled. Et pour en avoir suyvant ce
que sondit oncle luy avoit dit, se transporta en une maison deppen-
dant dudit prieuré de Chambon appellé Tresson, auquel lieu il feit
sortir à la portc [une] partie de ses gens. Et pource qu'il estoit nuyt
et craignant que l'on ne voulsist ouvrir, feist dire au receveur dudit
lieu qu'il vint audit hurtement, que c'estoit une lettre contenant que
ung nommé Desier luy mandoit qu'il luy envoyast son cheval. Et
pource qu'il feist reffuz faire ouverturc de ladite porte et que ledit
suppliant ne savoit où loger, declaira audit receveur que c'estoit luy.
Lors icelluy receveur feit ouverture de ladite porte. Et ce faict, pria
icelluy receveur ledit suppliant qu'il eust à frapper quelques coups
de congnée contre ladite porte, affin que icelluy receveur eust excuse envers son maistre ledit suppliant y avoir entré par force, ce
que ledit suppliant feist voulontairement pour complare à icelluy receveur et sans autre mal penser. Auquel lieu il feit prandre troys ou
quatre chars de bled suyvant que sondit oncle luy auroit dit auparavant et commandé. Et depuys, en apprenant par sondit oncle lesdites
prinses, auroit le tout alloué à ses fermiers et accenseurs.

Toutesfoys pour raison des cas dessusdits ou aucuns d'eulx, ledit suppliant a esté constitué prisonnier et mené en la conciergerie de nostre Palais à Paris, et depuys, par arrest de notre court de Parlement, auroit esté renvoyé par devant nostre senechal de Bourbonnais ou son lieutenant pour luy faire parfaire son proces, où il a tenu prison douze ou treize moys et y est encores de present en danger d'y finir miserablement ses jours, si noz grace et misericorde, etc. En nous humblement requerant que actendu ce que dit est et que lesdits cas sont advenuz plus pour la grant jeunesse dudit suppliant que autrement et que en iceulx faisant ne s'en est ensuyvy mort ne mutillation de membre, et que en tous autres cas, etc. Nous luy veullons sur ce impartir noz grace et misericorde, remission, et pardon, et en l'honneur et reverance de la glorieuse sacrée passion de nostre saulveur et redempteur Jhesus Crist, ou suysmes de present Pourquoy, etc. Si donnons en manche ces mesmes presentes à nostre bailly seneschal de Bourbonnais ou son lieutenant parce que les dessusdits cas ou la pluspart de ceux ont esté faictz en sa senechaussée et jurisdiction et que par arrest de nostredit court de Parlement ledit suppliant a esté renvoyé pardevant luy. Et à tous noz autres justiciers, etc. Donné à Paris au moys d'avril l'an de grace mil cinq cens trente-cinq et de nostre regne le vingt-deuxiesme, Moyennant la somme de dix livres tournois qu'il payera comptant pour en mectre en oeuvres pitoyables pour prier dieu pour l'ame des trespassez, laquelle somme de dix livres tournois a este paiée comptant, moy present faict comme dessus. Ainsi signé par le conseil, de Veyrac visa, contentor Aurillot.

3. Letter of remission for Guillaume Caranda (AN, JJ245B, 132^v–133^r; see pp. 30–31 above)

Françoys, etc. Savoir faisons à tous presens et advenir, Nous avons receu l'humble supplication de Guillaume Caranda, pouvre jeune homme de mestier de barbier, demourant en nostre ville de Senlis, aagé de vingt ans seullement ou environ, Contenant que le jour du Sainct Sacrement de l'Autel dernier passé, pour faire honneur à dieu et en recordacion et representacion de sa saincte Resurection, se seroyt ledit suppliant mys en ung tumbeau faisant et representant la figure de nostre seigneur, luy estant en son tumbeau, et avec luy estoient aucuns de ses voisins faisans et representans les figures d'autres des personnaiges assistans au tumbeau de nostre seigneur Jhesus

Christ, ou quel lieu et tumbeau ledit suppliant pendant le temps que la procession passa par la rue où il estoit.

Combien qu'il n'eust aucunement mesfaict ne mesdit à ung nommé Claude Caure, de mestier de taillandier, demourant en nostre ville de Senlis, ne eu jamais aucune question, noise ou debat entremis, neantmoins icelluy Caure, ledit jour du Sainct Sacrement environ l'heure de neuf heures du soir, estant à l'huys de la maison où il demouroit, lors comme ledit suppliant passoyt pardevant luy avec aucuns de ses voisins, qui alloient à l'esbat hors la porte de ladite ville de Senlis appellée la porte Sainct Rieulle, commance à dire et demander audit suppliant telz motz ou semblables, "Je voy le dieu sur terre. Avoys-tu print le membre virile et honteux royde en faisant le dieu?" Et proufferant lesdites parolles en motz deshonnestes arrogamment et contre l'honneur de chrestienté. A quoy ledit suppliant feist responce que "le sien n'estoit pas bien rasseré [that is, r-acéré] ne rechauffé et qu'il estoit hongre." En disant lesquelles parolles, icelluy suppliant et ceulx de sa compaignie allerent tousiours leur chemin, sans eulx arrester ne prandre garde ausdites parolles jusques hors ladite porte Sainct Rieulle, actendant l'heure de coucher et passant temps joyeusement.

Et en retournant et rapassant par ledit suppliant et autres de sa compaignie pardevant l'huys dudit Caure comme demye heure apres ou environ, icelluy estant encores près de sadite maison, s'addressa derechef audit suppliant plus austerement et arrogamment que devant, en luy reiterant lesdites parolles injurieuses et deshonnestes par irreverence de nostre seigneur Jhesus Christ et de la solempnité dudit jour. Ausquelles parolles icelluy suppliant feist semblable responce que dessus, en passant tousiours oultre et venant vers sa maison pour soy en aller coucher. Mais ledit Caure, qui estoyt homme fort noisif et souvent surprins de vin, ou contempt desdites parolles, suyvit et ala apres ledit suppliant et luy donna et frappa deux coups ou souffletz sur la teste et visaige, tellement que de l'ung desdits coups il fist tumber par terre le bonnet d'icelluy suppliant. Au moyen de quoy et pour obvier par ledit suppliant au danger de sa personne et à ce que ledit Caure ne l'oultrageast devantaige, de chaulde colle et son corps deffendant, tira ung petit cousteau qu'il avoit de coustume porter sur luy et d'icelluy frappa ledit suppliant ung coup sur l'oeil senestre dudit Caure, lequel cuyda mectre la main audevant. Au moyen de quoy fut ladite main blessée et touchée dudit cousteau, ne scet ledit suppliant par lequel endroyt. Ce fait se retira icelluy suppliant en sa maison, et tost apres fut adverty que ledit Caure au moyen dudit coup, faulte de bon apareil, bon gouvernement, ou autrement, estoyt et est allé de vie à trespas.

Au moyen du quel cas ledit suppliant, doubtant rigueur de Justice, se seroit absenté du pays auquel ne ailleurs en nostre royaulme, il n'oseroyt bonnement converser si noz grace, remission, et pardon ne luy estoyent sur ce imparties. En nous humblement requerant que actendu ce que dict est et la jeunesse dudit suppliant et que ledit cas est advenu de chaude colle et en son corps deffendant, et aussi que en tous autres cas ledit suppliant s'est tousiours bien et honnestement conduict et gouverné sans jamais avoir esté atainct ne convaincu d'aucun autre villain cas, blasme, ou reproche, Nous luy veullons sur ce impartir nosdits grace, remission, et pardon. Pourquoy, etc. Si donnons en mandement au bally de Senlis ou son lieutenant parce que ledit cas est advenu en sondit bailliage et à tous noz autres justiciers, etc. Donné à Paris au mois de juillet, l'an de grace mil cinq cens trente, et de notre regne le seiziesme. Ainsi signé par le conseil, Berthelemy visa, contentor de La Mare.

4. Letter of remission for Louis Paisant (AN, JJ238, 245ʳ–246ᵛ; see pp. 46–47 above)

Françoys, etc. Savoir faisons à tous presens et advenir, Nous avons receu l'humble supplicacion des parens et amys charnelz de Loys Paisant, pouvre homme boucher aagé de trente-six ans ou envyron, chargé de femme et trois petitz enfans, à present demourant en notre ville de Paris, Contenant que le dimanche xviiiᵉ jour de novembre dernier passé, apres avoir oy la messe que les bouchiers et estalliers du cimetiere Sainct Jehan ont acoustumé fere dire le jour de dimenche, s'en alla à la boucherye dudit cymetiere, où il trouva plusieurs compaignons, c'est assavoir, Anthoine Aubert, serviteur de Tameguy Aubery; Gilles Coingnet, serviteur de Claude Daumergue; Michel Seneschal, serviteur dudit Tameguy Aubry; Philippes Gaudart, serviteur dudit Dumergue; Jehan Boyer, serviteur de Jehan Aubert; Julien Texier, serviteur dudit Aubert. Où illecques, en la presence des dessusdits, fendit six beufz appartenant deux audit Tameguy Aubry, deux autres audit Daumergue, et les deux autres audit Aubert. Et apres qu'il eust ce faict, se partit de ladite boucherye en la compaignye de Guillaume Dambotz et s'en allerent ensemble à l'imaige Notre Dame devant le crucifix Sainct Jaques de la Boucherye, auquel lieu ilz trouverent Nicole Viel, Politon Aubourg, aussy compaignons bouchiers, et Jaques Godart, lesquelz beurent ensemble en icelle taverne. Et apres qu'ilz eurent desieuné, chacun paya son escot excepté ledit Paisant, qui paya dix-huit deniers tournois pour luy et pour Jaques Godart.

Et apres qu'ilz eurent desieuné, ilz s'en partirent d'icelle taverne et s'en allerent, c'est assavoir, ledit Paisant en l'escorcherye et les deux autres ne scet ledit Paisant en quel lieu. En laquelle boucherye ledit Paisant trouva Tameguy Obry, Jehan Cossron, Jaques Godart, Pierre Morin, Jaques Geoffroy, et Nicolas Gilbert, escorcheux en icelle escorcherye, où illec ledit Paisant habilla troys beufz appartenant audit Tameguy Aubry. Et apres qu'il eust iceulx habillez, en mena deux sur ung cheval à la boucherye dudit cymetiere Sainct Jehan, auquel lieu il beut en l'estal dudit Aubery avec ledit feu Real et Anthoine Aubry. Et incontinent qu'ilz eurent beu, ledit Paisant partit et retourna en icelle escorcherye, où il fist le reste dudit jour jusques environ heure de quatre heures de relevée.

A laquelle heure il se departit, luy et Philippes Boniface, Guillaumin Maillard, et un autre duquel il ne scet le nom. Et allerent en icelle taverne de l'ymaige Notre Dame, où illecques ilz se misrent à table pour soupper. Et peu apres arriverent en icelle taverne Jehan Geoffroy, Nicole Gilbert, Nicole Mesnaigier, et plusieurs autres compaignons desquelz il ne scet les noms ne surnoms, lesquelz tous soupperent ensemble excepté lesdits Gilbert et Mesnaigier, qui arriverent les derniers. Et apres qu'ilz eurent tous souppé, payerent chacun leurs escotz. Et ce fait, se partirent d'icelle taverne tous fors ledit Paisant, Philippes Bonficace, Jehan Geoffroy, Guillaume Mallard, Nicolas Mesnaigier, Nicolas Gilbert, et plusieurs autres compaignons lesquelz il ne congnoissoit et dont il n'est à present records. Lesquelz demourerent en icelle taverne et se misrent à jouer aux dez, c'est assavoir, ledit Boniface, Paisant, Nicolas Viel, et deux ou trois autres desquelz il n'est à present records. Et tellement jourerent que ledit Boniface perdit tout son argent en sorte que ledit Paisant luy bailla cinq solz tournois sur et tantino [?; for tantieme?] mys de quelques deniers qu'il avoit à eulx deux et vingt-cinq solz tournois. Et ce fait, laisserent ledit jeu.

Et alors ledit Gilbert fit ung mommon d'un douzain audit Jehan

Geoffroy, que ledit Jehan Gilbert gaigna, et le donna à boire. Et ce faict, ledit Boniface, qui est homme à la main lequel avoit ja tué et occis deux ou trois hommes comme l'on dict et reprins de Justice, dit audit Paisant que l'on baillast ledit manteau, jurant le sang dieu qu'il ne l'emporteroit pont. A quoy ledit Paisant fit responce qu'il ne luy bailleroit ledit manteau et qu'il le tenoit en gaige de vingt-cinq solz tournois, mais qu'il luy en bailleroit la moictié s'il vouloit, ce que ledit Boniface ne voulut. Surquoy se meurent plusieurs parolles entre eulx et desmentirent plusieurs fois l'un l'autre. Et en jurant par ledit Boniface par plusieurs foys le sang et la mort de nostre seigneur et le renonçant, donna sur la joue dudit Paisant [blank], en disant audit Jehan Geoffroy, illec present, qu'il luy baillast son cousteau. Quoy voyant par ledit Paisant, doubtant que ledit Boniface le voulses tuer et occire parce qu'il estoit soubdain à frapper, pour ad ce obvier et donner craincte audit Boniface de ce qu'il n'approchast, tira soubdainement l'un des cousteaulx de la gaine qu'il a acoustumé porter en sa saincture pour le faict de son mestier, duquel à chaulde colle donna ung coup audit Boniface, ne scet comment [*sic*; for bonnement?] ledit Paisant en quel lieu parce qu'il estoit eschauffé et courroucé desdites parolles qu'il et ledit Boniface avoyent ensemble. Duquel coup ledit Paisant auroit depuis oy dire que ledit Boniface par faulte d'appareil et mauvais gouvernement tantost apres est allé de vie à trespas.

Pour raison duquel cas icelluy Paisant a esté constitué prisonnier ès prisons de notre Chastelet, èsquelles il est encores de present, et doubte que soulz ombre de rigueur de Justice l'on voulsit contre luy proceder extraordinairement et fere son proces, si sur ce ne luy estoit notre misericorde impetré, sicomme ledit suppliant dict. En nous humblement requerant que actendu que ledit suppliant par cy-devant s'est bien et honnestement gouverné, sans jamais avoir esté reprins de Justice, etc. Pourquoy Nous ces choses considerez, voulans misericorde preferer à rigueur de Justice audit suppliant au cas dessusdit, avons quicté, remys, et pardonné, et par la teneur de ces presentes de grace especiale, pleine puissance, et auctorité royal quictons, remectons, et pardonnons, etc. Si donnons en mandement à notre prevost de Paris ou son lieutenant, en la jurisdiction duquel ledit cas est advenu. Et à tous noz autres justiciers, officers, et subiectz et chacun deulx sicomme à luy appartiendrez, etc. Donné à Paris au mois de decembre l'an de grace mil cinq cens vingt-cinq, et de notre regne le unziesme. Moiennat et promy que ledit suppliant a payé contant soixante souz tournois qui ont esté . . . et emploiez en euvres pytoiables pour prier dieu pour l'ame dudit defunct. Donné comme dessus, de Besze par le Conseil, de Besze visa, contentor Barthelemy.

5. Letter of remission for Jean Charbonnier dit Nain (AN, JJ236, 472 ^{v}–473 ^{v}; see p. 47 above)

François, etc. Savoir faisons que Nous avons recu l'umble supplicacion de Jehan Charbonnier dit Nain, pouvre simple homme de braz et labour, Contenant que de toute son aage il s'est bien et deuement gouverné, sans avoir reproche ne estre reprins d'aucuns villain cas, et a tousiours gaigné sa vie à busche et fagoter boys sans qu'il ait gueres faict autre estat. S'est marié au lieu de Flonville où il a tousiours faict sa residence et demourance, et esté chargé de femme et de plusieurs petitz enfans. Ung jour de mercredi depuis deux ans, mesmement ou mois d'avril y a ung an, se leva d'avec sa femme avec laquelle il avoit couché en sa maison. Et en se levant, demandant à sadicte femme si elle avoit de l'argent pour avoir du pain. Laquelle respondit qu'elle avoit deux lyars. Et apres luy dist ledit suppliant qu'il avoit deux karolus, et qu'elle luy baillast lesdits deux lyards et qu'il luy bailleroit lesdits deux karolus pour avoir du pain à ses enfans. A quoy, luy fut dit par sadite femme qu'il en desgaigeroit sa serpe qui avoit esté engaigée pour son frere Robin chez ung nommé Berquerel.

Et apres ces parolles, s'en partit, garny d'une congnie, et s'en alla au villaige de Mezieres, distant dudit Flonville d'une lieue, où illec abbatit demy arpent de boys pour Pierre Iantal, Sr de Le Plaigne. Et ce fait s'en alla en la maison de Le Plaigne, où il repeut et beut une pinte de vin, et luy prya ledit de Le Plaigne qu'il allast le lendemain fagoter ledit boys, ce qu'il fut accordé par ledit suppliant.

Et en issant dehors de ladite maison, trouva ung nommé Thibaut Corbon, qui luy demanda dont il venoit. A quoy, luy fut dit par ledit suppliant qu'il venoit de chez ledit Sr de Le Plaigne. Et alors ledit suppliant et Corbon s'en allerent chez Philibert Capperon, tavernier à Dreux, où ils beurent ung pot de vin et puis s'en allerent chacun de son costé. Assavoir, ledit suppliant devant la petite hale dudit Dreux, où il trouva son frere Thomas, qui luy demanda si le boys estoit abbatu. A quoy ledit suppliant repondit que oy. Et alors ledit Thomas demanda audit suppliant s'il vouloit aller aux nopces de son oncle Colin. Auquel il resondit "On yroit[?]. Je n'ay point d'argent. Voilà Robin, qui m'a mené aux tavernes et m'a fait despenser mon argent, et est ma serpe engaigée, et ne sçauroye de quoy besongner." Et alors s'en alla chez Francoys Berquerel, où ladite serpe estoit engaigée, et pria la femme dudit Berquerel qu'elle luy baillast ladite serpe et qu'il luy laisseroit sa congnée jusques à ce qu'il eust payé. A quoy elle respondit qu'elle ne la bailleroit point.

Et quant ledit suppliant vid qu'il n'avoit point sa serpe, de laquelle il devoit fagoter ledit boys dudit de Hantelle et gaingner sa vie et celle de ses enfans, il s'en alla tout desconforté, pensant passer par dedans le chasteau, ce qu'il ne peult faire parce que la porte estoit fermée et fut contraint se retourner par la porte du petit pont, où il trouva Denis Le Fevre et luy demanda s'il avoit veu ses freres. A quoy ledit Le Fevre respondit que oy, et qu'ilz n'estoient pas loing.

Et alors ledit suppliant comança à courir apres eulx et les[?] acouroit au lieu de la Loge Blanche. Et luy arrivé avec eulx, comença, à dire à Robin, "Pardieu, tu es ung vaillant seigneur." Lequel Robin respondit, "Pourquoy?" Et ledit suppliant dist, "Pour tant que pour ton plaisir tu m'a mené aux tavernes et m'avoit oy bien dit que tu me trahnoys." A quoy ledit Robin dist audit suppliant qu'il avoit menty. Et ledit suppliant dist que c'estoit luy, et que pourtant s'il avoit des biens de s'alymosnie et congé de son seigneur, qu'il ne laisseroit point à vivre s'il plaisoit à dieu.

Cela faict, marcherent ensemble. Et en marchant ledit suppliant dist audit Robin, "Cest que tu diz que tu bateras ma femme." A quoy repondit ledit Robin qu'il la galleroit bien et ledit suppliant avec. Et ledit suppliant luy dist ces parolles ou semblables, "Tu feras tes fievres quartaines." Et ledit Robin retourna et cuyda frapper de sa main ledit suppliant, lequel bailla de sa congnée sur la teste dudit Robin de la teste de ladite congnée, tellement qu'il fendit la teste et le versa à terre. Et depuis pour estre mal pensé ou autrement, allé de vie à trespas.

Pour raison duquel cas icelluy suppliant, craignant rigueur de Justice, s'est absenté du pays, auquel ne ailleurs en nostre royaume il n'oseroit bonnement retourner ne converser. En nous requerant humblement, attendu ce que dit est et que ledit suppliant a satisfait à parties interessées, et autres cas s'est tousiours bien conduict et gouverner, sans jamais avoir esté attainct ne convaincu, etc. Pourcquoy, etc. Si donnons en mandement par ces presentes aud. bailly de Dreux ou à son lieutenant au bailliage, ressort, ou jurisdiction duquel ledit cas est advenu, et à tous noz autres justiciers. Donne à Paris ou mois d'avril, l'an de grace mil cens xxiiii, et de nostre regne le dixiesme. Ainsi signé par le conseil, Debesze visa, contentor Barthelemy.

6. Letter of remission for Marguerite Vallée (AN, JJ252, 33ᵛ–34ʳ; see pp. 77–79 above)

François, etc. Scavoir faisons, etc. Nous avons recue l'humble supplication des parens et amys de Marguerite Vallée, vefve de feu Jaquemin Valenton, demourant à Villers-le-Sec en Partoys, aagée de trente-quatre ans ou environ, prisonniere ès prisons de Victry en Partoys, Contenant que dès xiii ou xiiii ans ou environ, elle fut conjoincte par mariage avec ledit deffunct Valenton son mary, et combien que audit mariage avec ledit deffunct Valenton son mary, combien que audit mariage ladite Marguerite se seroit tousiours bien conduicte et honnestement gouvernée, sans aucun reproche et mauvais renom de sa personne, et se soit tousiours aplicquée du tout à bien conduire et traicta sondict mary, enffans, et mesnaige au mieulx qu'elle avoit pu, sans faire mal ni desplaisir à sondit mary ne luy desobeyr, et que dudit mariage elle ait eu six enffans, mesme puis six ou sept moys en ça ayt eu deux filles, jumelles d'une ventre. Ce nonobstant, pendant ledit mariage sondit mary l'auroit tresmal traictée et icelle batue et oultraigée par plusieurs et diverses foys en plusieurs partyes de son corps, tant de coups de baston que aultres, dont elle auroit esté fort meurtrye et navrée. Et l'auroit si mal traictée et oultrageusement batue et mutilée journellement et continuellement qu'elle en auroit esté souventesfoys parturbée et divertye de son esperit et perdue l'entendement, en telle maniere que par plusieurs et diverses foys, temps, et années, elle et autres pour elle luy on faict ses offrandes et sa neufviesme devant Madame Sainte Berthe au lyeu et abbaye d'Aulnoy, qui est loingtain lieu dudit Villers et de la demeurance d'icelle Marguerite, pource que c'est ung lieu tresfort requis à telles personnes divertyes de leur esperit et entendement. Et au moyen de ses bapteries et mauvais traictement ladite Marguerite en seroit tumba quasi en desespoir et auroit desiré souventesfoys estre morte.

Et en continuant par ledit Valleton son mary ses mauvais traictemens, oultrages et batures, le samedy vingt-ungiesme jour d'octobre dernier passé, qui estoit environ huit jours apres que ladite Marguerite avoit esté relevée de la gesine de sesdites deux filles, et sur le soir, icelluy deffunct Valeton son mary, sans cause ne propos et sans ce qu'elle luy mesfaict ne mesdict, luy gecta ung godet de terre, dont elle fut actaincte, et apres luy rua ung plat de terre, duquel elle fut attaincte et fort meurtrye au bras. Depuys print ung grant tison de boys et apres le bichet de la ville, qui est ung vaisseau à mesurer grain grant, pesant et ferré en pluseurs endroits, desquelz et aussi de coups de poing l'auroit tant batue et oultraigée et mutilée au corps, bras, jambes, et par le visaige, qu'il l'auroit toute meurtrye, et mesmement par le visaige, en telle sorte qu'elle l'avoit tout noir de sang meurty.

Au moyen de quoy pour eviter à plus grant danger et peril de sa personne, apres avoir esté ainsi batue, mutillée, et meurtry, fut contrainte soy retirer et saulver sur l'un de leurs voisins, leur monstrant lesditz batures et oultraiges et en pleurant et en soy complaignant à sesdits voisins comme femme desesperée, disant qu'elle eust voullu estre morte. Lesquelsz voisins l'auroient consolée et reconfortée le mieux qu'ilz auroient peu, et pour la pityé de sesdits deux enffans, l'auroient persuadée de retourner en sondit hostel. Ce qu'elle auroit reffusé par plusieurs et diverses foys, disant qu'elle aymeroit myeulx mourir que d'y retourner et qu'elle ne faisoit que languir, desirant tousiours sa mort et la fin par desespoir, et que aussi bien sondit mary la tueroit d'une hache qu'il avoit et dont il la menassoit ordinairement.

Toutesfoys lesdits voisins, par la grande pitié de sesdites deux filles jumelles qu'elle nourrissoit, qui n'avoient que troys sepmaines ou environ, l'auroit tellement persuadée qu'ilz l'auroient ramenée en la maison de sondit mary, qui estoit ung homme furieux, subgect à vin, jureur et blasphemateur du nom de dieu, et qui estoit ja couché en ung petit lit près de feu, auquel lieu ladite Marguerite avoit nouvellement faict sa gesine. En continuant scs oultraiges, commença à injurier icelle Marguerite et la menasser d'oultraiges comme devant, blasphemant le nom de dieu, qu'elle ne couchoit d'ung moys avec luy. Quoy voyant, ladite Marguerite, laquelle au moyen de sesdits batures et oultraiges estoit ainsi parturbée de son esprit, divertye de son entendement et comme desesperée, dict par plusieurs foys audict Valeton son mary, "Voyla la hache dont tu me menasses tant. Tue moy, et ne me faict plus languir. Aussi bien ma vye me desplaist et ne sçauroys plus vivre en cest estat."

Lequel Valenton, apres que ceulx qui estoient aller remener et conduire ladite Marguerite en sadite maison se furent retirez et que icelle Marguerite demoura seulle avec ledit deffunct son mary, iceluy deffunct, en continuant sesdits oultraiges et perservant de mal en pire, soubdain et en grand fureur se seroit levé dudit petit lict où il estoit, et auroit prins ladite hache et, en jurant et blasphemant le nom de dieu plus que devant, dist à ladite Marguerite qu'il la garderoit bien de jamais parler ne aller hors ladite maison. Et en ce disant s'approcha d'elle et luy donna ung coup de ladite hache qu'elle destourna au moins mal qu'elle peut, et pource que ladite Margueritte pour soy saulver s'en fuyoit devant luy, rua impetueusement apres elle ladite hache tellement qu'elle passa par aupres de sa teste. Et voyant par icelle Margueritte la fureur dudit Valleton son mary et qu'il couroit pour relever ladite hache et luy frapper et oultraiger, icelle Margueritte, ainsi escurée et troublée desdits oultraiges et comme femme desesperée, se retourna et soubdain releva ladite hache, de laquelle, en repellant lesdits oultraiges et soy deffendant, elle rua deulx ou troys coups sur ledit Valeton, ne sçait ladite Marguerite bonnement en quel endroict, au moyen de ce qu'elle estoit si fort escuerée et troublée desdits battemens et oultraiges ainsi à elle faictz qu'elle ne sçavoit qu'elle faisoit.

Et pour obvier à la fureur de sondit mary seroit sortie de ladite chambre et, ainsi esmeue et desconfortée, se seroit retirée en la maison d'ung aultre de ses voisins, non pensant son mary estre fort blessé, où elle se seroit tenue et resposée iusques au lendemain qu'elle oyt dire qu'on avoit esté en leur maison et trouvé l'huys de la chambre apuyé par dedans d'un tizon et d'ung buchet et qu'on avoit trouvé son mary mort en icelle chambre.

A l'occasion duquel cas icelle Marguerite se absenta lors dudit lieu où ledit cas seroit advenu, et en seroit allée par plusieurs champs et villaiges par desespoir et en dueil et desplaisance, tant de ce qu'on disoit que sondit mary estoit ainsi mort que de ses pouvres enfans qui estoient demeurez seulz et despourveuz, et mesement lesdits petits iumeaulx qui estoient si jeunes, se seroit voullu noyer comme femme desesperée dont elle auroit esté gardée par gens qui la conduisoient. Et depuys, ayant memoire et recongnoissance de ses poures enfans qu'elle delaissoit en grand et merveilleux regret, se delibera retourner au lieu dont elle estoit partye pour les veoir et y pourveoir. Toutesvoyes que par les chemins en retournant, elle se mist quelquesfoys en effort de soy gecter dedans l'eaue pour soy noyer, dont elle fut tousiours gardée.

Et elle estant près du lieu de Betancourt, qui est continge et prochain dudit Villers, esté constitué [pri]sonniere par les officiers de la terre et seigneurie dudit Betancourt pour le Sieur ou Dame d'illec. Laquelle Marguerite auroit esté interrogée, et confrontée et commence à faire son proces pour raison dudit cas par nostre prevost dudit Victry. En quoy faisant, par crainte de Justice, elle auroit denyé avoir frappé ne touché ledit deffunct et faict plusieurs variations et denegations interrogatoires et confessions. Et doubtant lesdicts suppliants que pour raison dudit cas l'on veult procedder rigoreusement contre ladite Marguerite Vallée, si noz grace et misericorde ne luy estoient sur ce impartys, en nous humblement requerant lesdits suppliants pour ladite Margueritte, leur parente, et en faveur, pityé, et compassion de sesdits pauvres enfans, qui sont en voye de totale destruction et de mourir de faim et mesmement les deux petitz jumeaulz. Et attendu ce que dit est, mesmes que ledit cas est advenu par les faultes, coulpes, agressions, exces, et oultraiges dudit deffunct ainsi par luy faictz à ladite Margueritte sa femme et sans aucun propos et elle estant ainsi nouvellement relevée de sa gesine, et que ce qu'elle faict a esté en repellant par elle lesdits oultraiges et soy deffendant comme dit est dessus, et que tous autres cas ladite Marguerite s'est tousiours bien conduicte et gouvernée, sans jamais avoir esté actaincte ne convaincue d'aulcun autre villain cas, blasme, ou reproche, Nous luy voullons sur ce impartir noz grace et misericorde, pource est-il que nous voullons misericorde preferer à rigueur de justice à ladite Marguerite en ladite . . . pytié et compassion de sesdits pouvres enffans myneurs, avons quictée, etc. Si donnons en mandement par ces presentes à nostre bailly de Victry ou à son lieutenant audit Victry et à chacun d'eulx sicomme à luy appartiendra, pource que ledit cas est advenu en leur ressort et iuridicion. Et à tous, etc. Donné à Paris ou moys de febvrier l'an de grace mil cinq cens trente-six, et de nostre regne le vingttroysieme. Ainsi signé par le conseil, Delivre visa, contentor Aurillot. Approuvez sont ses motz en rature "ou à son lieutenant audit Victry et à chacun d'eulx" sur ce donné comme dessuz, Delivre.

7. Letter of remission for Bonne Goberde (AN, JJ253B, 118ᵛ; see pp. 93–94 above)

Françoys, etc. Savoir faisons, etc. Nous avons receue l'humble supplication de Bonne Goberde, vefve de feu Toussaintz Savary dit Baron, demeurant à Arnay-soubz-Viteaulx, aagée de trente-six ans ou environ, Contenant que le dymanche xxiiᵉ jour du moys de may dernier passé, ledit deffunct Savary prya de soupper avec luy Jehan Delynot, seigneur de Molins, Thomas de Heryot, seigneur de Cousy, et autres estant de la garnison tant dudit Viteaulx que dudit Arnay. Et dist ledit deffunct à ladite suppliante sa femme qu'elle apprestast le soupper pour eulx et qu'il s'en alloit à ses affaires.

Et revint ledit deffunct à l'hostel environ l'heure de troys heures apres-midy, où il trouva ladite suppliante sa femme et Michel Savary, leur fils, aagé de dix-huit ans ou environ, lequel Michel allumoit du feu pour accoustrer le soupper et ladite suppliante tenoit des poulletz, ausquelz elle couppoit la gorge pour les acoustrer avec autres choses pour ladite souper. Et sur ce arriva ledit deffunct, lequel, arrivé, commença à soy demener et courrousser, comme il estoit coustumier, et s'addressa audit Michel son filz, luy disant telles parolles ou semblables, "Meschant paillard, pourquoy n'as tu habillé le souper?" Et sur ce ladite suppliante print la parolle pour excuser leurdit filz en disant audit deffunct telles parolles ou semblables, "Baron, mon amy, l'heure de soupper n'est pas encores venue." Et en ce disant, ledit deffunct bailla ung grand coup de pied audit Michel son filz contre le costc, jurant, maulgreant, et blasphemant le nom, la chair, et la mere de nostre seigneur, disant qu'il affoleroit leurdit filz. Parquoy icelluy Michel leurdit filz s'esvada de la presence de sondit pere.

Et au regard de ladite suppliante, elle se haystoit de achepver de coupper la gorge ausdits poulletz, et s'addressa ledit deffunct par parolles de menasses et rigoreuses à ladite suppliante sa femme, laquelle luy dist derechef en telles parolles, "Baron, mon amy, ne vous courroussez poinct. L'heure de soupper n'est pas encore venue. Tout sera prest à heure. Vous avez tort d'avoir battu notre filz sans cause."

Et sans faire ne dire autre chose, ledit Thoussaint bailla à ladite suppliante deux souffletz de si grande roideur qu'elle tomba par terre. Puys elle se relleva et tumberent lesdits poulletz à terre, et avoit encores ledit cousteau tout sanglant en la main, et dist derechef ladite suppliante audit deffunct qu'il faisoit mal de la battre, veu qu'elle ne faisoit point de mal.

Et jaçoit ce que ladite suppliante ne peust en ce faisant avoir dict ne faict aucune chose audit deffunct qui luy deust desplaire, neant-moins par grande fureur iceluy deffunct print ung pallis de boys plain de chevilles estant illec, lequel palis l'on appelle coustumyere-ment "une chamberiere," servant à soustenir la bouche à rostir. Et d'icelle chamberyere ou palis frappa grandz coups sur ladite sup-pliante, mesmes par ung coste, tellement qu'elle tumba toute es-tourdye, les deux genoulx par terre avec l'un de ses bras et main, et de l'aultre main tenoit ledit cousteau sur sa teste, toute courbée et appuyée. Et dist lors ladite suppliante audit deffunct qu'il estoit bien meschant de la frapper ainsi sans cause. Estant ainsi ladite suppliante, ledit deffunct revint pour derechef frapper ladite suppliante et de roiddeur, en s'approchant d'elle, rencontra ledit cousteau que ladite suppliante tenoit encores sur sa teste, et en fut ledit deffunct enferré audessoulz de la mamelle gauche. Et jaçoit ce que ledit cousteau fust ung grand cousteau de cuysine poinctue, toutesfoys la playe et inci-sion dont ledit deffunct fust attainct estoit si petite que merveilles[?] et se recullit [*sic*; for se recula or se recuellit?] ung peu ledit deffunct.

Et au regard de ladite suppliante, non pensant que ledit deffunct fust frappé, elle se relleva autrement mal qu'elle peult, jaçoit ce qu'elle fust esnormement oultragée en son corps, et pour cuider bien faire, alla en leur jardin pour cueillir des grozelles pour appaiser ledit deffunct. Mais qu'elle oyt qu'il y avoit bruict en la maison, par-quoy elle revint soubdain et apperceut ledit deffunct son mary tumbé par terre, et disoit l'on qu'il estoit mort.

A ceste cause ladite suppliante, de crainte et frayeur dont elle fust surprinse, se evada et s'en fuinst du pays, ouquel ne ailleurs en notre royaulme elle ne seroit bonnemènt repairer, si noz grace et miseri-corde ne luy estoient sur ce impartiz. Et pendant son absence a este proceddé par saisye et transport de ses biens, deffaulx, banissement, et sentence contumace, dont elle a appellé si tost qu'elle est venue à sa congnoissance, en nous requerant humblement que, actendu que ledit cas est advenue sans precogitation au moyen des oultrages et aggressions dudit deffunct, et que ladite suppliante ne fist jamais au-dit defunct aucun tort ou oultrage, et que en tous autres cas icelle suppliante est bien fammée et reconnue sans jamais avoir esté actaincte ne convaincue d'aucun aultre vil cas, blasme ou reproche digne de pugnition, Nous luy veullons sur ce impartyr nosdites grace, pardon, et misericorde. Pourquoy, etc. Si donnons en mandement par ces mesmes au bailly d'Auxerre ou son lieutenant à Semur, pource que ledit cas est advenue en son bailliage, jurisdiction, et ressort dudit Semur, et à tous noz aultres, etc. Donné à Paris au moys d'octobre l'an de grace mil cinq cens quarante et de nostre regne le vingt-septieme. Ainsi signé par le conseil, Delivre visa, contentor Aurillot.

Sources on the Wife-Homicide of Claude Dater

On May 4, 1567, Claude Dater killed his wife, Anne Masson (see p. 21 above). Here are transcriptions of his letter of remission for that act and of his subsequent responses before the Consistory and the criminal lieutenant of Geneva some months later. They allow us to compare different tellings of the same event. As before, I have kept the orthography from the sixteenth century, but have added punctuation, capitalization, and some accents to facilitate twentieth-century reading.

1. Letter of remission for Claude Dater, dated July 1567 (AN, JJ265, 154^{r-v})

Charles, par la grace de dieu Roy de France, A tous presens et advenir salut. Sçavoir faisons, Nous avoir receu l'humble supplication de Claude Datel, pauvre fourbisseur demeurans en nostre ville de Lyon, chargé de deux enfans, Contenant que le iiiie jour du mois de may dernier, icelluy suppliant seroit sorty de sa maison pour aller à quelques affaires qu'il avoit. Et estant de retour environ huict heures du soir, il auroit ouy ung grand bruict que faisoient aucunes personnes estans en sadite maison. Et s'enquerant de la cause, on luy auroit dit qu'ilz s'estoient efforcez de saisir ung prebstre nommé Messire Claude Acarie, qui s'estoit enfermé avec la femme dudit suppliant nommée Anne Masson en la chambre du suppliant pour paillarder, et que le prebstre estoit sorty tout debraillé. Sur quoy le suppliant, surprins de collere, entra dans sa maison montant les marches et degrez d'icelle, serchant ledit prebstre, mais il s'estoit desia sauvé en une chambre prochaine, où son pere demouroit dans le mesme logis, et s'estoit mis et enfermé dans ung coffre où il fut trouvé apres. Et rencontrant ladite Anne Masson sa femme sur les degrez, laquelle faisoit contenance de s'en voulloir fuir, le suppliant luy auroit baillé deux coups d'espée, ne sçait en quel endroit pour la collere en laquelle il estoit. Desquelz coups elle seroit allée de vie à trespas le lendemain, laquelle auparavant auroit dict qu'elle pardonnoit audit suppliant.

Et le suppliant auroit esté mis prisonnier et procedé contre luy a divers attes[?], et ledit prebstre mis aussi prisonnier trouvé dans ledit coffre, lequel a dict, à ce que le suppliant a entendu, qu'il estoit allé en la chambre de ladite feue femme pour la confesser voullant retourner à l'eglise catholique. Et le suppliant craignant rigueur de Justice a humblement supplié et requier luy vouloir faire grace et pardon. . . .

2. Appearance of Claude Dater before the Consistory of Geneva, October 30, 1567 (AEG, Registres du Consistoire 24, 113$^{v)}$)

Claude Danther dict Cracquelin, fourbisseur, dict qu'il s'en alla à Lyon du temps des premiers troubles avecq sa femme, avecq laquelle il a bien et honnestement vescu, mais elle de son costé ne l'a pas faict et s'est addonnée à paillardise avecq ung prebstre. Il est vray qu'il ne la trouva pas avecq luy en luttc [*sic*; for l'acte] quand il luy bailla ung coupt d'espée du quel elle mourut, etc.

Advis de luy deffendre la cene pour avoir espanché le sang humain et le renvoyer à Messieurs à fin qu'ilz sçachent qu'ung tel homme est en leur ville. Apres il a dict en avoir sa grace, et qu'il a receu depuis la cene apres s'estre desclaré à ung diacre ou surveillant de Lyon, et dict que sa grace est à Lyon. Il confesse avoir donné à sa femme deux coups mortels. . . .

3. Interrogation of Claude Dater by the criminal lieutenant of Geneva, November 1567 (AEG, Procès criminels 1436 [1st series])

Responces de Claude Danter, fils de Thiolman, de Metz en Lorraine, fourbisseur, du 3 novembre 1567, aagé de 45 ans

Ayant juré, interrogé du temps et cause de sa detention.
Respond estre detenu dès maintenant, ne sçait pourquoy.

Interrogé s'il est marié.

Respond qu'il l'a esté, mais il ne l'est plus, car le 4 de may dernier sa femme fust trouvée en adultere avec un prestre par les voisins de la maison, dont il y ha quelques-uns en ceste ville.

Interrogé qu'il nomme ceux qui la trouverent.

Respond qu'il ne les sçauroyt nommer.

Interrogé s'il n'y la trouva en adultere.

Respond que non, car quand il y alla, le prestre en estoyt sorty.

Interrogé si elle fust poursuivie par la justice.

Respond que non, car luy revenant de souper de ville, les voisins luy dirent, "Montez, montez, vous trouverez beau mesnage chez vous" et luy estant declaré qu'on avoyt trouvé un prestre seul à seul enfermé avec sa femme. Ce que entendant il prinst son espée et voulut entrer en la chambre où estoyt le prestre, mais il ne peust et, s'en retirant, il rencontra sa femme par les degres et de colere la tua. Et en a esté prisonnier 15 semaines, tant qu'il y a fallu avoir grace du Roy, comme l'esleu Castelas, qui est en ceste ville, tesmoignera bien et Claude Le Lorrain.

Interrogé s'il a sa grace.

Respond que non, et qu'il ne l'a peu sortir de Lyon.

The Dismissal of Letters of Remission

When letters of remission were dismissed by judicial courts, the judges might let a previous sentence stand, or they might moderate it. The following list, showing the outcome of thirteen dismissed letters of remission, is offered as a suggestion of the range of possibilities, not as a carefully drawn sample. Execution was still a possibility for a supplicant whose letter was dismissed; thus, ratification was much to be desired. But a moderated sentence was also a possibility, and so supplicants were eager simply to get a letter signed in the first place: even if the pardon was not ratified, the king's name on the supplicant's story could give it a special status and contribute toward a more moderate penalty.

Dismissed by the Parlement of Toulouse

Two men, one woman (three cases): *remission* sought from death penalties for homicide; *condemned* to be executed. (Bernard de La Roche-Flavin, *Arrests notables du Parlement de Toulouse* [Toulouse, 1720], book 2, Lettres de Grace, title 5, article 3, p. 179; book 6, Des Homicides, title 53, article 2, pp. 460–61)

Dismissed by the Parlement of Paris

Master of the royal mint: *remission* sought from death penalty for homicide of brother-in-law; *condemned* to having head chopped off, display of head and corpse, confiscation of all goods, 400 livres for prayers for soul of the deceased, 2,000 livres to widow, 1,000 livres to brother. (BN, Ms. fr. 17527, 45^v–46^v, Oct. 14, 1527)

A man: *remission* sought from hanging for homicide, confiscation of all goods, 10 livres to pray for victim's soul, 60 livres to victim's fiancée; *condemned* to full penalty. (AN, X²ᴬ 89A, Nov. 24, 1539)

A gentleman: *remission* sought from the pillory and decapitation for acts of aggression, illicit assembly, and homicide of a royal sergeant; *condemned* to the pillory, permanent banishment from France, confiscation of all goods, 1,000 livres fine to king, 100 livres to widow, 20 livres to pray for victim's soul. (AN, X²ᴬ 86, Dec. 7, 1535)

A sausage seller: *remission* sought from death penalty for homicide; *condemned* to be banished from the bailliage of Sens for three years. (AN, X²ᴮ 53, Aug. 20, 1568)

A butcher: *remission* sought from being hanged for homicide in public market of Angers, 200 livres damages to widow, 200 livres to other kin; *condemned* to banishment from sénéchaussée of Angers forever, the same damages to widow and kin, and 20 livres fine to king. (AN, X²ᴮ 60, Apr. 24, 1574)

A man: *remission* sought from hanging for homicide, 120 écus to widow, and 100 écus to queen dowager Isabel; *condemned* to banishment from sénéchaussée of La Marche for nine years, 80 écus to widow, 120 écus to children, 10 écus to pray for soul of defunct, 10 écus to queen dowager. (AN, X²ᴮ 110, Sept. 20, 1580)

A lacemaker: *remission* sought from having hand cut off and hanging for homicide, 100 écus to widow, 20 écus to king; *condemned* to banishment from the sénéchaussée of Lyon for nine years and the same fines. (AN, X²ᴮ 114, Aug. 29, 1581)

"Jeune garçon": *remission* sought from unspecified penalty; *condemned* to be beaten and pay 10 écus to the complainant. (APP, Aᴮ6, 130ᵛ, Mar. 12, 1579)

A gentleman: *remission* sought from death sentence for homicide; *condemned* to nine years banishment from the kingdom and 100 écus in charitable works. (APP, Aᴮ6, 200ᵛ, Dec. 23, 1579)

Dismissed by the Sénéchaussée of Lyon

Printer's journeyman: *remission* sought from banishment from Lyon for five years and a 50 livres fine to the archbishop for wounding a proofreader; *condemned* to fulfill sentence. (ADR, BP445, 187ᵛ–191ʳ, Oct. 31, 1559)

Notes

Notes

The following abbreviations are used in the notes:

ADR Archives départementales du Rhône
AEG Archives d'Etat de Genève
AN Archives Nationales
APP Archives de la Préfecture de la Police, Paris
BN Bibliothèque Nationale

Note regarding dates: Until 1564, the new year in France was dated from Easter Sunday. In the text all dates are given by our reckoning. In the notes, however, any date between January 1 and Easter to 1564 is given in both reckonings, e.g., February 7, 1523/24.

Introduction

1. AN, JJ245B, 149^r–150^v.

2. A major collection of *lettres de remission* is in the Trésor des Chartes (AN, series JJ), a register of royal letters issued by chancellery offices from the fourteenth century through 1568. JJ is by no means a complete record—supplicants chose to have their letters of remission copied here at an extra cost, and furthermore some years are missing for the sixteenth century—but there are more than 9,500 letters from the years 1523 to 1568. See Michel François, "Note sur les lettres de rémission transcrites dans les registres du Trésor des Chartes," *Bibliothèque de l'Ecole des Chartes*, 103 (1942): 317–24, and, on the state of the Trésor des Chartes in the sixteenth century, Hélène Michaud, *La Grande Chancellerie et les écritures royales au seizième siècle (1515–1589)* (Paris, 1967), pp. 359–68. Letters of remission can also be found scattered throughout the criminal registers of the Parlement of Paris (AN, X^{2A}), as they were ratified by that court for persons in their

jurisdiction; some letters can be read on their original parchment in the cartons of the Parlementary arrêts for the late sixteenth century (AN, X 2B). Remissions ratified by lesser jurisdictions, such as the Sénéchaussée of Lyon, can be found in their registers (ADR, BP436 [1540–42] and subsequent years).

Evidently Paul Le Cacheux savored the storytelling quality of letters of remission some seventy years ago when he edited a collection of them pertaining to Normandy in the early fifteenth century: before each letter he put a summary resembling those introducing the stories of Boccaccio's *Decameron* and Marguerite de Navarre's *Heptaméron*. Paul Le Cacheux, ed., *Actes de la Chancellerie d'Henri VI concernant la Normandie sous la domination anglaise (1422–1435)*, 2 vols. (Rouen, 1908).

3. Pierre Braun, "La valeur documentaire des lettres de rémission," in *La Faute, la répression et le pardon*, vol. 1 of *Actes du 107e Congrès national des sociétés savantes, Brest 1982. Section de philologie et d'histoire jusqu'à 1610* (Paris, 1984), pp. 207–21.

4. For example, Léonce Celier, "Les moeurs rurales au XVe siècle d'après les lettres de rémission," *Bulletin philologique et historique jusqu'à 1715 du comité des travaux historiques et scientifiques, année 1958* (Paris, 1959): 411–19; Roger Vaultier, *Le Folklore pendant la Guerre de Cent Ans d'après les lettres de rémission du Trésor des Chartes* (Paris, 1965); and the collection of important essays based on letters of remission from the fourteenth and fifteenth centuries in *La Faute*: Claude Gauvard, "L'image du roi justicier en France à la fin du Moyen Age d'après les lettres de rémission," pp. 165–92; Pascal Texier, "La rémission au XIVe siècle: signification et fonctions," pp. 193–206; Braun, "La valeur documentaire"; Jacqueline Hoareau-Dodinau, "Les injures au roi dans les lettres de rémission," pp. 223–40; and Françoise Verdier-Castagne, "La délinquance universitaire dans les lettres de rémission," pp. 283–98, among others.

Robert Muchembled has used letters of remission from the Low Countries for studies of enormous richness on youth: "Les jeunes, les jeux et la violence en Artois au XVIe siècle," in Philippe Ariès and Jean-Claude Margolin, eds., *Les Jeux à la Renaissance* (Paris, 1982), pp. 563–79, and "Des jeunes dans la ville: Douai au XVIe siècle," *Mémoires de la société d'agriculture . . . de Douai*, 5th ser., 8 (1983): 89–96. His recent and still unpublished *thèse d'état* puts the letters to work for understanding broad cultural mentalities in Artois from the fifteenth through the seventeenth centuries ("Violence et société: Comportements et mentalités populaires en Artois, 1400–1660" [Thèse de Doctorat d'Etat, Université de Paris I, 1985]).

Gregory Hanlon has used information from letters of remission ratified from 1660 to 1703 by the sénéchaussée of Agen, along with other criminal records, for his excellent essay "Les rituels de l'agression en Aquitaine au XVIIe siècle," *Annales ESC*, 40 (1985): 244–68. A valuable analysis of letters of remission ratified by the Parlement of Navarre in the eighteenth century has been published by Christian Desplat, "La grâce royale: Lettres de grâce enregistrées par le Parlement de Navarre au XVIIIe siècle," *Revue de Pau et du Béarn*, 10 (1982): 83–99.

5. For this usage of "fictional," see Alvin B. Kernan, Peter Brooks, and J. Michael Holquist, eds., *Man and His Fictions: An Introduction to Fiction-Making, Its Forms and Uses* (New York, 1973), especially pp. 1–10. Hayden White, "The Value of Narrativity in the Representation of Reality," in W. J. T. Mitchell, ed., *On Narrative* (Chicago and London, 1981) p. 23. See also the discussion on this point by Louis O. Mink, "Everyman His or Her Own Annalist," ibid., pp. 238–39. Roland Barthes, "Historical Discourse," trans. Peter Wexler, in Michael Lane, ed., *Introduction to Structuralism* (New York, 1970), pp. 152–55; Paul Ricoeur, "Expliquer et comprendre. Sur quelques connexions remarquables entre la théorie du texte, la théorie de l'action, et la théorie de l'histoire," *Revue philosophique de Louvain*, 75 (1977): 126–47; Lionel Gossman, "History and Literature: Reproduction or Signification," in Robert H. Canary and Henry Kozicki, eds., *The Writing of History: Literary Form and Historical Understanding* (Madison, Wis., 1978), pp. 3–39. Other formulations on the presence of literary action in historical texts can be found in Wolfgang Iser, "Feigning in Fiction," in Mario J. Valdès and Owen Miller, eds., *Identity of the Literary Text* (Toronto, 1985), pp. 204–5, 214–23, and in Tzvetan Todorov, "Les catégories du récit littéraire," *Communications*, 8 (1966): 126–27. See also the helpful discussion in the Introduction to Suzanne Gearhart, *The Open Boundary of History and Fiction: A Critical Approach to the French Enlightenment* (Princeton, N.J., 1984).

6. Aristotle, *Rhetoric*, book I, chap. 3, 1358b–1359a on the three divisions of rhetoric (*The Basic Works of Aristotle*, ed. Richard McKeon [New York, 1941], pp. 1335–37). For a rigorous and interesting analysis of the early relation of thought about literature to philosophy on one hand and rhetoric on the other, see Wesley Trimpi, "The Ancient Hypothesis of Fiction: An Essay on the Origins of Literary Theory," *Traditio*, 27 (1971): 1–78. Daniel d'Augé, *Deux Dialogues De l'invention poetique, de la vraye congnoissance de l'histoire, de l'art Oratoire et de la fiction de la fable* (Paris: Richard Breton, 1560), 18ᵛ. On ideas about genre in the Renaissance, see Rosalie L. Colie, *The Resources of Kind: Genre-Theory in the Renaissance*, ed. Barbara Lewalski (Berkeley, Calif., 1973), chaps. 1, 3, and G. Mathieu-Castellani, "La notion de genre," in G. Demerson, ed., *La notion de genre à la Renaissance* (Geneva, 1984), pp. 17–34. For a discussion of the Renaissance definition of the word *feindre*, see François Rigolot, *Les Langages de Rabelais* (Geneva, 1972), p. 26, and *Le Texte de la Renaissance* (Geneva, 1982), pp. 28–31. A standard literary introduction to the relation of history and literature is William Nelson, *Fact or Fiction: The Dilemma of the Renaissance Storyteller* (Cambridge, Mass., 1973), chap. 2; see also Gossman, "History and Literature," pp. 3–10. The sixteenth-century legal humanist François Baudouin warns against inventing harangues to add to ancient texts and distinguishes between falsifying and adorning: "Nor should new material be added [to the testimony of the ancients] nor any words be substituted for theirs . . ., lest one seem not so much to adorn history as to make it faulty and mendacious" (Donald R. Kelley, *Foundations of Modern Historical Scholarship: Language, Law and History in the French Renaissance* [New York and London,

1970], pp. 132–33). A new essay by Marian Rothstein ("When Fiction Is Fact: Perceptions in Sixteenth-Century France," *Studies in Philology*, 83 [1986]: 359–75) points out that at the end of the sixteenth century French historical writing was intended "to serve truth," but also to give pleasure and serve "the life-experience of the user. . . . The implicit power and responsibility of historical accounts in such a system assigns considerable value to the affective qualities of the text, and by extension grants it some . . . degree of fictive license" (pp. 374–75).

For background and further bibliography on the "shifting boundary" between "history" and "fiction" in the medieval period, see Suzanne Fleischman, "On the Representation of History and Fiction in the Middle Ages," *History and Theory*, 22 (1983): 278–310.

7. Barbara Herrnstein-Smith, "Narrative Versions, Narrative Theories," *Critical Inquiry*, 7 (Autumn 1980): 213–36, especially pp. 231–36 for her way of conceptualizing narrative as a social transaction. See also Edward M. Bruner, "Ethnography as Narrative," in Victor Turner and Edward M. Bruner, eds., *The Anthropology of Experience* (Urbana, Ill., 1986), pp. 139–55, for an approach that draws both upon context and structure. A pioneering example of a historian's study of a folktale using context and *long-term* structures is Emmanuel Le Roy Ladurie, *Love, Death and Money in the Pays d'Oc*, trans. Alan Sheridan (New York, 1982). For approaches very helpful to a historian undertaking a literary analysis of texts like remission letters, see William Labov, *Language in the Inner City: Studies in the Black English Vernacular* (Philadelphia, 1972) and Mary Louise Pratt, *Toward a Speech Act Theory of Literary Discourse* (Bloomington, Ind., 1977).

Among instructive sources on narrative used for this project are Vladimir Propp, *Morphologie du conte*, trans. Marguerite Derrida (Paris, 1970), an essential classic, even though remission tales are quite unlike his "contes merveilleux" in structure; Roland Barthes, "Historical Discourse," and "Introduction to the Structural Analysis of Narratives," in Susan Sontag, ed., *A Barthes Reader* (New York, 1982), pp. 251–95; Wayne Booth, *The Rhetoric of Fiction* (2d ed.; Chicago, 1983); Hayden White, *Metahistory: The Historical Imagination in Nineteenth-Century Europe* (Baltimore, Md., 1973), pp. 1–42; Gérard Genette, *Narrative Discourse: An Essay in Method*, trans. Jane E. Lewin (Ithaca, N.Y., 1980); Peter Brooks, *Reading for the Plot: Design and Intention in Narrative* (New York, 1984), chap. 1.

In addition to monographs on sixteenth-century *contes* and *nouvelles*, which will be cited later in this study, there are studies of short forms which have a bearing on or are useful for comparison with the stories in letters of remission: André Jolles, *Formes simples*, trans. Antoine-Marie Buguet (Paris, 1972); Hans-Robert Jauss, "Une approche médiévale: les petits genres de l'exemplaire comme système littéraire de communication," in Demerson, *Notion de genre*, pp. 35–57; Claude Brémond, Jacques Le Goff, and Jean-Claude Schmitt, *L'Exemplum*, Typologie des sources du Moyen Age occidental, 40 (Turnhout, 1982); Jean-Claude Schmitt, ed., *Prêcher d'exemples. Récits de prédicateurs du Moyen Age* (Paris, 1985); Tzvetan Todorov, *Grammaire du Décameron* (The Hague and Paris, 1969); Roger Dubuis,

Notes to Pages 5–6

Les Cent Nouvelles Nouvelles et la tradition de la nouvelle en France au Moyen Age (Grenoble, 1973).

Yves Castan has devoted some marvelous pages to the construction of stories by the accused and by witnesses in criminal interrogations in the jurisdiction of the Parlement of Toulouse in the eighteenth century in *Honnêteté et relations sociales en Languedoc, 1715–1780* (Paris, 1974), pp. 90–94. Peter Linebaugh has included an analysis of the story element in published criminal reports in eighteenth-century England in "The Ordinary of Newgate and His *Account*," in J. S. Cockburn, ed., *Crime in England, 1440–1800* (Princeton, N.J., 1977), pp. 246–69, and Margaret Ann Doody has considered literary features of the accounts of murderesses in the Old Bailey Session Papers in "'Those Eyes Are Made So Killing': Eighteenth-Century Murderesses and the Law," *Princeton University Library Chronicle*, 46 (Autumn 1984): 49–80.

8. See, for example, the study of "Le discours testamentaire" in Parisian wills by Pierre Chaunu and his collaborators in *La mort à Paris, 16e, 17e, 18e siècles* (Paris, 1978), chap. 11.

9. AEG, Procès criminels 620 (2d series), depositions made before the *justice ordinaire* of Lyon in February 1545/46 against Antoinette Rossel, wife of master barber Jean Yvard. That these depositions survive at all is due to the fact that they were forwarded to Geneva, where Jean Yvard had repaired. Virtually all the sixteenth-century papers of the lower court of Lyon have disappeared. On interrogations, depositions, and confrontations between prisoners and witnesses preserved in the archives of the Parlement of Paris, see Monique Langlois, "Les archives criminelles du Parlement de Paris," in *La Faute*, pp. 7–14.

10. AEG, Procès criminels 1307 (1st series), excerpts from the interrogation of September 11, 1565. For background on this episode, see N. Z. Davis, "A Trade Union in Sixteenth-Century France," *Economic History Review*, 19 (1966): 48–69. For further examples of question and response in criminal interrogations, see the edition of minutes of meetings of the criminal chamber of the Parlement of Paris from September to November, 1562 AN, X²ᴬ 924), prepared by Paul Guérin and printed as "Délibérations politiques du Parlement et arrêts criminels au milieu de la première guerre de religion (1562)," *Mémoires de la société de l'histoire de Paris et de l'Ile-de-France*, 40 (1913): 1–116. See especially pp. 22–24, the interrogation of Claude Lemoyne, sergeant of Senlis:

Remonstré qu'il le trouva et luy voullut donner j. coup d'espée et luy en bailla sur le braz et que les tesmoings disent que, sans la présence de l'ung d'eulx, il l'eust tué.

A dict qu'il ne scet que c'est, et a dict que s'il ne l'eust voulu frapper, il ne l'eust frappé.

Remonstré qu'il ne luy demandoyt riens.

A dict que les tesmoings disent beaucoup plus qu'il ne feist. Et a dict qu'il a denyé.

11. AN, JJ265, 194ʳ. The various formulas can be found, for example,

in *Le grant stille et prothocolle de la Chancellerie de France nouvellement corrige* . . . (Paris: Galliot Du Pré, Feb. 8, 1514/15), 97ʳ; *Le grand Stille et prothocolle de la Chancellerie de France. De nouveau veu et corrige oultre les precedentes impressions faictes iusques en lan Mil Cinq cens xxxix* (Paris: printed by
Etienne Caveiller for Arnoul l'Angelier, January 1539/40), 119ᵛ; and *Le
Thresor du Nouveau Stille et Prothocolle de la Chancellerie de France. Et des
Chancelleries establies prez les Parlemens de ce Royaume* . . . *Oeuvre nouvellement mis en lumiere* (Paris: Abel l'Angelier, 1599), 26ʳ.

Chapter One

1. On letters of remission, see Jean Milles de Souvigny, *Praxis Criminis
Persequendi* (Paris: Simon de Colines, 1541), 55ʳ–60ᵛ; Jean Imbert, *Institutions Forenses, ou practique iudiciaire, translatée de Latin en François: Reveuë, et
grandement augmentée par M. Ian Imbert Lieutenant criminel au siege royal de
Fontenai Lecomte, autheur d'icelles* (Poitiers: Enguilbert de Marnef, 1563),
pp. 486–94; Jean Imbert, *Les Institutes de Praticque en matiere civile et criminelle, tant principalle que d'appel, briefvement extraicte en François des quatres
livres de Iean Imbert* (Lyon: Benoît Rigaud, 1566), 43ʳ–44ʳ; Jean Papon, *Secrets du Troisieme et Dernier Notaire de Iean Papon, Conseiller du Roy et Lieutenant general au Bailliage de Forests* (Lyon: Jean de Tournes, 1576), pp. 729–56;
Jean Papon, *Recueil d'arrests notables des cours souveraines de France* . . . *Aug-
menté en ceste derniere edition* (Cologny: Mathieu Berjon, 1616), book 24,
title 8 (De Graces et Remissions); Daniel Jousse, *Traité de la Justice criminelle
de France*, 4 vols. (Paris, 1771), vol. 2, part III, book 2, title 20, pp. 375–414;
Paul Guérin, "Introduction," *Recueil des documents concernant le Poitou contenus dans les registres de la Chancellerie de France*, vol. 6 (for 1390–1403), vol.
24 of *Archives historiques du Poitou* (1893); Jules Viard, ed., *Documents parisiens du règne de Philippe VI de Valois (1328–1350) extraits des registres de la
Chancellerie de France*, 2 vols. (Paris, 1900), pp. xix–xxiii; Le Cacheux, ed.,
Actes de la Chancellerie d'Henri IV (cited Introduction, n. 2), vol. 1, pp. xii–
xiv; Vaultier, *Le Folklore* (cited Introduction, n. 4), pp. ii–iv; Pascal Texier,
"La remission au XIVe siècle," in *La Faute* (cited Introduction, n. 3),
pp. 193–205; André Laingui and Arlette Lebigre, *Histoire du droit pénal*, 2
vols. (Paris, 1979), vol. 1, pp. 63–65, 150.

2. AN, JJ238, 23ʳ–24ᵛ (false witness); JJ256C, 47ᵛ (a clerk for a Sénéchaussée allowing opposing parties to see papers in a case); JJ257C, 118ʳ⁻ᵛ
(theft of money); JJ265, 110ʳ⁻ᵛ (theft of sheep); JJ257B, 46ᵛ (receiving stolen
ecclesiastical goods); AN, X²ᴬ 86, Nov. 17, 1535 (defloration of a virgin);
AN, JJ253B, 114ᵛ (tax riot); APP, Aᴮ2, 26ᵛ ("pour Rebellion faicte a Justice"); AN, JJ263B, 10ᵛ–11ᵛ (for "le fait de la religion"); AN, X²ᴬ 95,
863ʳ–868ᵛ (publishing heretical books); Bernard de La Roche-Flavin, *Arrests Notables du Parlement de Toulouse* (Toulouse, 1720), book 2, title 7,
Graces, p. 152 (heresy); AN, JJ263A, 271ʳ–272ʳ (alleged complicity in es-
pionage for Spain); *Le Journal d'un bourgeois de Paris sous le règne de François
Ier (1515–1536)*, ed. V.-L. Bourilly (Paris, 1910), pp. 360–61 (heresy: those
prosecuted after the Affaires des Placards of 1534, pardon with intervention

from the pope), p. 396 (forgery). See also Papon, *Troisieme Notaire*, pp. 729–30 and below, p. 12, on the capital cases for which remission was allowed. Penalties of banishment were not supposed to be remitted (p. 730), but in occasional examples they were (APP, A^{B}1, 154^{r}), as were some condemnations to life in the galleys (APP, A^{B}1, 92^{v}).

3. Example of the Parlement of Paris urging a prisoner to seek a letter of remission in AN, X^{2A} 918, April 23, 1560: "Arresté à luy faire obtenir remission qui luy sera enterinée" (I am grateful to Alfred Soman for this reference). Example of the Parlement of Toulouse urging prisoners to obtain letters of remission in Bernard de La Roche-Flavin, *Treize livres des Parlemens de France* (Geneva: M. Berjon, 1621), book 13, chap. 69, paragraph 6, p. 1107.

4. AN, JJ245B, 150^{r}; JJ238, 204^{r}; JJ247, 138^{v}–139^{r}; APP, A^{B}1, 289^{v}. Minutes from a meeting of the criminal chamber of the Parlement of Paris in October 1562 suggest how a man might burst into a plea for pardon in the middle of his interrogation. Asked about why he had killed a man, the grain thresher Jacques Bruneau said he had been "out of his mind" ("hors d'entendement") and fell on his knees and begged for pardon. In this case, the court thought it inappropriate; he did not seek a remission and was condemned to death (Guérin, ed., "Délibérations politiques" [cited Introduction, n. 10], p. 79).

5. AN, JJ248, 12^{r}, letter of remission, dated January 1534/35, for Pierre Guillot.

6. AN, JJ238, 244^{r}–245^{r}; JJ249B, 1^{r-v}, 118^{r-v}, 30^{v}–31^{v}; JJ257C, 111^{v}–112^{r}; JJ249B, 21^{v}–22^{r}. Sometimes suppliants became fugitives not directly after the homicide or death of the victim, but after an escape from prison: AN, JJ248, 3^{r-v}; JJ259, 38^{r-v}. Etienne Dolet's poetic supplication for a letter of remission in connection with his heresy charges in 1544 was composed in the Piedmont after his jailbreak from Lyon (*Le Second Enfer*, ed. Claude Longeon [Geneva, 1978, based on the 2d ed., Troyes: Nicole Paris, 1544], pp. 22–27).

7. Etienne Dolet, *Carminum Libri Quatuor* (Lyon, 1538), book 2, Carmen 1, pp. 60–61. Richard Copley Christie, *Etienne Dolet, the Martyr of the Renaissance, 1508–1546* (London, 1899), pp. 308–9.

8. By 1561 there were Petites Chancelleries at the Parlements of Paris, Toulouse, Bordeaux, Rouen, Dijon, Aix, Grenoble, and Rennes (Abraham Tessereau, *Histoire Chronologique de la Grande Chancellerie de France* [Paris, 1676], p. 126; Roger Doucet, *Les Institutions de la France au XVIe siècle*, 2 vols. (Paris, 1948), vol. 1, pp. 104–11. For an excellent study of the chancellery in all its aspects, see Michaud, *Grande Chancellerie* (cited Introduction, n. 2).

On the *jussio*, see ibid., part II, chap. 2, and p. 256 n. 5 ("Toutes lettres de rémission, grace, pardon . . . doivent estre de commandement"). Royal secretaries did sometimes prepare letters without proper commands (Papon, *Troisieme Notaire*, p. 7), and this presumably happened with letters of remission. But the anxiety of Dolet and others about this first phase of the pardon process and the role of patrons in it shows the importance of the command. See below, p. 49, on the high financial officer whom the king kept dangling for weeks till he sent the order that his letter be drafted.

In principle, homicides that involved straight self-defense would be taken to a Little Chancellery office; more complicated excuses, to a Grand Chancellery officer or to the king himself. In fact, self-defense is one of the arguments used in most supplications, along with other remissible excuses, so this neat distinction does not hold. For letters of remission requested from the Petite Chancellerie at Bordeaux, see AN, JJ256B; from the Petite Chancellerie at Paris, JJ256C (correcting references in Michaud, *Grande Chancellerie*, p. 360 nn. 3–4).

9. Dolet, *Second Enfer*, pp. 116–18; Christie, *Dolet*, pp. 309–13; Marc Chassaigne, *Etienne Dolet* (Paris, 1930), pp. 136–40. In 1543, Dolet's second letter of remission—for the crime of heresy and publishing heretical books—was discussed by the privy council (Claude Longeon, *Documents d'archives sur Etienne Dolet* [Saint Etienne, 1977], p. 31). Another example of a letter of remission being discussed by the privy council can be found in BN, ms. fr. 5905, 53^r–54^v, Dec. 2, 1559. Here the victim's relatives, one of whom was a royal almoner, were protesting the letter of remission granted to Christophe de Gonnier, seigneur du Brul; the privy council decided to send the matter to the Parlement of Paris. For intervention on behalf of the swordcutler, see AEG, Procès criminels 1436 (1st series), Nov. 4, 1567: "Et les Informations prinses furent envoyées en la cour et baillées au chancellier par La Croix solliciteur et deputé de l'eglise de Lion."

10. Papon, *Troisieme Notaire*, pp. 728, 745–47. *Le grand Stille* (1539–40) (cited Introduction, n. 11), 123^v–124^r: "Remission pour le ioyeulx advenement du roy en une ville." On this feature of the Royal Entry, see the new book by Lawrence Bryant, *The King and the City in the Parisian Royal Entry Ceremony: Politics, Art and Ritual in the Renaissance* (Geneva, 1986), pp. 24–26. Examples of pardons granted in connection with the Joyous Entry of Henri II in Dijon: AN, JJ258B, 110^v; in connection with his Entries in Rouen and Fécamp: ADR, BP441, Sentence of June 15, 1551 (letter of remission, Oct. 1550) and Sentence of Nov. 5, 1551 (letter of remission, Oct. 1550); in connection with the Entry of Charles IX in Compiegne in 1567: AN, JJ265, 164^v–165^r.

11. AN, JJ249B, 21^v–22^r. Marguerite de Navarre, who knew the remission process well, tells a story in the *Heptaméron* about an attorney of Alençon seeking a pardon for a homicide and starting off by writing a letter to the chancellor: "Et envoya à la court en diligence demander sa grace. . . . Mais il ne peut si tost despecher sa lettre à la chancellerie," when she intervened (*L'Heptaméron*, ed. Michel François [Paris, 1967], nouvelle 1, p. 15). On this episode, based on a real case in Alençon, see pp. 58–59 below.

12. Michaud, *Grande Chancellerie*, pp. 253–66, 49–50, and p. 50 n. 5. A letter of remission given to a widow of Orléans, Apr. 1545/46 "in honor of and reverence for the death and passion of our Lord," AN, JJ257B, 46^v. Marguerite de Navarre has a Good Friday pardon granted in Nouvelle 23 (*Heptaméron*, pp. 186–93). The Parlement of Paris sometimes chose

Holy Week to ratify a letter of remission with special consideration for the supplicant: AN, X²ᴬ 98, 123ʳ⁻ᵛ, Apr. 21, 1545/46. The supplicant was ordered freed from prison and told to prepare well for Easter, to pray for the health of the king and the dauphin, and henceforth to live in peace with his neighbors.

13. Milles de Souvigny, *Praxis Criminis Persequendi*, 57ᵛ. Papon, *Troisieme Notaire*, pp. 729–30. F. A. Isambert et al., eds., *Recueil général des anciennes lois françaises*, 29 vols. (Paris, 1822–33): vol. 12, pp. 635–36, "Ordonnance sur le fait de la justice," Villers-Cotterêts, Aug. 1539, articles 168, 172; vol. 14, p. 83, Edict of Orléans, Jan. 1560/61, article 75; vol. 14, p. 198, Edict of Moulins, Feb. 1566, article 34; vol. 14, p. 477: Edict of Blois, May 1579, article 194. Imbert, *Institutions Forenses*, p. 487. Michaud, *Grande Chancellerie*, pp. 324–36.

Letters of pardon technically fell into categories of "remission," "pardon," and "abolition"; "pardon" referred to a case where a person had been present at a homicide, but had not actually given the blow, and "abolition" to a situation where a prosecution had not yet been started in a homicide case (Guérin, "Introduction," p. x; Imbert, *Institutions Forenses*, pp. 487–88; Papon, *Troisieme Notaire*, pp. 756–61). Most of the letters found in the archives are in the "remission" category, and they make up the bulk of the sources used in this study.

14. Chancellery letters were paid for by category, and the letter of remission fell into the category of a *charte*, a decision "d'effet perpetuel" (*Le Grand Stile et Prothocolle de la Chancellerie de France. De nouveau veu et recorrige oultre les precedentes impressions* [Paris: Jean Ruelle, 1548], 126ʳ; Michaud, *Grande Chancellerie*, pp. 212, 335). In principle, the cost of a charte was the same in the early sixteenth century as it had been in the late fourteenth century, namely 3 livres or 60 sous, to be divided between the king, the royal notary, and the wax-melter. In fact, Michaud shows that the price of a charte had risen to about 6 livres in the reign of François Ier. Despite the protests of the Third Estate at the Estates of Orléans, a royal edict of 1561 raised the cost of a letter of remission to 8 livres 8 sous, but a chancellery list of prices from the mid-1550's already gives 10 livres 10 sous as the cost for a charte, while Jean Imbert, a criminal judge in Poitou, says a remission required 11 livres in 1563. A royal edict of 1570 raised the price of a remission letter further to 14 livres 8 sous. Michaud, *Grande Chancellerie*, pp. 335–36, 341–43; Octave Morel, *La Grande Chancellerie Royale et l'expédition des lettres royaux de l'avènement de Philippe de Valois à la fin du XIVe siècle (1328–1400)* (Paris, 1900), p. 358; C. Lalourcé, ed., *Recueil des Cahiers Généraux des Trois Ordres aux Etats-Généraux*, 4 vols. (Paris, 1789), vol. 1, pp. 380–81, article 220; "Taulx des Seaulx es chanceleries de France faict par Monsʳ Deslandes" (written after Jan. 1554/55), BN, ms. fr. 5085, 317ᵛ; Imbert, *Institutions Forenses*, p. 387, *Institutes*, 43ʳ; Tessereau, *Grande Chancellerie*, pp. 130, 145.

On additional payments in connection with letters of remission, see Isambert, ed., *Recueil général*, vol. 11, pp. 369, 371: Edict of Blois, Mar. 1498/

99, articles 128, 138; and Laingui and Lebigre, *Histoire du droit pénal*, vol. 1, p. 150. On payments to secretaries beyond their wages from the king, see Michaud, *Grande Chancellerie*, pp. 113, 295 n. 8.

15. La Roche-Flavin, *Treize Livres*, book 13, chap. 69, paragraph 6, p. 1107: "et si l'accusé estoit pauvre [les juges] ordonnoyent que [les lettres de rémission et pardon] lui seroyent gratuitement expediées." Morel, *Grande Chancellerie*, pp. 366–69; Michaud, *Grande Chancellerie*, p. 335 n. 5. Examples of letters with "gratis" written on them: AN, X²ᴮ 53, Aug. 20, 1568, letter of remission for Jean Harson "pauvre homme charcutier," "Gratis par pouvreté"; X²ᴮ 40, Oct. 8, 1565, letter of remission for Jean Mynard "gratis par pauvreté." AEG, *Procès criminels* 1436 (1st series), Nov. 4, 1567, testimony of swordcutler Hugues Jordan.

16. Isambert, ed., *Recueil général*: vol. 11, pp. 368–69, Edict of Blois, Mar. 1498/99, article 126; vol. 14, p. 198, Edict of Moulins, Feb. 1566, article 35. The Edict of Amboise, in Jan. 1572, prescribed that henceforth gentlemen and officers must address themselves with their letters of remission to the Parlement in the jurisdiction where the crime occurred, because of the "facility" with which they were able to get remissions ratified by judges in the sénéchaussée or presidial courts (ibid., vol. 14, p. 250, article 9). Papon, *Arrests notables*, book 24, title 8, pp. 1351, 1354. On the one-year time limit for submitting for ratification, *Le grand Stille* (1539/40), 124ʳ⁻ᵛ gives special letters of relief for not having submitted the remission for ratification within the year. On the new law requiring submission for ratification within three months, *Le Thresor du Nouveau Stille* (1599) (cited Introduction, n. 11), 15ᵛ.

17. A supplicant presented the letter for ratification either as a prisoner at some stage of a criminal trial, or as a former fugitive surrendering herself or himself voluntarily as a prisoner to ask for entérinement (for example, existing prisoners in APP, Aᴮ1, Aug. 20, 1564, June 11, 1566: surrendered voluntarily as prisoner, APP, Aᴮ1, Feb. 19, 1567, Oct. 21, 1568).

18. Portrait of the entérinement of letters of remission put together from Milles de Souvigny, *Praxis Criminis Persequendi*, 55ʳ–60ʳ; Pierre Lizet, *Brieve et succincte maniere de proceder tant a l'institution et decision des causes criminelles que civiles et forme d'informer en icelles* (Paris: Vincent Sertenas, 1555), 31ᵛ–33ʳ; Jean Imbert, *Institutions Forenses*, pp. 492–94; Alfred Soman, "Procès pour homicide d'une sorcière au XVIIe siècle," *L'Histoire*, 1 (May 1978): 74–75; and from sentences of ratification or nonratification found in AN, X²ᴬ 79, 86, 87, 89, 98; X²ᴮ 40, 44, 53, 60, 103; and ADR, BP441, 443, 444.

Ratification proceedings in a regional court would often occur in the presence of the kin of the deceased; when they took place before a Parlementary tribunal in a city distant from the scene of the crime, then a copy of the letter of remission would be forwarded to the kin, and their responses and those of witnesses would be sent for. The first stage of the ratification hearing before the Parlement of Paris always involved the king's attorney and often an attorney for the victim's kin. After the supplicant had humbly requested to be availed of the king's grace, the king's attorney formally requested the letter of remission and any records from the criminal trial so he could study them, and the attorney for the aggrieved family asked for a copy of the letter of remission. If there was much doubt about the story alleged in the letter of remission, then witnesses might be brought to the Parlement of Paris at the supplicant's expense (AN, X²ᴬ 89A, Nov. 14, 1539). Otherwise, they would be questioned by a local judge and a report made to Parlement (AN, X²ᴬ 98, 21ᵛ, Apr. 14, 1545/46). Witnesses were named, of course, by the supplicant as well as by the victim's kin.

Some examples of time intervals in pardon cases: Lyon dyer Claude Cleppoing killed a printer's journeyman in a fight in July 1550, got his letter of remission in October, surrendered himself to the Sénéchaussée of Lyon in January 1550/51, and had his letter ratified in November 1551 (ADR, BP441, sentence of Nov. 5, 1551). Lyon boatman Jean Bas killed a cook in a fight on Easter Monday 1558, then accidentally killed a boatman's little boy in November 1558, got his letter of remission in Paris that same month, and had his letter ratified in Lyon on Dec. 24 without having to be a voluntary prisoner (ADR, BP444, 201ᵛ–202ᵛ, 212ᵛ–215ᵛ). Of 100 persons who were prisoners at the Conciergerie at Paris in the 1560's and 1570's while their letters were being reviewed (APP, Aᴮ1–6), almost a third had their cases disposed of in a month or less, and another 40 percent had to wait three to six months. Two persons had to wait more than a year, one of them having his remission finally ratified, but with an unusually large fine to his victim's kin, the other having his remission dismissed (APP, Aᴮ4, 225ʳ; Aᴮ6, 294ʳ).

19. Any time the deceased left a widow and heirs or other close kin who had a legitimate claim, the letter of remission might include the formula "satisfaction faite à sa partie civile." Examples of remissions ratified with specified payments: solicitor Pierre Gosse of Pontoise is pardoned provided he pay a pastrymaker's widow the 24 livres agreed upon before his victim's death and 30 livres more (AN, X²ᴬ 89A, Jan. 31, 1539/40); hatter Laurent Sabourin, who had been condemned to death for his homicide and to pay 80 livres to the widow and children of his victim as well as a 100 livres fine to the seigneur of his *châtellenie*, or local jurisdiction, in Poitou, is pardoned provided he pay the widow and children 64 livres (AN, X²ᴮ 53, Sept. 14, 1568). Example of a remission ratified with charitable payments specified: a textile worker of Amiens, who killed his master in a drunken fight, is pardoned provided he pay 100 sous to the Cordeliers of Paris and 100 sous in other alms (AN, JJ249B, 1ᵛ–2ʳ).

Examples of remissions ratified with provisions of banishment: a poor gardener from Ribeauville in Picardy banished from France for two years; a legal officer of Nogaro banished from the sénéchaussée of Toulouse for two years (JJ265 170ᵛ–171ʳ, 193ʳ–194ʳ). Both were Protestants who had killed Catholics in the tense year 1567. Example of a remission ratified with provision that the supplicant serve in the army: a surgeon of Bléré in Touraine pardoned in 1572 for his homicide provided he serve the king three years in the town of Metz (presumably as an army surgeon) and pay 600 livres to the kin of the deceased (APP, Aᴮ4, 44ʳ).

20. Thomas A. Green, *Verdict According to Conscience: Perspectives on the*

English Criminal Trial Jury, 1200–1800 (Chicago, 1985), pp. 106–97, and see below, chap. 2, pp. 74–75. Jousse, *Justice criminelle* (1771), vol. 3, pp. 480–554 on Homicide. Under the single rubric, Jousse distinguishes four "manners" of homicide (by necessity, by accident, by imprudence, voluntarily) and discusses them and further distinctions with greater logical fineness than in the sixteenth-century texts. He also opens his section on penalty by saying that it depends on the quality and circumstances of the case. But he still gives the general maxim that "tout homicide, même involontaire ou à son corps défendant, mérite la peine de mort à moins qu'on n'obtienne les lettres de grace du Prince" (p. 482). On the general history of criminal responsibility in Old Regime France and its transformation by the Napoleonic Code, see Laingui and Lebigre, *Histoire du droit pénal*, vol. 1, especially pp. 26–103, 147–58.

21. La Roche-Flavin, *Arrests notables*, book 6, title 53, Des Homicides, article 1, p. 460 (reference to the ire of God and Deut. 21:1–9). *Le Guydon des Practiciens contenant tout le faict de practique comme lon se doibt conduyre en exerceant icelle*, ed. Etienne Dolet (Lyon: Scipion de Gabiano, 1538), 345ʳ. Jean Papon, *Trias Iudiciel du Second Notaire* (Lyon: Jean de Tournes, 1575), pp. 460–73: "D'Homicide"; *Troisieme Notaire*, pp. 741–44. The humanist jurist André Tiraqueau wrote an important treatise on the Roman law of punishments and the circumstances under which they could be mitigated, but it was not addressed to the practical issues approached by the judges' texts (*De Poenis Legum* [Lyon: Claude Senneton, 1559]).

22. *Guydon des Practiciens*, 345ʳ.

23. Bernard Schnapper, "La justice criminelle rendue par le Parlement de Paris sous le règne de François Ier," *Revue historique de droit français et étranger*, 4th series, 52 (1974): 269–74; Alfred Soman, "La justice criminelle aux XVIe et XVIIe siècles: le Parlement de Paris et les sièges subalternes," in *La Faute*, pp. 20–22, 34–38. Imbert, *Institutions Forenses*, p. 491; La Roche-Flavin, *Treize Livres*, book 13, chap. 69, paragraph 6, p. 1107: "Et de faict i'ay veu quelquefois, que la Cour par grande et accoustumee equité, auparavant que proceder au iugement de ceux qui estoyent accusés d'homicide fait en se defendant, leur on enioinct d'obtenir du Roy, ou de sa Chancellerie, lettres de remission et pardon."

24. On the procedures of French criminal justice in the sixteenth century, see Imbert, *Institutions Forenses* and Lizet, *Brieve et succincte maniere* for contemporary sources. In addition to the early work of A. Esmein, *Histoire de la procédure criminelle en France* (Paris, 1882), see Jean Imbert and Georges Levasseur, *Le Pouvoir, les juges et les bourreaux* (Paris, 1972); John H. Langbein's examination of legislation in *Prosecuting Crime in the Renaissance* (Cambridge, Mass., 1974), pp. 223–51; and the important essay of Soman, "La justice criminelle" in *La Faute*, pp. 15–52. I have given a picture of the procedure in a single criminal trial in N. Z. Davis, *The Return of Martin Guerre* (Cambridge, Mass., 1983), chaps. 7–8. Also useful is Raymond A. Mentzec, Jr., "The Self-Image of the Magistrate in Sixteenth-Century France," *Criminal Justice History*, 5 (1984): 23–43.

25. Schnapper, "La justice criminelle," p. 270. AN, X²ᴬ 86, Nov. 17,

1535. Another example of a supplicant who felt he had not been able to get out the true story behind his homicide in the course of his criminal trial is François Boussier, a hired plowman of a village in Anjou, who killed a man making noise in the garden in the middle of the night (AN, X²ᴬ 98, 183ᵛ, May 15, 1546).

26. Lizet, *Brieve et succincte maniere*, 32ʳ⁻ᵛ; Imbert, *Institutions Forenses*, pp. 492–93; AN, X²ᴬ 89A, Nov. 24, 1539; ADR, BP441, sentence of Sept. 14, 1551. In deciding whether to ratify the letter of remission of Jean de Mores, seigneur de Rocheux—a letter hotly contested by the widow of his victim—the Parlement of Paris said there would be a formal confrontation with witnesses "if need be" ("si besoing est"), but it did not occur, and the letter was ratified (AN, X²ᴬ 98, 296ʳ, June 7, 1546). An example where ratification hearings moved to formal "confrontation et recollement" (*sic*; in fact, the récolement, or the rereading of a deposition to a witness to make sure he or she verified it, preceded the confrontation with the accused): AN, X²ᴬ 98, 71ᵛ–72ᵛ. Plowman François Boussier was questioned under torture before his letter of remission was ratified by the Parlement, although this may have occurred in connection with his appeal of his death sentence and before he had obtained his letter of grace (AN X²ᴬ 98, 183ᵛ).

27. Roger D. Abrahams, *Between the Living and the Dead* (FF Communications 225; Helsinki, 1980), a study of neck-riddles. On Samson, see Judges 14:14. In the collection of medieval riddles, or "devinettes," published by Bruno Roy, none has the exact motif of the traditional neck-riddles, but several require the same complicated narrative answer for their solution (*Devinettes françaises du Moyen Age*, ed. Bruno Roy [Cahiers d'études médiévales 3; Montréal, 1977], nos. 215, 269, 550, 551). Cf. the "neck-verse" of the late medieval clergy, the Latin Biblical text (often the opening of Psalm 151), which, if the accused could read it, would give them benefit of clergy in a criminal case and save their necks.

28. Papon, *Troisieme Notaire*, pp. 1–2, 6–7. François de Billon, *Le Fort inexpugnable de l'honneur du sexe Femenin* (Paris, 1555; facsimile, New York, 1970), chap. 14: "Requeste que la plume fait aux Dames en faveur des Secretaires," especially 241ʳ–242ʳ. *Le Thresor du Nouveau Stille* (1599), 4ᵛ–5ᵛ: the king has decorated the royal notaries with "Noblesse et infinis beaux privileges."

29. Michaud, *Grande Chancellerie*, part I, chap. 3 and p. 293 n. 9. Book 2 of Tessereau's *Grande Chancellerie* gives all the major legislation concerning the royal secretaries and the names of many of them from the reign of Louis XI through the reign of Henri III.

30. On the cultural connections and activities of the royal secretaries, see Michaud, *Grande Chancellerie*, pp. 178–86, and Papon, *Troisieme Notaire*, pp. 40–42. A. H. Schutz, *Vernacular Books in Parisian Private Libraries of the Sixteenth Century According to the Notarial Inventories* (University of North Carolina Studies in the Romance Languages and Literatures, 25; Chapel Hill, N.C., 1955), pp. 38, 83, 86: the *Decameron* in French in the libraries of royal secretary Jacques Perdrier and of Anne Tronson, wife of royal secretary Robert de Saint Germain. R. Doucet, *Les Bibliothèques parisiennes au*

XVIe siècle (Paris, 1956), pp. 83–89: Nicole Gilles, notaire et secrétaire du roi, had in his library in 1499 *Les Cent Nouvelles Nouvelles*, a 1485 translation of the *Decameron*, and *La Mer des Histoires* among his 64 titles.

31. *Le grant stille* (1514/15; cited Introduction, n. 11), 96ᵛ–98ᵛ; *Le grand Stille* (1539/40), 119ʳ⁻ᵛ; *Le Grand Stile* (1548), 125ʳ–126ʳ. The copy of the 1939/40 edition in Special Collections at the University of Pennsylvania Library has a sixteenth-century inscription saying that the book was a gift of merchant Christophe Brunel to notary A. Souillart. Some royal secretaries compiled or had a scribe compile their own formularies: Hélène Michaud, *Les Formulaires de Grande Chancellerie, 1500–1580* (Paris, 1972), remissions mentioned pp. 63, 68, 158, 166. A formulary compiled in 1570–71 is BN, ms. Dupuy 273, with a "Forme de remission" on 160ᵛ–161bisᵛ; it gives lengthy variants on the legal formulas for the last sentences of the remission letter. Printed formulas for letters of remission are also given by Milles de Souvigny, *Praxis Criminis Persequendi*, 56ᵛ–58ᵛ, and by Papon, *Troisieme Notaire*, p. 753. In general on sixteenth-century preambles, see Michaud, *Grande Chancellerie*, pp. 212–14.

32. AN, JJ238, 23ʳ; JJ257C, 7ᵛ; JJ238, 171ʳ; JJ247, 138ᵛ. Also "pouvre simple femme" (JJ253B, 114ᵛ), "povre simple homme" (JJ256B, 37ᵛ); "pauvre homme vieulx et caducque" (JJ263A, 271ʳ); "paintre chargé de sa mere et sept filles à marier, ses soeurs" (JJ257C, 141ʳ).

33. AN, JJ248, 3ʳ. The reference to military service also draws upon an old Roman consideration for pardon, service to the republic (Imbert, *Institutions Forenses*, pp. 486–87). Cf. the supplication of Claude Le Charron, student at the University of Bourges, "son of the late master Claude Charron, when alive doctor of laws and lieutenant in the Sénéchaussée of Lyon" (JJ245B, 62ʳ).

34. *Le grant stille* (1514/15), 97ʳ; *Le grand Stille* (1539/40), 119ʳ⁻ᵛ; *Le Grand Stile* (1548), 125ʳ⁻ᵛ. The 1539/40 and 1548 formularies changed the phrase "ne convaincu d'aucun aultre vilain cas blasme ou reproche" to "aultre vilain cas blaspheme ou reproche," perhaps reflecting growing concern for heresy. Milles de Souvigny, *Praxis Criminis Persequendi*, 57ᵛ; Papon, *Troisieme Notaire*, p. 753.

35. On solicitors picking up royal letters for their clients, see Michaud, *Grande Chancellerie*, p. 352. On a preliminary letter sent for a prisoner requesting the ratification of his letter of remission, see AN, X²ᴮ 53, Aug. 20, 1569, letter for Jean Harson to the Parlement of Paris.

36. ADR, BP441, sentences of June 15, Sept. 14, and Dec. 22, 1551; BP444, 201ᵛ–202ʳ, 212ᵛ–215ᵛ, 263ᵛ–266ᵛ. One can find a similar variation in the presence of attorneys when supplicants asked for ratification of letters of remission before the Parlement of Paris. Supplicants appearing without an attorney as they sought entérinement: AN, X²ᴬ 98, 28ᵛ, 64ᵛ; supplicants appearing with an attorney: AN, X²ᴬ 98, 73ᵛ; X²ᴬ 87, Jan. 18, 1535/36. Isambert, ed., *Recueil général*, vol. 14, p. 633, article 162. See the discussion of this article—"En matières criminelles, ne seront les parties aucunement ouïes et par le conseil ne ministère d'aucunes personnes, mais répondront par leur bouche des cas dont ils seront accusés"—in Langbein,

Prosecuting Crime, pp. 235–37. On the continuing access of the accused to attorneys, see Soman, "La Justice criminelle," p. 50; and on the claim that advocates can plead in criminal cases on points of law, see Claude Expilly, *Plaidoyez de Me Claude Expilly . . . President au Parlement de Grenoble* (Lyon, 1662), Plaidoyé 39. Examples of advocates pleading for the ratification of a letter of remission are in ibid., Plaidoyé 32 (1595); *Journal d'un bourgeois de Paris*, p. 157 (1523); and AN, X²ᴬ 98, 73ᵛ–74ʳ.

37. Michaud, *Grande Chancellerie*, p. 355, quoting AN, X²ᴬ 114, June 2, 1553. "Minute de lettres de grace ou pardon sur icelle dressez en bonne et deue forme Les lettres de grace et pardon pour Jacob et David Momin Vacquies freres/pour Jacob comme ayant commis le meurtre et pour David comme assistant" (1616). Archives Perries-Labarthe, Mas-Grenier, document on loan to Jean-Philippe Labrousse. Michaud reports that some royal secretaries had an attorney on their staff for legal advice on drafting letters (*Grande Chancellerie*, p. 289).

38. Philippe Canaye, *Remonstrances et Discours faicts et prononcez en la Cour et Chambre de l'Edict, establie à Castres d'Albigeois* (Paris: Adrian Perier, 1598), p. 33. Albert Labarre, *Le Livre dans la vie amiénoise du seizième siècle* (Paris, 1971), pp. 272–77; the Amiens procureurs as a group possessed fewer books than the avocats (pp. 112–13). La Roche-Flavin, *Treize Livres*, book 2, chap. 18, "Des solliciteurs et praticiens," and pp. 239–40 on the Basoche. Adolphe Fabre, *Les Clercs du Palais. Recherches historiques sur les Bazoches des Parlements* (Lyon, 1875); Howard G. Harvey, *The Theatre of the Basoche* (Cambridge, Mass., 1941).

39. La Roche-Flavin, *Treize Livres*, book 3, chaps. 1–3, "Des Advocats," and book 2, pp. 239–40. Catherine L. Holmes, *L'Eloquence judiciaire de 1620 à 1660* (Paris, 1967), pp. 13–40, 292–98. On forensic eloquence, see the superb study of Marc Fumaroli, *L'Age de l'Eloquence. Rhétorique et 'res literaria' de la Renaissance au seuil de l'époque classique* (Geneva, 1980), especially pp. 427–521. Jacques Faye, *Recueil des Remonstrances faites en la cour de Parlement de Paris aux ouvertures des Plaidoiries* (La Rochelle: Hierosme Haultin, 1592), Remonstrance 1 (1581), pp. 1–18, on Advocates who plead and their eloquence. On advocates pleading "cas gras," see Pierre Grolier, *Plaide pour un amoureux iniustement detenu prisonner, Appellant au siege Royal criminel de Lyon, Faict par Monsieur Grolier Advocat* (Lyon: Macé Bonhomme, 1556); Expilly, *Plaidoyez*, Plaidoyé 8, Mardi gras, 1605; La Roche-Flavin, *Treize Livres*, book 4, pp. 391–92. An example of a plea for pardon is published in Expilly, *Plaidoyez*, Plaidoyé 32 (1595).

40. Noël du Fail was still an advocate at Rennes in 1547 when his *Propos Rustiques* first appeared. On men of law and humanist scholarship, see Kelley, *Foundations of Modern Historical Scholarship* (cited Introduction, n. 6). An example of love intrigues written up as sentences in a law case is Martial d'Auvergne, *Aresta amorum* (Lyon: Sébastien Gryphius, 1533) with commentaries by the Lyonnais jurist Benoît Court. On the libraries of avocats, see Labarre, *Le Livre*, pp. 112–13, 243–49, 281–305; Doucet, *Bibliothèques parisiennes*, pp. 105–64 (inventory of the books of Jean Le Féron, avocat in the Parlement of Paris: 670 items, including several medieval romances);

Schutz, *Vernacular Books*, pp. 38, 66, 78–79, 82 (copies of Boccaccio's *Decameron* in the library of Léon Godeffroy, avocat in the Parlement of Paris, and in that of François Fournier, avocat in the bailliage of Amiens).

41. Papon, *Troisieme Notaire*, p. 748. Papon was talking here about a letter of remission that was controversial, with some recommending its ratification and some its dismissal.

42. In criminal matters, jurisdiction over members of the clergy was divided between the church and the king, the royal justice always trying to increase its control (Doucet, *Les Institutions*, pp. 690–91), clerics usually trying to take their case to an ecclesiastical tribunal, where a death penalty would not be given unless the accused was relaxed to the secular arm. Priests are present, but not extremely numerous, among sixteenth-century pardon recipients. Of three cases specially analyzed for this study, all concerning homicide, a parish priest in Auvergne had action taken against him both by royal officers and by the Bishop of Clermont (AN, JJ238, 165 $^{r-v}$); while the cases of a religious of the order of Fontrevaulx, living in Picardy, and a Benedictine monk of Carcassonne seem to have gone directly to royal courts (JJ237, 31 ^{r}; JJ257B, 67 $^{r-v}$).

43. On the veillées, see Vaultier, *Le Folklore*, pp. 111–14. On storytelling in shops, see the ruling for the textile industry in a French town cited by Levasseur: the journeymen, while working, are not to tell "aucun discours d'histoires, d'aventures ou d'autres entretiens qui détourne les ouvriers" (E. Levasseur, *Histoire des classes ouvrières et l'industrie en France avant 1789*, 2 vols. [Paris, 1900], vol. 2, pp. 423–44). On the local composition of songs, see AN, X ^{2A} 44, Dec. 9, 1479 (Jeanne Corsele of Paris accused of composing a defamatory song about the adventures of Agnès du Pin, her neighbor, and having it sung in several places, including on Agnès's street) and N. Z. Davis, "Charivari, Honor and Community in Seventeenth-Century Lyon and Geneva," in John J. MacAloon, ed., *Rite, Drama, Festival, Spectacle: Rehearsals Toward a Theory of Cultural Performance* (Philadelphia, 1984), pp. 42–57 (songs made up by male and female artisans about their neighbors' activities in Lyon in 1668 and in Geneva in 1669). On songs about neighborhood events in eighteenth-century Languedoc, see Nicole Castan, *Les Criminels de Languedoc: Les exigences d'ordre et les voies du ressentiment dans une société pré-révolutionnaire (1750–1790)* (Toulouse, 1980), p. 244. On medieval storytelling aloud and its relation to the *nouvelle*, see Dubuis, *Les Cent Nouvelles nouvelles*, pp. 559–61, and on the relation of oral accounts of "news" and "faits divers" to written "nouvelles," see Gabriel A. Pérouse, *Nouvelles françaises du XVIe siècle. Images de la vie du temps* (Lille, 1978), pp. 26–37. On life histories, oral and written, see N. Z. Davis, "Ghosts, Kin and Progeny: Some Features of Family Life in Early Modern France," in Alice S. Rossi et al., *The Family* (New York, 1977), pp. 96–99 and n. 31. AN, JJ256C, 41 $^{r-v}$, letter of remission, dated Apr. 1544, for Fiacre Marglier of Brie.

44. In general on confession, Thomas N. Tentler, *Sin and Confession on the Eve of the Reformation* (Princeton, N.J., 1977), pp. 57–134, and Jacques Toussaert, *Le Sentiment religieux en Flandre à la fin du Moyen Age* (Paris,

1963), pp. 104–21. *Statuta ecclesie Lugduni* (Lyon, no date [ca. 1488], b ii^r–b iiii^r; *Statuts et Ordonnances synodales de l'Eglise metropolitaine de Lyon* (Lyon, 1578), chap. 9 on Confession. *Heures a lusage de Mascon . . . et plusieurs Oraisons de nouveau adioustees* (Lyon: Thibaud Payen, 1554), concludes with an Examen de Conscience, organized by sins of thoughts and will, sins of tongue and action. Emond Auger, *La manière d'ouir la messe avec dévotion . . . Ensemble la manière de bien confesser ses pechez* (Paris, 1571), D iii^r–F i^r: urges self-examination by the Ten Commandments, the seven branches of sin, the acts of mercy. Adrien du Hecquet, *Les Enseignemens des Paroisses* (Lyon: Benoît Rigaud, 1583), 33^r–44^r: exhortations to prepare for confession starting the first Sunday of Lent.

Jean Benedicti, *La Somme des Pechez et le Remede d'iceux* (Paris: Denis Binet, 1595), book 5, chap. 4 on Confession, especially pp. 645, 647. In advising the priest how to conduct confession, Benedicti returns to the same point: confession was not supposed to be a place to "narrer une histoire" and the confessor should try to discourage people from doing it (book 5, chap. 2, p. 576).

45. Jean Cotreau, *Commentaires, en forme de sermons, exposans les dix Commandemens de Dieu* (Paris: Guillaume Chaudiere, 1576), Sermon 19, 176^r–185^v.

46. Philippe de Vigneulles, *Les Cent Nouvelles Nouvelles*, ed. Charles Livingston (Geneva, 1972), no. 73, pp. 292–93. AN, JJ247, 127^{r-v}, letter of remission, dated Sept. 1534, for Jeanne, wife of Jean Galzy, sergeant of Saint Victor in Rouergue. AN, X^{2A} 44, Nov. 18, 1479. Lyon dyer Claude Cleppoing killed a printer's journeyman in a street fight btween craft groups on July 19, 1550. He fled the city and went to Fécamp to surrender himself as a prisoner and was there to be granted a pardon at the Joyous Entry of Henri II in October (ADR, BP441, sentence of Nov. 5, 1551). Henri II had made his Joyous Entry into Lyon in late September 1548. The pardons listed in note 10 to this chapter are all for persons who fled from one place to a town wherc the king was to enter, including a woman, Barbe Milly, a peasant's wife living near Troyes, who fled to Dijon to surrender herself for the Joyous Entry of Henri II earlier that September (AN, JJ258B, 110^v, Sept. 1548).

47. *L'Histoire Memorable de la Conversion de Iean Guy parricide, et la constance de sa mort: natif de Chastillon sur Loing, et executé audict lieu* (Orléans: Eloi Gibier, 1566), pp. 5–7.

48. Imbert, *Institutions Forenses*, p. 492.

49. Michel de Montaigne, *Essais*, book 3, chap. 9, "De la vanité," in *Oeuvres complètes*, ed. Albert Thibaudet and Maurice Rat (Bibliothèque de la Pléiade; Paris, 1962), p. 940.

50. The series AN, X^{2A}, of the Parlement of Paris (Arrêts) and ADR, BP, of the Sénéchaussée of Lyon (Sentences) do not include a transcription of the testimony of the supplicant at the time of ratification, but merely the finding of the court, the reactions of the kin of the deceased, a copy of the letter of remission and other legal detail. In the Paris series X^{2B} 1 and following (Minutes d'Arrêts), there are fuller records in connection with the

hearings, including the original parchment of the letter of remission, but I found no transcription of ratification testimony for the 1560's through 1580's. Formal interrogations of pardon seekers would normally have been preserved in the subseries X²ᴮ 1174–1318 (pièces d'instructions), but they are fragmentary for the sixteenth century; cartons 1174 (1569–71) and 1175 (1579–83) did not, alas, yield any transcriptions of hearings on letters of ratification. Further sleuthing by others might uncover sixteenth-century examples of full ratification testimony.

51. AN, JJ265, 154ʳ⁻ᵛ; AEG, Procès criminels 1436 (1st series), Nov. 3, 1567. A native of Metz, Dater's name is given as Datel in the letter of remission; as Dater in the Livre des habitants de Geneva in 1551 and 1572 (Paul-F. Geisendorf, ed., *Livres des habitants de Genève*, 2 vols. [Geneva, 1957–1963], vol. 1, p. 20, vol. 2, p. 12); as Dather in a Lyon apprenticeship contract of 1566 (ADR, 3E4061, Nov. 18, 1566) and variously as Danter and Dattel in his Geneva trial.

52. Soman, "Procès pour homicide d'une sorcière." AN, X²ᴬ 178, 604ᵛ–607ʳ (I am very grateful to Alfred Soman for providing me with his transcription of this document to compare with the interrogation published in his article).

53. Papon, *Troisieme Notaire*, p. 7.

54. *Theorique de l'Art des Notaires . . . Traduite de Latin en François et succinctement adaptee aux Ordonnances Royaux par Pardoux du Prat Docteur es droits* (Lyon: Basile Bouquet, 1582), pp. 32–33. Papon, *Troisieme Notaire*, pp. 28–32.

55. Ibid., p. 750; Milles de Souvigny, *Praxis Criminis Persequendi*, 56ᵛ–57ʳ. Toward the end of the century, two formularies say not only that the letter of remission is to describe what actually happened, but also that it is supposed to conform to the "informations," that is, to the sworn depositions already taken about the case: the phrase in the 1570–71 manuscript formulary is "sera desduict le faict aupres de la verité et juxte les informations" (BN, ms. Dupuy 273, 161ʳ) and in the 1599 printed formulary, "soit mis le cas comme il est advenu et selon et en ensuivant les informations de point en point" (*Le Thresor du Nouveau Stille*, 25ᵛ). It is difficult to envisage situations where the notary or the supplicant had copies of the "informations" to use during a recording session; in fact, the results of the formal judicial inquiry were secret. Rather this phrase must be another way of insisting that the supplicant avoid "obreption" and "subreption," that is, avoid putting in things he can not prove and omitting things he knows can be established by witnesses, the things that he would assume would have been recorded in the "informations." In any event, the letter recorded the supplicant's story, not all the evidence in the case.

56. AN, JJ245B, 150ʳ⁻ᵛ; JJ247, 139ʳ; JJ248, 11ᵛ–12ʳ; JJ256B, 36ᵛ (letter of remission for Peyronteau Delebrere of the jurisdiction of Mondieu in Le Brouilh, Comté d'Armagnac, Dec. 1542).

57. AN, JJ245B, 149ᵛ–150ᵛ (see Appendix A for transcription of Manny's letter of remission); X²ᴬ 178, 604ᵛ–607ʳ; Soman, "Procès pour homicide d'une sorcière," p. 74. Secretaries also added the legal word

"ledit" or "ladite," that is "the said," for specificity. Some of them added the adjective "feu," "the late," before the first mention of the victim's name in the letter, but many of them let the suspense build up. The reader may not know for sure who is going to be killed till the event is described.

Here is the account from the journal of Sire Gilles de Gouberville, gentleman and lieutenant of streams and forests in the Cotentin of Normandy, of having a letter drawn up by a royal secretary. It was not a letter of remission, but this picture suggests how the process worked for a literate person:

Saturday, Feb. 8, 1555/56: "Je m'en allé chez Monsr Le Chandelier, segrétayre du Roy, affin qu'il me dressast une requeste. . . . Au soyer je retourné chez led. s^r Chandelier quérir ma requeste. Je luy baillé deux escus sol et ung teston à son clerc pour la mettre au net."

Sunday, Feb. 9: "Sur le soyer, je fus quérir ma requeste chez Monsr Chandelier. Je donné à son cler, qui l'avoyt mise au net, encor ii s."

Monday, Feb. 10: "Je corrigé ma requeste pour ce qu'elle me sembloyt trop prolixe."

Tuesday, Feb. 11: "Je montré ma requeste à Monsr Le Chandelier, qui la trouva bien. Je baillé à son cler, pour la remettre au net, viii s." (Gilles de Gouberville, *Le Journal du Sire de Gouberville*, ed. Eugène de Robillard de Beaurepaire [Caen, Rouen and Paris, 1893], p. 248.)

58. It does not seem possible to sort the letters of remission according to the royal secretary who, together with his clerks, actually drew them up. There are signatures reported in the copies made in AN, JJ and X^{2A}, but they come from the person who has signed the act for the Chancellery, the secretary who has "seen" the act and takes responsibility for it and its contents, and the officer who has collected the fee and is responsible for dispersing it. As Michaud points out, these persons are not the same as the person who has drawn up the letter (*Grande Chancellerie*, pp. 228–29, 306–10). The repetition of the same names in many letters of remission after the words "Visa" and "Contentor" confirms the supposition that these men are playing special roles for the Chancellery. Michaud says that the signature of the person who has actually drawn up the letter can sometimes be found on the verso of the parchment (p. 308), but I found too few signatures on the original parchments to be able to pinpoint a secretarial author. In any case, the argument being made here is that even if we knew the secretary's name, the content and style of the letter can not be attributed to him alone.

59. AN, JJ245B, 149^r–150^v; X^{2A} 95, 863^r–868^v, reprinted in Longeon, ed., *Documents sur Etienne Dolet*, pp. 25–30. Dolet's third and last request for a letter of remission was also for publishing and selling heretical books. It was a poem in rhymed couplets, *Le Second Enfer*, written from his refuge in the Piedmont in 1544, after he had escaped from a Lyon prison, and partly inspired by Clément Marot's pardon poems, "L'Enfer" and "Au Roy, au temps de son exil à Ferrare." Dolet's poem has the same arguments as the 1543 letter of remission: blame laid on jealous enemies who have framed him; a consideration of his motives and whether he could reasonably have

sent bales of prohibited books with his name prominently displayed on them; a self-portrait as a good merchant-printer, a man whose "naturel est d'apprendre tousjours" and who wishes to serve Eloquence (*Second Enfer*, pp. 70–88). This similarity argues further for the presence of the supplicant in the text of the letter of remission.

60. AN, JJ253A, 139ᵛ–140ʳ, 147ʳ⁻ᵛ, letters of remission for Claude Perrot, sergeant in the Sénéchaussée of Lyon, and for Pierre Chavaignat, dit Le Pelle, lieutenant of the prévôt and captain of the watch, Aug. 1539. AN, JJ238, 202ᵛ–204ʳ, letter of remission, dated Nov. 1525, for Regnault Gregoire of Chartres.

61. AN, JJ255B, 22ᵛ–23ʳ, 30ʳ⁻ᵛ, letters of remission, dated Feb. 1540/41 and Mar. 1540/41, for Guillaume Fournier of Lyon for the homicide of Ysambert de Clamal.

62. For examples of earlier advocates' pleas in criminal cases that include narratives of the events as well as matters of law, see AN, X²ᴬ 44, Nov. 18, 1479, Mar. 3, 1479/80; X²ᴬ 53, Nov. 16, 1484 to Sept. 12, 1485, *passim*; X²ᴬ 72, 3ʳ, Nov. 23, 1524; X²ᴬ 79, Apr. 4, 1527/28; X²ᴬ 87, Feb. 5, 1535/36, and especially July 8, 1536, the account of a surgeon accused of a false cure. On the lawyers' roles in criminal cases after the edict of Villers-Cotterêts, see note 36 above and Alfred Soman, "La décriminalisation de la sorcellerie en France," *Histoire, économie et société*, 4, no. 2 (1985): 200–202. One can read some of these later criminal plaidoyers in registers devoted to sessions known as audiences—for example, AN, X²ᴬ 1392, a registre d'audience for 1582: 13ʳ and 16ʳ for facts organized around legal claims rather than around a story line; 25ᵛ–28ᵛ for an advocate elaborating in French and Latin on the frequency of murder in France and the tardiness of punishment ("dict que les assassinatz sont aujourdhuy si communz en la France. . . . Et neantmoins la punition en est si lente") before he finally turns to the "fait particulier."

63. AN, X²ᴬ 98, 73ᵛ–74ʳ, Apr. 15, 1545/46, Delaporte pleading for the ratification of the letter of remission of Jean de Villeneufve, seigneur de Villeneufve. Expilly, *Plaidoyez*, Plaidoyé 32, "Sur une presentation de lettres de grace," pp. 264–71. Three other pleas on criminal cases (Plaidoyés 22, 24, 39) get quickly to points of law and give little or no narrative. In some of his pleas in civil cases, Expilly opens with a concise and clear history of the "fait" and then moves to a wide philosophical, legal, and moral consideration of the issues (e.g., Plaidoyé 3 on the clockmaker of Romans). But Expilly does not indulge in excessive storytelling, a style that would have received criticism as a "plaidoyer embarrassé . . . par tant de faicts et allegations superflues" (La Roche-Flavin, *Treize Livres*, book 3, chap. 3, paragraph 5, p. 306). On the Plutarchan "rhétorique des citations," see the excellent discussion in Fumaroli, *L'Age de l'Eloquence*, pp. 444–46.

64. AN, JJ249B 51ʳ–52ᵛ (letter of remission, dated Apr. 1535/36, for Charles de Villelume).

65. On the popularity of chivalric romances in the early sixteenth century, see John J. O'Connor, *Amadis de Gaule and Its Influence on Elizabethan Literature* (New Brunswick, N.J., 1970), pp. 3–13; Labarre, *Le Livre,*

pp. 210–11. On reading *Amadis de Gaule* aloud at the Cotentin manor house of the Sire de Gouberville in February 1554/55, see Gouberville, *Journal*, p. 156.

66. On rural disorder in the Bourbonnais in the 1520's and on the dramatic clash between Charles de Bourbon, connétable of France, and François Ier as viewed by a contemporary in Paris, see *Journal d'un bourgeois de Paris*, pp. 125–32, 140. The administrative integration of the Bourbonnais began in 1523. To be sure, there was royal intervention in the duchy going back to the fourteenth century: the king sometimes issued letters of remission to persons there and sometimes cases were appealed to Parlement from ducal judicial courts. But Charles de Villeneuve's case would have been a strictly ducal matter before the 1520's. On the Bourbonnais in the fifteenth and early sixteenth centuries, see André Leguai, *De la Seigneurie à l'Etat: Le Bourbonnais pendant la Guerre de Cent Ans* (Moulins, 1969), chaps. 7, 9, 18–19, and by the same author, *Histoire du Bourbonnais* (Paris, 1960), pp. 47–67. Among recent studies of the situation and values of the country nobility in sixteenth-century France, see George Huppert, *Les Bourgeois Gentilshommes: An Essay on the Definition of Elites in Renaissance France* (Chicago, 1977); James B. Wood, *The Nobility of the "Election" of Bayeux, 1463–1666: Continuity Through Change* (Princeton, N.J., 1980).

67. AN, JJ124, 188^v, printed in Léon Mirot, *Les Insurrections urbaines au début du règne de Charles VI (1380–1383)* (Paris, 1905), p. 116 n. 1.

68. AN, JJ86, 89^r, printed in Siméon Luce, *Histoire de la Jacquerie d'après des documents inédits* (Paris, 1859), pp. 217–18; and see several other remissions in the Pièces Justificatives published by Luce.

69. AN, JJ170, no. 106, printed in L. Douët d'Arcq, *Choix de pièces inédites relatives au règne de Charles VI*, 2 vols. (Paris, 1864), vol. 2, pp. 180–82.

70. AN, JJ243, 100^r, printed in Georges Guiffrey, *Procès criminel de Iehan de Poytiers, Seigneur de Saint-Vallier* (Paris, 1867), pp. 155–72. This book is a study of the entire case and reproduces all its documents.

71. AN, JJ238, 165^{r-v}. The village was Montaigut-le-Blanc in Auvergne.

72. AN, JJ253A, 139^v, letter of remission, dated Aug. 1539, for Claude Perrot, sergeant in the Sénéchaussée of Lyon; JJ254, 6^r, letter of remission, dated Jan. 1537/38, for Barthélemy Pain, poor *poissonier* of Lyon, for the homicide of Antoine Beraud dit Perceval.

73. AN, JJ253B, 114^v, letter of remission, dated Oct. 1540 and sent to the bailiff of Laon, for Jeanne, wife of Perret Hennequin, of the village of Ramieville[?] near Coucy. Jeanne quotes the women as shouting, "Ces meschans rompent nos huys et maisons et emportent tous nos biens." This is a valuable text for the history of women's collective action.

74. AN, JJ257B, 107^{r-v}, letter of remission, dated July 1546, for Pierre Francete, of a village in the Agenois and currently in the prisons of Cognac, for having killed a seigneur who was using violence against the priest to prevent his carrying the host in the Corpus Christi procession. Francete was one of the priest's servants. AN, X^{2A} 178, 604^v–607^r (transcription kindly provided by Alfred Soman); this is the 1611 letter of remission of Pierre Marion, in which, as we have already noticed, the royal notary must

have inserted the word "frustratoires." AN, JJ256C, 30ᵛ–31ʳ, letter of remission, dated Apr. 1543/44, for Jeanne Pasquellet of Lyon.

75. Philippe de Vigneulles, *Gedenkbuch des Metzger Bürgers Philippe von
Vigneulles aus den Jahren 1471 bis 1522*, ed. Heinrich Michelant (Stuttgart,
1852, reprinted Amsterdam, 1968), p. 8, and see also the "cas de fortune"
on p. 261. Armine Avakian Kotin, *The Narrative Imagination: Comic Tales by
Philippe de Vigneulles* (Lexington, Ky., 1977), pp. 86–87 and p. 118 n. 5.
Among the numerous tales with historical settings, nouvelle 19B is one of
the few where the situation—a wartime prohibition on the export of provisions—is central to the events of the story; nouvelle 99 is an example of a
tale taken directly from an earlier Italian collection and reset as an expe-
dition of the Duke of Lorraine (Vigneulles, *Cent Nouvelles Nouvelles*,
pp. 109–11, 397–406). On the use of historical reference to make tales
seem "recent" and "authentic," whether or not they were, see Dubuis, *Les
Cent Nouvelles nouvelles*, pp. 19–33.

Le Grand Parangon des Nouvelles Nouvelles (1535–37) of the saddler Nicolas de Troyes also uses names drawn from the region of Tours, where he
lived, and bases itself both on local events and on stories remade from earlier collections. But it too does not give an *explanatory* historical frame to
the tales. See the edition prepared by Krystyna Kasprzyk (Paris, 1970) and
Kasprzyk's study *Nicolas de Troyes et le genre narratif en France au XVIe siècle*
(Warsaw and Paris, 1963).

76. Marcel Tetel, *Marguerite de Navarre's Heptameron: Themes, Language,
and Structure* (Durham, N.C., 1973), pp. 195–96. Thomas Platter, *Autobiographie*, trans. Marie Helmer (Cahier des Annales, 22; Paris, 1964).

77. Keith Thomas, *Religion and the Decline of Magic* (London, 1971), pp.
223, 285, 295; Madeleine Jeay, *Savoir Faire: Une Analyse des croyances des "Evangiles des Quenouilles" (XVe siècle)* (Le Moyen Age Français, 10; Montréal,
1982), *passim*. Benedicti, *Somme des Pechez*, pp. 47–48, on "special days."

78. There is much evidence on the occurrence of homicide on feast days
in the fourteenth and fifteenth centuries in Vaultier, *Le Folklore*, in the six-
teenth century in Muchembled, "Les jeunes, les jeux et la violence" (cited
Introduction, n. 4), pp. 568–69, and in the eighteenth century in Pascal
Mallen, "La criminalité dans le Comté de Crussol au 18e siècle," *Bulletin du
Centre d'histoire économique et sociale de la Région lyonnaise*, 4 (1984): 54–55.
On insults and quarrels on feast days in eighteenth-century Languedoc, see
N. Castan, *Criminels de Languedoc*, pp. 262–65. My stress here is not on the
factual correlation between homicides and feast days, but on how subse-
quent accounts of the homicides make use of the timing.

79. AN, JJ262, 196ʳ–197ᵛ, letter of remission, dated July 1553, for
Pierre Bodin, docteur ès droits and advocate in the Parlement of Aix. Also
JJ236, 462ʳ–463ʳ, letter of remission, dated Apr. 1524, for Pierre Martin,
young peasant of Cuire in Lyonnais (preparations for Mardi Gras); JJ255B,
53ʳ⁻ᵛ, letter of remission, dated May 1541, for Etienne Preyle, baker of
Lyon (ball game on Lundi Gras); JJ263A, 89ʳ⁻ᵛ, letter of remission, dated
Feb. 1555/56, for Nicolas Bodin, eighteen-year-old youth from a village in

the Comté de Roussillon (on the day of Carême-Prenant a shoe full of urine was thrown at him by the late Pierre Pinot); JJ263A, 207ʳ–208ʳ, letter of remission, dated May 1556, for Pierre Regnault, a young married man of Lyon, for wounding an unknown person on the Sunday of Carême-Prenant. On carnival and collective violence, see Emmanuel Le Roy Ladurie, *Le Carnaval de Romans* (Paris, 1979).

80. AN, JJ261B, 192ᵛ–193ʳ, letter of remission, dated July 1552, for Jean Macaigne of Rethondes; both Rethondes and Berneuil, the village of his victim, are in Picardy. Also see JJ238B, 1ᵛ, letter of remission, dated Jan. 1524/25, for Pierre de Bresil, merchant of Vézelay (feast of the parish on Saint Peter's day); JJ249B, 23ᵛ–24ʳ, letter of remission, dated Feb. 1535/36, for Antoine Roche of Néronde in Forez (feast day of Saint John the Baptist; his victim was from the village of Saint Paul d'Esperence); JJ261B, 224ʳ–225ᵛ, letter of remission, dated Aug. 1552, for Jean Brissanade of the village of Trinitat in Auvergne (feast of the Assumption, a fight with a priest from another village).

81. AN, JJ249B, 30ᵛ–31ᵛ, letter of remission, dated Feb. 1535/36, for Jean Couldray, winegrower of "Lay" near Paris.

82. AN, JJ245B, 132ᵛ–133ʳ, letter of remission, dated July 1530, for Guillaume Caranda, barber of Senlis. See Appendix A.

83. Giovanni Boccaccio, *The Decameron,* trans. John Payne (New York, 1931), Third Day, Story Ten, p. 291. (Payne, whose translation first appeared in 1886, left this passage in the original Italian.) In the French translation of the *Decameron* made for Marguerite de Navarre by Antoine Le Maçon and first published in Paris in 1545, the sentence reads: "Et estant ainsi Rusticque bruslant plus que devant pour la veoir ainsi nuë, et belle, la resurrection de la chair va venir" (*Le Decameron de Missire Iehan Bocace, Florentin* [Paris: la veufve Maurice de La Porte, 1553], 124ʳ).

François Rabelais, *Tiers Livres,* in *Oeuvres complètes,* ed. J. Boulenger (Bibliothèque de la Pléiade; Paris, 1955), chap. 27, p. 428. Leo Steinberg, *The Sexuality of Christ in Renaissance Art and Modern Oblivion* (New York, 1984), pp. 82–108, and for the discussion of John W. O'Malley, S.J. on the relation of this theme to the treatment of the Incarnation in Renaissance sermons, see pp. 199–203.

84. C. L. Barber, *Shakespeare's Festive Comedy: A Study of Dramatic Form and Its Relation to Social Custom* (Princeton, N.J., 1959). Mikhail Bakhtin, *Rabelais and His World,* trans. Helene Iswolsky (Cambridge, Mass., 1968). V. A. Kolve, *The Play Called Corpus Christi* (Stanford, Calif., 1966). Jean Jacquot and Elie Konigson, eds., *Les Fêtes de la Renaissance,* III (Quinzième colloque international d'études humanistes, Tours, 10–22 juillet 1972; Paris, 1975). Michael D. Bristol, *Carnival and Theater: Plebeian Culture and the Structure of Authority in Renaissance England* (New York and London, 1985).

85. N. Z. Davis, "The Rites of Violence," in *Society and Culture in Early Modern France* (Stanford, Calif., 1975); Yves-Marie Bercé, *Fête et révolte. Des mentalités populaires du XVIe au XVIIIe siècle* (Paris, 1976); Le Roy Ladurie, *Carnaval de Romans.*

86. Jean Guéraud, *La Chronique lyonnaise de Jean Guéraud, 1536–1562*, ed. Jean Tricou (Lyon, 1929), pp. 91–92. Oranges were part of Mardi Gras games at Montpellier, noted the Swiss medical student Felix Platter in 1553, adding "the fruit is sold ridiculously cheap" in the area (*Beloved Son Felix: The Journal of Felix Platter,* trans. Sean Jeannett [London, 1961], p. 52). In Lyon, oranges would have been more expensive and a desirable food for gagnedeniers.

87. Guéraud, *Chronique*, p. 92. I have not found a remission in connection with this homicide in AN, JJ263A (1556), but these copies made for the Chancellery records are only a fraction of all remissions granted. The years from 1557 to 1565 are missing in the JJ series. See also *Journal d'un bourgeois de Paris,* p. 367 for the treatment of a homicide by a financial officer of his brother-in-law at a dinner in honor of the feast of the Annunciation in 1526.

88. See, for example, the fine treatment of accounts of public celebrations in 1651 as part of the "Fronde des mots" in Christian Jouhaud, *Mazarinades: la Fronde des mots* (Paris, 1985), chap. 5.

89. On the contrast between Protestant and Catholic sense of time, see N. Z. Davis, "The Sacred and the Body Social in Sixteenth-Century Lyon," *Past and Present*, 90 (Feb. 1981): 40–70, and Gerard T. Moran, "Conceptions of Time in Early Modern France. An Approach to the History of Collective Mentalities," *Sixteenth Century Journal*, 12, no. 4 (1981): 3–19. I have not a large enough selection of letters of remission from persons identifiable as Protestants for the years after 1565 to see whether this speculation has any validity.

90. *Advertissement et Discours des chefs d'Accusation et Points Principaux du proces criminel fai[t] à Maistre Iean Poisle, Conseiller en la Cour de Parlement. A la requeste de Maistre René le Rouillier, aussi Conseiller en icelle Cour partie civile Monsieur le Procureur General du Roy ioinct avec luy* (n.p., 1582), p. 9.

91. AN, JJ264, 129ʳ, letter of remission, dated Mar. 1566, for Mathieu Loste, merchant of Lyon, for the homicide of Etienne Martin. JJ265, 83ᵛ–84ᵛ, letter of remission, dated Apr. 1567, for François de Rozer, écuyer, for the homicide of François Gauffre alias Le Cappitaine La Magne. JJ265, 231ʳˉᵛ, letter of remission, dated Dec. 1567, for François de Bucamps, merchant of Beauvais. See also JJ266, 55ᵛ, letter of remission, dated Apr. 1568, for Etienne de Vancontault, écuyer, for the homicide of Etienne Raymond, sergeant of Cusset, "estans lesdites villes [of Cusset and Vichy] en division l'une avec l'autre."

92. AN, JJ265, 193ʳ–194ʳ, letter of remission, dated Sept. 1567, for Me Pierre Prugno, procureur d'office of the Queen of Navarre in the Basse Court of Armagnac.

93. AN, JJ266, 146ʳ–147ʳ, letter of remission, dated Oct. 1568, for Bertrand Pulveret, captain of the chateau of Pierre-Scize at Lyon. When the Baron des Adrets came to Lyon in May 1562 to direct the Huguenot seizure of the city, he had lodged with Captain Latour (Pierre de Vaissière, *Le Baron des Adrets* [Paris, 1950], p. 30). Latour and Lacombe had been important captains during the Protestant regime of 1562–63.

Chapter Two

1. Benedicti, *Somme des Pechez* (cited chap. 1, n. 44), book 2, chap. 4, on the commandment "Thou shalt not kill," pp. 103–8. Benedicti also put limitations on the rightfulness of killing a thief who came in the night: though the civil law allowed it, it was prohibited by divine law if one had the possibility of apprehending the person alive (p. 108). Cotreau, *Commentaires* (cited chap. 1, n. 45), 176^r–177^r; Deut. 19:1–6. It was also permitted for the state to kill evildoers found guilty by the procedures of justice and for soldiers to kill in a just war (Benedicti, p. 107).

2. *Le Compost et Kalendrier des Bergiers. Reproduction en facsimile de l'édition de Guy Marchant* [Paris, 1493], ed. Pierre Champion (Paris, 1926), d iii^v; Hecquet, *Les Enseignemens des Paroisses* (cited chap. 1, n. 44), 84^v–86^v; Benedicti, *Somme des Pechez,* book 3, chap. 12, on "Ire," pp. 356–67. Jean Calvin, *Institution de la religion chrestienne* (Geneva, 1541), 4 vols., ed. Jacques Pannier (Paris, 1961), vol. 1, p. 254, on the commandment "Tu n'occiras point." See also the very interesting discussion of the tension between the "relative laxism in civil law" and the "apparent rigor in the moral law" of the Church in regard to letters of remission ratified by the Parlement of Navarre in the eighteenth century in Desplat, "La grâce royale" (cited Introduction, n. 4), pp. 86–88.

3. Morton W. Bloomfield, *The Seven Deadly Sins* (East Lansing, Mich., 1952, reprinted 1967), pp. 147, 165, 242. Benedicti, *Somme des Pechez,* book 4, chap. 13, pp. 367–76 on "Gourmandise," especially pp. 369–71 on "Yvrongnerie." Papon, *Second Notaire* (cited chap. 1, n. 21), p. 470; *Troisieme Notaire* (cited chap. 1, n. 1), pp. 741–44. Examples of the drunkenness plea: AN, JJ249B, 1^v–2^r, 31^r.

4. AN, JJ248, 3^{r-v}, 11^v–12^v; JJ256B, 28^v–29^v; JJ256C, 30^r; JJ265, 159^{r-v}, 170^v–171^r; JJ266, 57^v–58^v. ADR, BP441, sentence of June 15, 1551 (letter of remission, Oct. 1550).

5. AN, JJ249B, 26^{r-v}. The supplicant and his fellows had the duty to defend themselves "comme sont serviteurs de Sr de Saint George." This may refer to a local confraternity of which Saint George was the patron, but Saint George's exploits were well known through *The Golden Legend* and other sources (Jacobus de Voragine, *The Golden Legend,* trans. Granger Ryan and Helmut Ripperger [New York, 1969]). This letter of remission is discussed more fully later in this chapter.

6. Le Cacheux, ed., *Actes de la Chancellerie d'Henri VI* (cited Introduction, n. 2), vol. 1, p. 3, #1: "par chaleur et temptacion de l'ennemi"; p. 5, #2: "moult courroucié . . . tempté de l'annemi"; vol. 2, p. 253, #228; p. 276, #235. Paul Guérin, ed., *Recueil des documents concernant le Poitou contenus dans les registres de la Chancellerie de France,* vol. 11 (for 1454–74), vol. 38 of *Archives historiques du Poitou* (1909), pp. 86–87, #1433: "temptacion de l'ennemy." Alfred Soman informs me that he has found "tenté de l'Ennemi" often in the *plumitifs,* or recordkeepers' notes, of criminal interrogations by the Parlement of Paris in the sixteenth century and after (letter of Feb. 15, 1987), and I have found a man in a sodomy case in Geneva saying

in the course of his interrogation that he was "conduit de Sathan et de maulvais espritz" (AEG, Procés criminels 517 [1st series], interrogation of Jan. 9, 1555). However, I have not come upon the phrase in the letters of remission.

7. *Traicté des elements, temperaments, humeurs et facultés naturelles, selon la doctrine d'Hippocrates, et de Galien* (Lyon: Guillaume Rouillé, 1555), pp. 76, 84. *Dictionnaire Francoislatin, autrement dict Les mots Francois, avec les manieres duser diceulx, tournez en Latin* (Paris: Robert Estienne, 1549), p. 108: "Chole ou cole, ire, courroux . . . Il est en chaulde chole, id est, Il est en son ire." Edmond Huguet, *Dictionnaire de la langue française du seizième siècle*, 7 vols. (Paris, 1925–67), vol. 2, pp. 274–75, gives many examples of the usage of "chaude chole" or "chaude colle" in diverse settings. It was by no means a restricted legal term.

8. AN, JJ249A, 80^{r-v}; JJ265, 154^{r-v}, 159^{r-v}. JJ249B, 28^v–29^r: "gens querelleux, mal vivans et mal renommez au pays." JJ258B, 122^{r-v}: "un mauvais homme publiquement blasmé d'avoir commis plusieurs homicides, homme mal famé et renommé vivre en toute dissolution de vie et de mauvaise conversation."

9. Booth, *Rhetoric of Fiction* (cited Introduction, n. 7), pp. 3–6, 437–41. Erich Auerbach, *Mimesis: The Representation of Reality in Western Literature,* trans. Willard Trask (Princeton, N.J., 1953), chap. 1, especially pp. 19–23. Genette, *Narrative Discourse* (cited Introduction, n. 7), pp. 161–85. Papon, *Troisieme Notaire*, p. 750. With the letter of remission, the "illusion of mimesis" is not just a matter of moving from a living scene to signifying narrative words (Genette, p. 164), but also of adopting a realistic style that conceals concealment. See the discussion of "gaps" in those stories below.

10. AN, JJ238, 171^r–172^v, letter of remission, dated Sept. 1525, for Pierre Marie, master shoemaker of Paris, aged about 60. Another example of the insanity plea coupled with a story is in AN, X^{2B} 44, arrêt of Sept. 13, 1566: letter of remission, dated June 1566, for Coulin Guyborat, laboureur of Troissy, aged 70 or 72. Whereas the madness of the shoemaker was attributed to a high fever about two years before, as a result of which he would occasionally "go out of his mind," the Champagne peasant was described as "furieux" due to old age. The shoemaker's supplication was made by himself, the peasant's by his family. Another example: AN, JJ257C, 42^r: an orphaned youth, aged 23, "troublé de son esprit et entendement," that is, of unsound mind.

11. AN, JJ251, 93^r–94^r, letter of remission, dated Aug. 1538, for Nicolas de Regnel, factor in Lyon for two merchants of Paris. Other examples: JJ247, 54^v (a young Lyon merchant with a group of friends on a feast day accidentally killed his host's servant while playing with a loaded harquebus); JJ253A, 150^v (a young villager in the Lyonnais, playing around with swords with his friends after celebrating the local "kingdom" of Saint Peter's day, accidentally wounded and killed his friend); JJ257B, 7^v (two twelve-year-old boys of the town of Montmorillon, playing with a harquebus they thought unloaded, shot someone accidentally); JJ249B, 65^r (a Parisian craftswoman claims to have killed her female apprentice acciden-

tally, having touched her with a fireplace tool without even being aware of it). In each case the story is used to build a tranquil or merry atmosphere, and show how sorry the killer was, weeping after the accident, etc.

12. AN, JJ238, 244^r–245^v, letter of remission, dated Dec. 1525, for Gueryn Marnat of the village of Voigny in Champagne; JJ253B, 16^v–17^v, letter of remission, dated Feb. 1539/40 for Euvard de Boys, young hatmaker of Reims. Muchembled, "Les jeunes, les jeux et la violence" (cited Introduction, n. 4), pp. 568–69, gives several examples of rural wedding fights.

13. AN, JJ256C, 1^{r-v}, letter of remission, dated Jan. 1543/44, for Nicolas Raslon of the village of Roaonne (Craonne?) in Picardy; JJ258B, 122^{r-v}, letter of remission, dated Oct. 1548, for Louis Jouchet, master mason of Lyon; JJ266, 94^{r-v}, letter of remission, dated June 1568, for Vincent de La Balle, laboureur of Canteleu in Normandy. The hat symbol has a long history through the Quakers, who refused to doff their hats, to Sigmund Freud, who was humiliated at his father's story of having his hat knocked off by a Christian and doing nothing but quietly pick up the hat from the road ("unheroic conduct"; Sigmund Freud, *The Interpretation of Dreams*, trans. James Strachey [New York, 1960], p. 197). On concern for honor among commoners in the eighteenth century, see N. Castan, *Criminels de Languedoc* (cited chap. 1, n. 43), pp. 160–62.

14. AN, JJ249B, 1^{r-v}, letter of remission, dated Jan. 1535/36, for Antoine Simon dit Lesponte, vigneron of a village in the bailliage of Senlis. This is an especially well-constructed story, with opening detail about Simon serving the supper (the custom for the groom), then overhearing his sister and brother-in-law talking as he is eating at the end of the table with the other servers and they are warming themselves at the fire. The quotations from his nephews—"Mon oncle, je vous crye mercy" and "Voicy mon oncle qui me veult tuer"—cast the supplicant in a less than favorable light; the story shows some effort at fairness.

15. AN, JJ256B, 36^v–37^r; JJ256C, 37^v–38^r, letter of remission, dated Apr. 1544, for Simon Le Chantre of Corbeny in Picardy, concerning a fight with his brother in the course of dividing their father's inheritance; JJ257B, 91^r, letter of remission, dated July 1546, for Remy Oudin, of a village in Picardy, on a quarrel with his half-sister and her husband about a property belonging to his aged mother.

16. AN, JJ248, 3^{r-v}, letter of remission, dated Jan. 1534/35 and addressed to the bailiff of Berry, for Huguet Baraton, écuyer, "homme d'armes de noz ordonnances" under the command of the Marquis de Saluces.

17. François Billcois, *Le duel dans la société française des XVIe–XVIIe siècles. Essai de psychologie historique* (Paris, 1986), chap. 2. This judicial combat was immediately written up in a pamphlet: *L'ordre du combat de deux gentilshommes faict en la ville de Moulins accordé par le roy nostre Sire* (in ibid., pp. 20–21).

18. AN, JJ249B, 2^{r-v}, letter of remission, dated Jan. 1535/36 for Jean de Gilques, écuyer. Another example of a gentleman's homicide of a commoner is in JJ257C, 103^v–104^r, letter of remission, dated Mar. 1546/47,

for Adam Prard, young gentleman of Mouliherne in Anjou. The commoner had developed a "mortal hatred" of Prard in a conflict over properties, which Prard claimed he had inherited and the commoner claimed belonged to him. The quarrel took the form of an attack on the gentleman's honor: the commoner called him a "thief," each charged the other with lying, and Prard then reached for his dagger. For an interesting new study of self-definitions of noble virtue in the sixteenth century, see Ellery Schalk, *From Valor to Pedigree: Ideas of Nobility in France in the Sixteenth and Seventeenth Centuries* (Princeton, N.J., 1986). The letters of remission inevitably show more vigilance in defense of noble status among country gentlemen in the first half of the sixteenth century than do the texts used for Schalk's work (cf. pp. 31–32).

19. AN, JJ257C, 127^r–128^r, letter of remission, dated Apr. 1546/47, for François de Villeprounée, seigneur de Quinée in Anjou. The homicide occurred on Mar. 25 and the letter of remission was signed before Easter day, Apr. 10.

20. AN, JJ253B, 28^v–29^r, letter of remission, dated Mar. 1539/40, for Claude de Montafe, baker of Crépy-en-Valois. The baker claimed that he had hit the apprentice on the head only "to correct him," as a master must do to his servant. JJ257C, 115^v, letter of remission, dated Apr. 1546/47, for Simon Cailland, tapissier of Châtellerault.

21. Rabelais, *Tiers Livre*, chap. 3, in *Oeuvres complètes* (cited Chap. 1, n. 83), pp. 339–40.

22. AN, JJ257A, 95^{r-v}, letter of remission, dated May 1546, for Legier Barbier, carpenter, for the homicide of Pierre du Sault, seigneur of La Touche in Touraine. Other creditors who kill their debtors: JJ249B, 49^v–50^v, letter of remission for a fish salesman of Abbeville for the homicide during Lent 1532/33 of a client in Clermont-de-l'Oise, who refused to pay for past purchases and instead asked for more; JJ266, 49^v–50^v, letter of remission, dated Apr. 1568, for Louis Frambourg, "revendeur et cabaratier" at Paris, for the homicide of the muleteer of the Duke of Nemours after Frambourg sent his wife to collect and the muleteer, saying he owed nothing, hit the wife, etc.

23. AN, JJ257C, 144^{r-v}, letter of remission, dated May 1547.

24. AN, JJ256C, 34^r, letter of remission, dated Apr. 1543/44, for Antoine Pinatel, jeune compagnon of Lyon.

25. AN, JJ256C, 48^{r-v}, letter of remission, dated May 1544, for Antoine Giney, journeyman butcher of Paris.

26. ADR, BP441, sentence of Sept. 14, 1551, ratifying a letter of remission, dated June 1551, for Christofle Farfannchy, courier of Lyon.

27. Billacois, *Le duel*, p. 23.

28. AN, JJ256B, 39^{r-v}, letter of remission, sealed at the Petite Chancellerie of the Parlement of Bordeaux, Dec. 1542, for Maistre Seur de Lucas, avocat in the court of the Sénéchaussée des Landes in Saint-Sever.

29. AN, JJ257C, 200^v–201^r, letter of remission, dated Aug. 1547, for Yzabel Ondinet, peasant in a joint household in the Bourbonnais, for the homicide of a hired harvest hand who, Ondinet claimed, owed him money.

JJ257B, 30ᵛ, letter of remission, dated Feb. 1545/46, for Philbert Aconnez, vigneron and occasional taverner in the village of Mosson in Burgundy. He said he had extended credit for food to his victim; when he came to collect payment, the peasant and his wife said they owed him nothing and insulted him as a "fine moneylender" ("tu es ung bon presteur d'argent") and as a "leper and son of a lepress," then hit his face and pulled off his hat. AN, X²ᴬ 98, 296ʳ–299ᵛ, letter of remission, dated Dec. 1545, for Jean de Mores, seigneur de Rocheux, for the homicide of Adam de Hodon, seigneur de Mayet in the Blésois. The supplicant said he had "sold" Hodon a seigneury with permission to repurchase (that is, the equivalent of a loan) and then had repaid Hodon, who claimed he couldn't find the sale papers to return. Over dinner two years later, Hodon claimed the property had never been repurchased and said "he feared nothing" from Mores. Mores went out to get his horse, but thinking he could be reproached as "pusillanimous" if he left after such remarks from a man "not of his quality," and seeing Hodon about to unsheath his sword, he killed him "in the fury of anger." In June 1546 the Parlement of Paris ratified the letter of remission, which had been challenged by the widow, on condition that Mores pay her 4500 livres in damages and establish a weekly mass in the church of Beauvilliers for the repose of Hodon's soul.

  30. AN, JJ265, 170ᵛ–171ʳ, letter of remission, dated Aug. 1567, for Nicaize Gabez, gardener of the village of Ribeauville, for killing the curé of Wassigny who, "knowing the supplicant to be of the Religion," had quarreled with him about the preaching of the Reformed minister in Cambrésis and about the meaning of the Trinity, said he was lying, and then thrown a pot at him.

  31. Jill Mann, *Chaucer and Medieval Estates Satire: The Literature of Social Class and the General Prologue to the Canterbury Tales* (Cambridge, Eng., 1973).

  32. Vigneulles, *Cent Nouvelles Nouvelles* (cited chap. 1, n. 46); Kotin, *Narrative Imagination* (cited chap. 1, n. 75), chap. 4.

  33. Noël du Fail, *Les Propos Rustiques (Texte original de 1547)*, ed. Arthur de La Borderie (Geneva, 1970). Bonaventure Des Periers, *Nouvelles récréations et joyeux devis,* 2 vols., ed. Louis Lacour (Paris, 1874).

  34. AN, JJ249B, 13ʳ–14ᵛ, letter of remission, dated Jan. 1535/36, for Pierre Roche "pauvre homme de la terre" of the village of Montmartre. Other examples of supplications which open with a feud or previous quarrel: JJ236, 308ʳ–309ʳ, letter of remission, dated Dec. 1523, for stonecarver Louis Jobey, who said that about a year earlier two other stonecarvers had conceived "a mortal hatred" for him and his brother; JJ265, 185ᵛ–186ʳ, letter of remission, dated Sept. 1567, for solicitor Jacques Binet of L'Ile-Bouchard, who said that a local seigneur had a "mortal hatred" for his father and him because of litigation over a rent of three measures of rye and two capons owed by the seigneur to the supplicant's father.

  35. AN, JJ256B, 36ᵛ, letter of remission, dated Dec. 1542, for Peyronteau Delebrere from the parish of Mondieu in Le Brouilh in Armagnac.

  36. AN, JJ256B, 28ᵛ–29ᵛ, letter of remission, dated Nov. 1542, for Jean

de La Forcade dit de Verdun, "povre homme de labour" of Malaussanne in the Béarnais. "Loup-garou," or werewolf, was a frequent male insult in the sixteenth century; La Forcade's friend seems to have been accusing him of werewolf activity.

37. AN, JJ249A, 43^r, letter of remission, dated Sept. 1536, for Etienne Mechault, carpenter and cabinetmaker of Lyon.

38. AN, JJ249B, 1^{r-v}: "Mon oncle, je vous crye mercy" (see note 14 above). Among many examples of the pacifying phrase, "Je ne vous demande rien" or "Je ne te demande rien": JJ249B, 5^r–6^r, 28^v–29^v; JJ256C, 37^v–38^r; ADR, BP441, sentence of Dec. 22, 1551, ratifying the letter of remission, dated Feb. 1548/49, of Pierre Goyon, "pauvre homme de labeur" living in the Lyonnais. Individual variants on the pacifying phrase: from a young male inhabitant of Honnecourt-sur-Escaut in Picardy to a Feast of Kings reveler, "Mon amy, c'est assez, croy moy" (AN, JJ249B, 21^v–22^r); from a young Lyon shoemaker to a butcher whom he did not know and who made fun of his red bonnet on a country road, "Mon amy, nous ne voulons point de debat" (JJ253B, 61^v–62^r); from a seigneur in Anjou in a conflict with a commoner about Lent, "Retire toy et ne me poursuiz plus. Je ne te serche point et ne t'avoyr jamais veu ne cogneu" (JJ257C, 127^r–128^r).

39. Barthes, "Introduction to the Structural Analysis of Narratives" (cited Introduction, n. 7), p. 266. See also the rich pages of Paul Ricoeur on the essential connection between explaining why something happened and telling the story of its happening in "Expliquer et comprendre" (cited Introduction, n. 5), especially pp. 143–44, a theme more fully developed in his *Temps et récit*, 3 vols. (Paris, 1983–85), vol. 1; in English, *Time and Narrative,* trans. Kathleen McLaughlin and David Pellaveur (Chicago, 1984–85).

40. AN, JJ257C, 19^v–20^v, letter of remission, dated Jan. 1546/47, for André de Bourges, tailleur de pierre of Paris. I am grateful to Alfred Soman, now completing a *thèse d'état* on the prosecution of magic and sorcery before the Parlement of Paris, for his comments on this case. He notes that the "maladie des enfleurs," for which André was seeking his mother's remedy, was especially likely to be treated by magical technique.

41. A ratification procedure of letters of remission, dated Oct. 1558, for a young Lyon clerk Falco Jarricot, shows Jarricot being asked to name witnesses to "verify" his statements about his victim's aggression, wounds, and deathbed pardon (ADR, BP444, 208^v–209^r, 299^v–302^v). Some witnesses so named at the hearing were not among the people mentioned in the letter of remission; this suggests that the names in the narrative are partly given to create vraisemblance, to add concreteness to the tale. Roland Barthes, "The Reality Effect," in Tzvetan Todorov, ed., *French Literary Theory Today: A Reader* (Cambridge, Eng., and Paris, 1982), pp. 11–17.

42. "Pour estre creu par serment du contenu en une remission quant on ne peult prouver," in *Le Grand Stile* (1548) (cited chap. 1, n. 14), 128^{r-v}. *Guydon des Practiciens* (cited chap. 1, n. 21), 167^r–173^v: "Des probations."

43. AN, JJ257C, 179^v–180^r, letters of remission, dated June 1547, for Jean Faurier of the town of Mirande in Gascony.

44. Rabelais, *Pantagruel*, chap. 28, in *Oeuvres complètes*, pp. 287–88.

45. AN, JJ238, 245ʳ–246ᵛ, letter of remission, dated Dec. 1525, for Louis Paisant, butcher of Paris.

46. Benedicti, *Somme des Pechez*, book 1, chap. 10, on the Third Commandment, p. 81. Benedicti regretted that the Church allowed butchering on Sunday. Of course, dicing on the Sabbath was completely forbidden (p. 83).

47. AN, JJ236, 472ᵛ–473ᵛ, letter of remission, dated Apr. 1524, for Jean Charbonnier dit Nain of Flonville in the bailliage of Dreux, for the homicide of his brother Robin.

48. AN, JJ257B, 16ʳ, letter of remission, dated Jan. 1545/46, for Guillaume Guillon, laboureur of Mareil-sur-Mauldre in the Ile-de-France, for the homicide of Philippe Simon.

49. AN, JJ245B, 109ᵛ–110ᵛ, letter of remission, dated June 1530, for Jean Acarie, student at the University of Orléans, for the homicide of Jeanne de Bourg. Acarie was pardoned provided he pay 12 livres for prayers for her soul.

50. As I finish writing this book, there comes to my hands Thomas M. Greene's *The Vulnerable Text: Essays on Renaissance Literature* (New York, 1986), a splendid study of Renaissance texts from Petrarch to Ben Jonson. The "wounds" in his texts have somewhat different sources from the "wounds" in the pardon tales; he relates their vulnerability to "four basic conditions of language: its historicity, its dialogic function, its referential function, and its dependence on figuration" (pp. 100–103). The "wounds" in the pardon tales have to do with their problematic relation to real wounds, but, insofar as they call attention to their own partiality, they have a "dialogic function."

51. AN, JJ256C, 32ʳ, letter of remission, dated Apr. 1543/44, for Philippe Fortespaulle, a sixteen-year-old shepherd of Ostenay in Beauce; 37ᵛ–38ʳ, letter of remission, dated Apr. 1544, for Simon Le Chantre, "paovre simple homme" living at Corbeny near Laon, for the homicide of Jean Le Chantre dit Byot, his brother.

52. AN, JJ255A, 61ᵛ, letter of remission, dated Nov. 1541, for Pierre de Moustin dit Sarraguc. By this date Lazare de Baïf had published his *De re navali libellus* and his *De vasculis libellus*. He became maître des requêtes de l'Hôtel in 1538 (Bernard Quilliet, *Les corps d'officiers de la prévôté et vicomté de Paris et de l'Ile-de-France de la fin de la Guerre des Cents Ans au début des Guerres de Religion, Etude sociale* [Lille, 1982], pp. 698–700).

53. *Journal d'un bourgeois de Paris* (cited chap. 1, n. 2), pp. 285–86. The man in question was Claude Laurencin, Baron de Riverie, from a very wealthy Lyon commercial family, cousin of another Claude Laurencin, receveur des tailles in the Lyonnais, and himself *panetier du roi*. His letter of remission, dated Mar. 1527/28, traces his homicide of François Dupré to "parolles injurieuses" said by Dupré about the supplicant in connection with efforts to establish a Parlement in Lyon. The letter is frank: Laurencin describes himself as looking for Dupré to avenge the insult, and the wife's relation to the viceroy of Naples and also to a *gentilhomme ordinaire* of the

king's chamber is made explicit. The Parlement's ratification was during Easter week. AN, JJ243, 121^r–122^r; X^{2A} 79, Mar. 19, 1527/28.

54. *Journal d'un bourgeois de Paris,* p. 367. The treacherous dinner was held on Lady Day, Mar. 25, 1526/27, and the man was executed in Oct. 1527. This same case is described in like terms in the anonymous chronicle of another Parisian close to the legal world (BN, ms. fr. 17527, 45^v–46^v), who reproduces the Oct. 14 sentence of the Parlement of Paris dismissing the letters. Other pardons are reported by the Bourgeois de Paris on pp. 83–86, 156–57, 159, 258, 263, 363, 369–70, 387.

55. Papon, *Troisieme Notaire,* pp. 745–46.

56. Lalourcé, ed., *Recueil des Cahiers Généraux* (cited chap. 1, n. 14), vol. 1: "Etats d'Orléans en 1560," article 115 of the Clergy (p. 47); articles 101–2 of the Third Estate on the subject of the Nobility (pp. 324–35); vol. 2: "Etats de Blois en 1576," article 170 of the Remonstrance of the Third Estate (pp. 250–51). The king's mercy was especially to be displayed in his pardons at a Joyous Entry or on Good Friday: here he could be at his most gracious in interpreting the cases beyond self-defense and homicide to avenge a wife caught in the act of adultery. But his subjects still did not want him to go beyond the remissible circumstances described by Papon (see p. 12 above) and pardon ambushes, premeditated murders, and the like.

57. Pierre de L'Estoile, *Journal de L'Estoile pour le règne de Henri III (1574–1589),* ed. Louis-Raymond Lefèvre (Paris, 1943), pp. 275–76 (Sept. 1581), 221 (Aug. 1579). The target of the Italian financial officer was no other than Bertrand Pulveret, whom we met at the end of Chapter 1 receiving a pardon from the king for his allowing homicides at the chateau of Pierre Scize. Other pardons or efforts at pardon are reported by L'Estoile on pp. 80–81, 151–52, 245. See also the story given by Brantôme of a grace granted by Charles IX to the Baron of Bournazel of Gascony. He had killed another gentleman—"on disoit que c'estoit par grande supercherie"—but the ladies and gentlemen of the court urged he be pardoned. The widow of the victim and the chancellor both opposed grace, but "he was among the gallants of the court" and was given his pardon just as he was leaving prison for execution. Pierre de Bourdeille, seigneur de Brantôme, *Les Dames galantes,* ed. Pascal Pia (Paris, 1981), pp. 417–18.

58. Gouberville, *Journal* (cited chap. 1, n. 57), pp. 719–20. Even when a letter of remission and a homicide were discussed by the privy council, the cases were sent to Parlementary bodies for consideraton (BN, ms. fr. 5905, arrêts of the privy council, Dec. 2, 1559, 53^r–54^v; July 12, 1566, 91^v–92^v).

59. Isambert, *Recueil général* (cited chap. 1, n. 13), vol. 11, p. 369, ordinance of Blois, Mar. 1498/99, article 128; vol. 14, p. 250, edict of Amboise, Mar. 1572, article 9: because of the complaints from his subjects about the "ease" with which gentlemen and royal officers were getting their letters of remission ratified by local courts, the king orders that they must present them in person on their knees before the Parlement in the jurisdiction in which the act was committed. Only then would they return to the local court for challenge by the victim's kin. Papon, *Arrests notables* (cited chap. 1, n. 1), book 24, title 8, p. 1354. [Parlement of Brittany], *Instructions et ar-*

ticles pour labbreviaton des proces . . . Faict a Vennes le parlement y tenant le V jour Doctobre mil cinq cens quarante (Rennes: Thomas Mestrard, n.d. [1540], 3ᵛ, article 11: "Cy devant plusieurs remissionnaires voullans eviter pugnition de crime et delictz par eulz perpetrez et commis ont faict intimer par ung sergent les remissions par eulx obtenues aux iuges procureurs du roy et parties civilles sans comparoir ny presenter en personne ny en iugement lesdites remissions, si non trois et quatre ans apres qu'ilz veuient [*sic*] les tesmoings mortz et qu'ilz les ayent faict absenter en maniere que les cas dont ilz sont chargez ne se peuvent verifier." Until the reign of Charles IX the time limit for presenting letters of remission for entérinement was one year; under Charles IX it was limited to three months (*Le Thresor du Nouveau Stille,* 1599 [cited Introduction, n. 11], 15ᵛ).

60. AN, JJ257B, 30ᵛ–31ʳ, letter of remission, dated Feb. 1545/46, for Jean Clavier, marchand voiturier of Lyon. Clavier put the counterclaims of witnesses in his supplication and tried to answer them.

61. Dolet, *Carminum Libri Quatuor* (cited chap. 1, n. 7), book 1, carmen 1, pp. 59–60. Franciscus Floridus Sabinus, *Adversus Stephani Doleti Aurelii Calumnias* (Rome, 1541), quoted by Christie, *Dolet* (cited chap. 1, n. 7), p. 307 n. 1.

62. Occasionally the Chancellery copy of letters of remission in series JJ includes the payment or other provisions required by the ratifying court, and then we know the fate of the letters. But in many cases this is absent, and one has only the copy of the letter without indication of whether it was ratified or dismissed. In any case, registering letters of remission with the Chancellery was not obligatory and required an additional payment.

63. APP, Aᴮ 1–Aᴮ 6 (1564–1580, though some months and most of the year 1574 are missing). One hundred persons involved in 92 cases were found awaiting review of their letters of remission; letters were dismissed in only six cases. These figures are offered simply to give an impression of rates of ratification: while 431 letters of remission are copied in JJ from many jurisdictions of the years 1565–68, only 19 persons were in the Paris Conciergerie in those same years awaiting ratification or dismissal of their letters.

64. I have especially looked at AN, X²ᴬ 86, 87, 89A, 98, and ADR, BP441, 444, 445. A full-scale legal study of pardons would, of course, make a systematic examination of ratification and dismissal through many such judicial registers.

65. There were sometimes cases where it was not appropriate for the recipient of pardon to make a payment to the victim's kin, as when the dead person had been completely at fault or there were no appropriate claimants. For example, clerk Pierre Rambaud of Lyon was not required to make any payment to the family of a priest named Gueynard, whom he alleged to have slain in self-defense. No relatives of Gueynard appeared at the ratification hearing; moreover, Gueynard was claimed to have had a "mortal hatred" against Rambaud because the latter was the attorney for a chambermaid seeking damages against the priest—an unsavory case (ADR, BP444, 263ᵛ–266ᵛ, sentence of Feb. 14, 1558/59).

66. ADR, BP445, 187^v–191^r, sentence of Oct. 31, 1559. Two years later the journeyman Jacques Baillon got letters of abolition and recall from his banishment (ADR, BP446, 195^v–198^r).

67. ADR, BP444, 202^{r-v}.

68. For a firsthand description of how the king compelled ratification of the Concordat, see Jean Barrillon, *Journal du Jean Barrillon, secrétaire du Chancelier Duprat, 1515–1521*, ed. Pierre Vaissière (Paris, 1899), vol. 2, pp. 77–80. On the king's insisting on the ratification of the letters of abolition for Marie Quatrelivres, wife of Me Louis Ruzé, see *Journal d'un bourgeois de Paris*, pp. 83–86, and Nicolas Versoris, *Livre de Raison de Me Nicolas Versoris avocat au Parlement de Paris, 1519–1530*, ed. G. Fagniez (Paris, 1885), p. 28. See on this case, Barbara B. Diefendorf, *Paris City Councillors in the Sixteenth Century: The Politics of Patrimony* (Princeton, N.J., 1983), pp. 171–73.

69. AN, X^{2A} 95, 870^r–871^r and X^{2A} 98, 535^v–536^r, reprinted in Longeon, ed., *Documents sur Etienne Dolet* (cited chap. 1, n. 9), nos. 6, 13. Dolet, *Carminum Libri Quatuor*, book 2, carmina 5, 11, pp. 67–68, 72–73. Christie, *Dolet*, p. 314.

70. Isambert, ed., *Recueil général*, vol. 11, pp. 353–54: ordinance of Blois, Mar. 1498/99, article 70. Papon, *Arrests notables*, book 24, title 8, "De graces et remissions," pp. 1350–51. La Roche-Flavin, *Treize Livres* (cited chap. 1, n. 3), book 13, ch. 69, "Sur la Chambre de la Tournelle et iurisdiction criminelle," paragraphs 2, 6, 35, pp. 1106–14. Jean Bodin, *Les Six Livres de la Republique* (Paris: Jacques du Puys, 1577), book 1, chap. 10, pp. 173–76; though Bodin was insistent that the king must not share the right to pardon, he thought grace must never be offered in violation of divine law, and specifically never for an irremissible murder (p. 175).

Expilly, *Plaidoyez* (cited chap. 1, n. 36), p. 268. Jousse, *Justice criminelle* (cited chap. 1, n. 1), vol. 2, pp. 381, 400–404. Texier, "La rémission au XIVe siècle" (cited Introduction, n. 4), especially pp. 200–203. During the procession of Emperor Charles V through France in 1539, the François Ier gave him the right to grant Entry pardons (AN, X^{2A} 89A, Jan. 29, 1539/40), but this was perceived as an extension of the king's sovereignty, as it was when he allowed the queen to grant Entry pardons. In 1515, when François Ier gave the Queen Mother the power to pardon apart from the time of an Entry, the Parlement of Paris protested, and she renounced her privilege (Isambert, ed., *Recueil général*, vol. 12, pp. 18–19; Bodin, *Republique*, p. 174).

71. Bodin, *Republique*, p. 174, *The Six Bookes of a Commonweale*, ed. K. D. McRae (Cambridge, Mass., 1962), book 1, chap. 10, p. 172. Expilly, *Plaidoyez*, Plaidoyé 32: "Sur une presentation de lettres de Grace," Dec. 12, 1594, pp. 286–87 (from Pierre Ronsard's *Institution pour l'Adolescence du Roy treschrestien Charles Neufviesme de ce nom*, first published in 1562).

72. Papon, *Troisieme Notaire*, p. 728: the Prince ordinarily has the rights of pardon by justice and extraordinarily has them by special privilege at his entry to the crown, "according to which he can sometimes go beyond the limits of justice, and this to let it be known that he must not

start, nor want to start his reign with severity, penalties, and punishments but with clemency, gentleness, and grace." On the king's pardoning at Entries, see Bryant, *The King and the City* (cited chap. 1, n. 10), pp. 24–26. Bryant argues that at the end of the sixteenth century, the king was establishing a constitutional right to pardon after his succession whether or not he was physically present at an Entry. On the king's touching for scrofula at his Entry to Lyon, see *La Magnificence de la superbe et triumphante entree de la noble et antique Cité de Lyon faicte au Treschrestien Roy de France Henry deuxiesme de ce Nom,* ed. Georges Guigue (Lyon, 1927), p. 79. The king could also touch at times other than his Entry (Marc Bloch, *Les Rois Thaumaturges* (Paris, 1961), book 2, chap. 5.

73. Isambert, ed., *Recueil général,* vol. 11, pp. 368–69: ordinance of Blois, Mar. 1498/99, article 126; Papon, *Arrests notables,* book 24, title 8, p. 1351; Milles de Souvigny, *Praxis Criminis Persequendi* (cited chap. 1, n. 1), 55ᵛ–56ʳ. Michel Foucault, *Surveiller et punir. Naissance de la prison* (Paris, 1975), part I; in English, *Discipline and Punish: The Birth of the Prison,* trans. Alan Sheridan (New York, 1977).

74. *Journal d'un bourgeois de Paris,* p. 159. BN, ms. fr. 17527, 53ᵛ–54ᵛ. Guiffrey, *Procès criminel de Iehan de Poytiers* (cited chap. 1, n. 70), pp. 143–45.

75. Versoris, *Livre de Raison,* p. 41.

76. *Discours de l'abus des iustices de village. Tiré du traité des offices de C.L.P.* (Paris: Abel l'Angelier, 1603), 56ʳ–57ᵛ.

77. AEG, Procès criminels 1307 (1st series), testimony of printer Claude Masson, Aug. 29, 1565. The most celebrated example of insouciance in regard to homicide is *The Life of Benvenuto Cellini,* trans. John Addington Symonds (4th ed., London, 1896), pp. 130–33, 141–62, 308, 318, 329; but see also the self-righteous tone taken by Théodore Agrippa d'Aubigné in describing his fights in "Sa Vie à ses enfants" in *Oeuvres complètes,* 6 vols., ed. E. Réaume and F. de Caussade (Paris, 1873–1892), vol. 1, pp. 20, 25–31.

78. Montaigne, *Essais* (cited chap. 1, n. 49), book 3, chap. 12, "De la phisionomie," pp. 1030–31. Billacois, *Le Duel,* pp. 89–91, 191.

79. Lalourcé, ed., *Recueil des Cahiers Généraux,* vol. 1, Etats d'Orléans, p. 382: the king's response to articles 220–24 of the Third Estate's remonstrance on royal letters. In his *Republic,* Jean Bodin shows the royal justification for giving grace beyond what was remissible by the laws: how else can the Prince show mercy if he can not remit penalties established by God's law? Monarchs "believe that the grace they give is all the more agreeable to God as the crime is heinous and detestable" (*Republique,* p. 175).

80. Marguerite de Navarre, *Heptaméron* (cited chap. 1, n. 11), nouvelle 23, pp. 186–93, nouvelle 1, pp. 11–18.

81. Des Periers, *Nouvelles récréations et joyeux devis,* vol. 2, nouvelle 111, pp. 152–55. The story was also picked up by Henri Estienne in his *Apologie pour Hérodote,* 2 vols., ed. P. Ristelhuber (Paris, 1879), chap. 15, pp. 216–17. Estienne gives the name of the thief as Simon Dagoubert, the son of a royal advocate of Issoudun, and the name of the seigneur as Monsieur de Nevers, a noble of high status.

82. *L'Histoire Memorable* (cited chap. 1, n. 47). Châtillon-sur-Loing, to-

day known as Châtillon-Coligny, was the ancestral home of the Coligny brothers and a base for their religious and military activities in these years (Robert Kingdon, *Geneva and the Consolidation of the French Protestant Movement, 1564–1572* [Madison, Wis., and Geneva, 1967], pp. 74–75, 164–65). The printer of the pamphlet, Eloi Gibier of Orléans, played an important role in publishing Protestant tracts in the 1560's, though he also printed royal edicts, including one in the spring of 1572 that touched on remissions (Louis Desgraves, *Eloi Gibier, imprimeur à Orléans* [Geneva, 1966], and Eugénie Droz, "Deux études sur Eloi Gibier," *Chemins de l'hérésie. Textes et documents*, 4 vols. [Geneva, 1970–76], vol. 4, pp. 101–34; J.-F. Gilmont, "Eloi Gibier, éditeur de théologie réformée," *Bibliothèque d'humanisme et renaissance*, 47 [1985]: 395–404). The story of Jean Guy was taken from Gibier's edition by the Protestant scholar-publisher Henri Estienne and used in an exemplary way in his *Apologie pour Hérodote*, in the chapter "Des homicides de nostre temps," pp. 385–91.

83. Calvin, *Institution de la religion chrestienne* (1541), chap. 5, "De penitence," vol. 2, pp. 204–9.

84. E. William Monter, *Studies in Genevan Government (1536–1605)* (Geneva, 1964), pp. 63–65.

85. AEG, Registres du Conseil 58, 91^v–92^r, 96^r–97^r, 98^v; Procès criminels 1136 (1st series). *Registres de la Compagnie des Pasteurs de Genève,* 6 vols. (Geneva, 1962–1980), vol. 4 (1575–1582), ed. Olivier Labarthe and Bernard Lescaze, pp. 331–32.

86. AEG, Registres du Conseil 75, 53^r–55^r, Mar. 21, 1580 (debate about pardoning the banished adulterers). *Registres de la Compagnie des Pasteurs,* vol. 3 (1565–1574), ed. Olivier Fatio and Olivier Labarthe, pp. 126–29, 287–90 (the Pastors reproach both Councils for giving grace to Jean Louvencourt for a first offense of adultery with a serving girl; the punishment remitted was being displayed publicly in a carcan, an iron pillory: "Nul ne peu dispenser des loix divines, perpetuelles et universelles"); vol. 4, pp. 323–35 (opposition of the Company of Pastors to grace for murderers and adulterers, 1580); vol. 6 (1589–1594), ed. Sabine Citron and Marie-Claude Junod, pp. 91–94 (opposition of the pastors to grace for Captain Mongin, convicted of murder at Orange, 1592). On these cases, see Eugène Choisy, *L'Etat chrétien calviniste à Genève au temps de Théodore de Bèze* (Geneva and Paris, n.d. [1902]), pp. 179–86, 201–4, 294–300.

87. *Registres de la Compagnie des Pasteurs,* vol. 3, pp. 122–23: Pastor Beza warns the Council of Two Hundred that heretics will tell any kind of story to get their grace and then go on and do worse. Calvin gave a portrait of the moderate mixing of justice and clemency in his *Institutes*: "Mais il fault qu'un magistrat se donne garde de tous les deux: c'est à sçavoir, que par sévérité désordonnée il ne navre plus qu'il ne médecine; ou que par folle et superstitieuse affectation de clémence, il ne soit cruel en son humanité, en abandonnant toutes choses par sa facilité, avec le grand detriment de plusieurs" (*Institution de la religion chrestienne* [1541], chap. 16, "Du gouvernement civil," vol. 4, p. 212). In many ways Calvin was carrying over Seneca's preference for clemency over pardon or indulgence, for *clementia* over *venia,*

which he had discussed in his 1532 Commentary on the *De Clementia,* without being as rigid as Seneca and without agreeing with Seneca that a wise man should avoid "pity" (*Calvin's Commentary on Seneca's "De Clementia,"* trans. and ed. Ford Lewis Battles and André Malan Hugo [Leiden, 1969], book 2, chaps. 3–4, 6–7, pp. 351–61, 369–81). In the *Institutes,* Calvin was working not only within a Christian frame, but within a Reformed frame, where divine pardon and remission tower over human justice and clemency. See also Calvin's portrait of the just judge in his sermon on Deut. 19 (*Sermons sur le Deutéronome,* in *Opera Omnia,* ed. G. Baum, E. Cunitz, and E. Reuss [Corpus Reformatorum, 55; Brunswick, 1884], vol. 27, sermon 115, pp. 587–88).

In his essay "Divers evenemens de mesme conseil," Montaigne makes a contrast between a Protestant nobleman who tried to kill the Catholic prince François de Guise for the justice of the Protestant cause, and Guise, who decided to forgive him: "Now I want to show you," says the latter in Montaigne's quotation, "how much gentler is the religion I hold than the one that you profess. Yours has advised you to kill me without a hearing, having received no harm from me; and mine commands me to pardon you, convicted though you are of having wanted to murder me without reason" (*Essays,* in *The Complete Works of Montaigne,* trans. Donald M. Frame [Stanford, Calif., 1948], book 1, chap. 24, p. 91).

88. *Registres de la Compagnie des Pasteurs,* vol. 6, p. 94. Different Protestant views on remission are shown in the case of the swordcutler Claude Dater, who killed his wife for adultery in 1567. The Reformed Church of Lyon helped him get his pardon by sending a representative to court. When Dater came to Geneva a few months later, the Consistory denied him the Lord's Supper "for having spilled human blood" and sent his case to the Small Council, "so they know that such a man is in their town." Dater was given a criminal trial in which the facts of his homicide and of his receiving pardon were verified, and he was freed with a remonstrance (AEG, Registres du Consistoire 24, 113ᵛ; Procès criminels 1436 [1st series]; see Appendix B).

89. For the medieval background on miraculous survivals during execution through the action of Jesus and especially of Mary and the saints, see Baudouin de Gaiffier, "Un thème hagiographique: le pendu miraculeusement sauvé," *Revue belge d'archéologie et d'histoire de l'art,* 13 (1943): 123–48, reprinted in his *Etudes critiques d'hagiographie et d'iconologie* (Brussels, 1967), pp. 194–226. Voragine, *The Golden Legend,* pp. 373–74. A statement of the belief in the late sixteenth century is found in the "Conversations" of the Poitiers merchant-storyteller Guillaume Bouchet, *Les Serées de Guillaume Bouchet, Sieur de Brocourt,* 6 vols., ed. C. E. Roybet (Paris, 1873–1882), vol. 3, p. 65, Quatorziesme Seree: "Le peuple aussi, estant misericordieux, a souvent voulu sauver de pauvres criminels, quand en les pendant la corde venoit à rompre, ou que le bourreau eust failly à les faire mourir promptement: mesmes qu'il y a des Iurisconsultes qui tiennent qu'on doit absoudre les pauvres patiens qui eschapent ainsi de la mort, si le criminel a tousiours protesté de son innocence, pensans ce soit un miracle."

90. *Journal d'un bourgeois de Paris*, pp. 313–14; Versoris, *Livre de Raison*, p. 116.

91. *Discours veritable de la miraculeuse delivrance d'une fille de chambre condamnée à la mort, laquelle avoit esté faussement accusée d'un homicide par un qui luy vouloit ravir son honneur. Avec la punition exemplaire qui fut faicte de l'accusateur le 15 Iuin 1606 à S. Didier proche de Nancy en l'Orrayne* (Aix: Claude Rore, 1606). Roger Chartier has made a fascinating study of two pamphlets, dating from 1588 and 1589, that describe the miraculous survival during execution of a young woman falsely accused of infanticide in a town near Rennes ("La pendue miraculeusement sauvée. Etude d'un occasionnel," in R. Chartier, ed., *Les Usages de l'imprimerie* [Paris, 1987], pp. 83–127).

92. D'Augé, *Deux Dialogues De l'invention poetique* (cited Introduction, n. 6), 18^v. Lee A. Sonnino, *A Handbook to Sixteenth-Century Rhetoric* (London, 1968), pp. 152–53: "Purgatorio" as a distinct "mode of conducting speech." Montaigne, *Essais*, book 2, chap. 10, "Des livres," pp. 399–400.

93. For a general introduction to sixteenth-century pamphlets, see J.-P. Seguin, *L'information en France avant le périodique. 517 canards imprimés entre 1529 et 1631* (Paris, 1964): a bibliography of crime pamphlets is found on pp. 69–82. Pardon themes also seem to figure very little in popular visual representation of crime except in the case of the miraculous survival of an execution (see the study of Gaiffier, cited in note 89 above). In contrast to the few pardon scenes found for this book, the pictorial representation of execution is very rich indeed: David Kunzle, *The Early Comic Strip: Narrative Strips and Picture Stories in the European Broadsheet from c. 1450 to 1825* (Berkeley, Calif., 1973), pp. 157–96; Samuel Y. Edgerton, Jr., *Art and Criminal Prosecution During the Florentine Renaissance* (Ithaca, N.Y., and London, 1985).

94. Among the texts used for these generalizations are [Guillaume Le Sueur], *Histoire Admirable d'un Faux et Supposé Mary, advenue en Languedoc, l'an mil cinq cens soixante* (Paris: Vincent Sertenas, 1561); Martial Deschamps, *Histoire tragique et miraculeuse d'un vol et assassinat commis au païs de Berri, en la personne de M. Martial Deschamps Medecin de l'Université de Paris, et ordinaire de la Maison et Ville de Bourdeaux, escripte et presentée par luimesmes au Treschrestien Roi de France et de Poloigne Henri Troisieme du nom, avec l'Arrest de la Court de Parlement de Paris sur ce intervenu. Plus, Contemplation Chrestienne et Philosophique contre ceulx qui nient la Providence de Dieu* (Paris: Jean Bienné, 1576); *Histoire sanguinaire, cruelle et emerveillable, d'une femme de Cahors en Quercy pres Montauban, qui desesperée pour le mauvais Gouvernement et menage de son mary, et pour ne pouvoir apaiser la famine insuportable de sa Famille, massacra inhumainement ses deux petis enffans. Et consecutivement sondict mary, pour lesquelz Meurdres, elle fut exécutée à mort par ordonnance de justice le cinquiesme jour de Febvrier, mil V.C.IIII XX Trois dernier passé. Avec la Remontrance qu'elle fit publiquement au dernier suplice, sur le devoir des hommes mariez, envers leurs Femmes et enffans* (suivant la copie imprimee a Thelouze [*sic*] par J. Columbier, 1584); *Histoire prodigieuse d'un detestable parricide entrepris en la personne du Roy, par Pierre Barriere, dit la Barre, et comme sa Majesté en fut miraculeusement garentie. Avec l'extraict du proces criminel faict audict*

Barriere (n.p., 1594); *Arrest memorable de la Cour de Parlement de Dole, contre Gilles Garnier, Lyonnois, pour avoir en forme de Loup garou devoré plusieurs enfans, et commis autres crimes: enrichy d'aucuns poinct recueilliz de divers autheurs pour esclaircir la matiere de telles transformations* (Angers: Jean Hernault, 1598, jouxte la Coppie imprimée à Orleans; the trial allegedly took place in 1573); *Discours tres-veritable, de deux meurtres et massacres merveilleux advenus depuis n'agueres en deux et divers mariages* (Iouxte la copie imprimee à Langres, Par Iean des Preys Imprimeur du Roy, 1603); *Les larmes de repentance d'une jeune fille Prisonniere, dans les Prisons de Lyon, qui a pery son fruict* (Lyon: Pierre Roussin, 1606); *Histoire merveilleuse et veritable Des homicides, voleries, et assassinats infinis et detestables, commis par le Capitaine la Noye, tenant logis au village de la Chaume, pres de la ville de Geant sur Loyre: ensemble le moyen comme il fut descouvert, et sa prinse et l'execution qui en fut faite, tant de luy que de sa femme et enfans, et un sien serviteur, consentant des forfaits, le samedy 3 Mars 1608* (Lyon: Louis Clavel, n.d. [1608]).

95. Excerpts from legal records are given in the pamphlet by Deschamps, *Histoire tragique et miraculeuse*; in the *Histoire prodigieuse d'un detestable parricide*; and in the werewolf story, *Arrest memorable de la Cour de Parlement de Dole*.

96. The Parlement of Paris condemned Foucault and his female accomplice to be beheaded and the two hired assassins to be broken on the wheel, but since they had all long since fled, the punishment was to be carried out in effigy (*Histoire tragique et miraculeuse*, pp. 59–62). This is precisely the kind of situation in which the condemned might ultimately seek letters of remission, but which the aggrieved physician could try to foreclose by publishing his account of what happened. But also Deschamps had a religious purpose: his introductory "Epistre au Roy" and closing "Contemplation Chrestienne" both talk about God's providence first and foremost, and only secondarily about the importance of royal justice. Interestingly enough, a 1627 crime pamphlet stresses governmental action more than it does divine intervention. In *Histoire veritable, d'un assassinat commis en la personne d'un ieune gentil-homme de Provence, par un ieune homme, qui a esté executé en la place de Greve, avec ses complices, le 19 Iuin 1627* (Paris: Claude Morlot, 1627), the murderers of a young man, who have deceived him into thinking he can find lost documents through magic, are swiftly apprehended by the action of the Duc de Guise once he gets the report from a secret witness. It would be interesting to examine other seventeenth-century crime pamphlets to see whether they also give added weight to governmental initiative.

97. *Histoire merveilleuse et veritable Des homicides . . . commis par le Capitaine de Noye.*

98. *Discours au vray de la cruauté plus que barbare exercé par le Capitaine la Noue, lequel tenoit logis entre Bayonne et Bourdeaux, et esgorgeoit miserablement les marchands qui y venoient loger, luy, sa femme, ses deux fils, et sa fille, et son valet: Avec leur prinse et lamentable deffaite à Bourdeaux, le 7 Iuin, 1610* (A Poiters, Par Pierre La Fosse, Iouxte la copie imprimé [*sic*] à Bourdeaux).

99. Bouchet, *Serees*, vol. 3, pp. 41–42, Quatorziesme Seree: "Des Decapitez, des Pendus, des Fouëttez, des Essoreillez, et des Bannis."

100. Rabelais, *Tiers Livre*, chaps. 39–44, in *Oeuvres complètes*, pp. 468–

84. See the discussion of these chapters in M. A. Screech, *Rabelais* (London, 1979), pp. 265–72.

101. Nicolas de Troyes, *Le Grand Parangon des Nouvelles Nouvelles* (cited chap. 1, n. 75), no. 40, pp. 108–10. Kasprzyk thinks this is one of de Troyes' tales based on real events (*Nicolas de Troyes* [cited chap. 1, n. 75], p. 104). In his edition of the mid-fifteenth-century Burgundian *Cent Nouvelles Nouvelles,* Pierre Champion gave examples from the letters of remission of the Dukes of Burgundy to show how individual motifs or story lines, such as "the jealous husband" or "the fight among mummers and maskers," are reflected in the *Nouvelles* (*Les Cent Nouvelles Nouvelles,* ed. Pierre Champion [Paris, 1928], pp. lxvviii–xcv). There is only one nouvelle, however, that ends in a remission: nouvelle 56, discussed below in chap. 3, p. 108n.

102. Marguerite de Navarre, *Heptaméron,* 2d day, nouvelle 12, pp. 90–97; 4th day, nouvelle 36, pp. 261–66. Both of these stories are serious and allow the revenger to escape, but they also lead to very interesting discussion among the listeners. Of course, there are numerous comic tales of revenge where the perpetrator gets away with it. On revenge tragedy, see Elliott Forsyth, *De Jodelle à Corneille (1553–1640): Le Thème de Vengeance* (Paris, 1962), especially chaps. 2–7; Fredson T. Bowers, *Elizabethan Revenge Tragedy, 1587–1642* (Gloucester, Mass., 1959).

103. Marguerite de Navarre, *Heptaméron,* 3d day, nouvelle 23, pp. 186–93.

104. Emmanuel Philipot, *La vie et l'oeuvre littéraire de Noël du Fail gentilhomme breton* (Paris, 1914), pp. 74–88.

105. Ibid., pp. 85–86. Du Fail locates his story in time exactly during the period of his stay in Bourges in 1546. He says of the two law cases with which the tale ends, "I think they will be settled at the Grands Jours de Riom," that is, at the end of the special session of the Parlement of Paris held at Riom in the autumn of 1546.

106. On the aguilanneuf, see Vaultier, *Le Folklore* (cited Introduction, n. 4), pp. 94–95, and Mr. Du Tilliot, *Mémoires pour servir à l'histoire de la fête des foux* (Lausanne and Geneva, 1751), pp. 68–73.

107. AN, JJ249B, 26ʳ⁻ᵛ, letter of remission, dated Feb. 1535/36, and addressed to the bailiff of Berry, for Benoît Dorgnat.

108. Philipot, *Noël du Fail,* pp. 175–97.

109. Du Fail, *Propos Rustiques,* pp. 75–84: "Mistoudin se venge de ceux de Vindelles, qui lavoyent battu, allants à Haguilleneuf."

110. Du Fail's chapter on the Aguilanneuf fight takes some of its general inspiration, as Philipot has pointed out (*Noël du Fail,* p. 164), from an episode in Rabelais' *Gargantua:* the scornful and unexpected rudeness and even violence of the flat-bun bakers of Lerné toward Grandgousier's courteous shepherds, to which the shepherds respond with a vigorous and successful fight (chap. 25). The bakers then incite their king, Picrochole, to war on Grandgousier, and Picrochole is ultimately defeated. There are clearly differences between the two treatments in tone and in central preoccupation. All the Anger is on one side in Rabelais' fight, and it is a permanent Bitter

Anger (Picrochole) rather than pardonable Hot Anger (chaude chole). There is a gap between what happened and what is told by the bakers and the shepherds to their respective kings (chaps. 26, 28), but eventually the shepherds admit that they had kept the quarrel going by bloodshed (chap. 32). Rabelais' targets are grander than those of du Fail, including the imperial designs of the emperor Charles V (Screech, *Rabelais,* pp. 164–70) and the character of war. Philipot went on to say of du Fail's chapter "the whole account is du Fail's, and certainly rests on real events" (p. 164). We have in the angry men of remission tales those "real events" that offered substance and narrative for du Fail's recreation.

111. *Histoires Tragiques extraictes des oeuvres italiennes de Bandel, et mises en nostre langue Françoise, par Pierre Boaistuau surnommé Launay, natif de Bretaigne* (Paris: Vincent Sertenas, 1559); modern edition prepared by Richard A. Carr (Paris, 1977). For a study of this text, see Richard A. Carr, *Pierre Boaistuau's "Histoires Tragiques": A Study of Narrative Form and Tragic Vision* (North Carolina Studies in the Romance Languages and Literatures, 210; Chapel Hill, N.C., 1979). The story of Romeo and Juliet also circulated in France in the years 1560–80 in the form of a play, now lost, by Cosme la Gambe dit Chateauvieux (Raymond Lebègue, *La Tragédie française de la Renaissance* [Paris, 1954], p. 42 n. 4, p. 69).

112. "Edits contre les mariages clandestins," Feb. 1556/57 in Isambert, ed., *Recueil général,* vol. 13, pp. 469–71. Jean de Coras published a widely read text on this law in 1557: *Des Mariages clandestinement et irreverement contractes par les enfans de famille au deceu ou contre le gré, vouloir et consentement de leurs Peres et Meres* (Toulouse: Pierre du Puis). Coras had taught Boaistuau law at the University of Valence (Michel Simonin, "Notes sur Pierre Boaistuau," *Bibliothèque d'humanisme et renaissance,* 38 [1976]: 325).

113. Boaistuau, "Histoire troisiesme, De deux amans, dont l'un mourut de venin, l'autre de tristesse," in *Histoires Tragiques,* ed. Carr, pp. 63–119; see especially pp. 64, 77, 82–85, 88–92. Cf. Matteo Bandello, *Tutte le Opere,* ed. Francesco Flora (Milan, 1966), vol. 1, novella 9, especially pp. 741–43. In a major study of Bandello's novellas, Adelin Charles Fiorato has shown that they too draw heavily on observed experience and history (*Bandello entre l'histoire et l'écriture. La vie, l'expérience sociale, l'évolution culturelle d'un conteur de la Renaissance* [Florence, 1979], pp. 579–618).

114. Boaistuau, "Histoire troisiesme," pp. 114–19. All of this last speech by Friar Laurens and the various sentences are added by Boaistuau. Bandello simply says that Il signor Bartolomeo had the story told him in great detail and pardoned Friar Lorenzo and Romeo's servant Pietro (novella 9, p. 765). Some of the differences between the versions of Bandello and Boaistuau are described in Geoffrey Bullough, *Narrative and Dramatic Sources of Shakespeare,* 8 vols. (London and New York, 1957–75), vol. 1, pp. 272–74.

115. Carr, *Boaistuau's "Histoires Tragiques,"* p. 127. Simonin, "Notes sur Pierre Boaistuau," pp. 325, 328–30. On the contribution of Jean de Coras to the theory of sovereignty, see A. London Fell, *Origins of Legislative Sovereignty and the Legislative State* (Königstein and Cambridge, Mass., 1983).

116. For the continental sources of Shakespeare's play and the poem by Arthur Brooke, *The Tragicall Historye of Romeo and Juliet* (1562), drawn from Bandello and Boaistuau, see Bullough, *Narrative and Dramatic Sources,* pp. 269–363. I am, of course, interested here in the way in which all of these sources are nourished by or respond to actual remission tales.

117. Shakespeare, *Romeo and Juliet,* ed. T. J. B. Spencer (The New Penguin Shakespeare; Harmondsworth, Eng., 1967), I.1.

118. Ibid., I.2, I.4–5, II.4.

119. Ibid., III.1, III.3.

120. There are several examples in the French letters of remission of male servants committing homicide while going about their master's or mistress's business (e.g., AN, JJ253B, 7ʳ⁻ᵛ; JJ257B, 107ʳ⁻ᵛ; ADR, BP445, 327ʳ–331ʳ). None of them represent themselves as joking around the way Sampson and Gregory do, but they all identify with the causes of their master and mistress and are insulted when their employer's interests are not served.

121. Two studies that look afresh at male anger in *Romeo and Juliet* are Coppélia Kahn, *Man's Estate: Masculine Identity in Shakespeare* (Berkeley, Calif., 1981), pp. 82–103, and Marianne L. Novy, *Love's Argument: Gender Relations in Shakespeare* (Chapel Hill, N.C., 1984), pp. 106–7.

122. Naomi D. Hurnard, *The King's Pardon for Homicide Before A.D. 1307* (Oxford, 1969). John Bellamy, *Crime and Public Order in England in the Later Middle Ages* (London and Toronto, 1973), pp. 192–98. Thomas A. Green, "The Jury and the English Law of Homicide," *Michigan Law Review,* 74 (1976): 414–72. Green, *Verdict* (cited chap. 1, n. 20), part I, *passim* and especially pp. 32–46 on the difference between accounts in the coroners' rolls and accounts in the juries' enrollments. One other important difference exists between the English law of homicide and the French. In England certain kinds of homicide were justifiable and could lead to an acquittal by the jury: these were defined as "executions pursuant to a royal order and . . . slaying thieves caught escaping with the goods and outlaws who resisted capture," to which were added in the fourteenth century "the slay[ing] of felons caught in the act of burglary, arson, or robbery" and in the sixteenth century "slayers of would-be murderers" (Green, "English Law of Homicide," pp. 419, 436; *Verdict,* pp. 79–86, 122). In France, these were remissible homicides, but still had to go through the pardon procedure, as we have seen in Chapter 1.

123. Green, *Verdict,* pp. 116–17. Lawrence Stone, *The Crisis of the Aristocracy, 1558–1641* (Oxford, 1965), pp. 235–40.

124. J. M. Kaye, "The Early History of Murder and Manslaughter," *Law Quarterly Review,* 83 (1967): 569–601; Thomas Glyn Watkin, "Hamlet and the Law of Homicide," *Law Quarterly Review,* 100 (1984): 282–310 (Watkin makes a compelling case for Shakespeare's familiarity with current changes and problems in the law of homicide and shows how new concerns with the "defendant's state of mind"—Was there malice aforethought or not?—are reflected in *Hamlet*). Green, "English Law of Homicide," pp. 472–99, and *Verdict,* pp. 106–7, 117–29. James S. Cockburn, *Calendar*

of *Assize Records: Home Circuit Indictments, Elizabeth I and James I, Introduction* (London, 1985), pp. 117–21. Given what we have seen in Geneva, perhaps there is some influence from Protestant sensibility in England on the emergence of the manslaughter category.

125. Cockburn provides a beautifully detailed picture of this legal system in action in the late sixteenth and early seventeenth century in ibid. Pardons were still being given (pp. 198–208), but the area of expansion was in pleas of benefit of clergy. In the late seventeenth and eighteenth centuries, the role of pardons was more central, as John M. Beattie has shown in his *Crime and the Courts in England 1660–1800* (Princeton, N.J., 1986), pp. 430–36: "pardons had become a fundamental element in the administration of the criminal law" (p. 431). Cynthia Herrup is now undertaking a major new study on royal pardons in early modern England.

126. *Romeo and Juliet*, V.3, lines 229–69.

127. Ibid., V.3, lines 294–95, 307–8. The prince's self-reflection here is in contrast with the ease with which the Duke hands out pardons at the end of *Measure for Measure*, but both plays raise questions about the uses of mercy. In *The Merchant of Venice*, the pardon granted by the Duke of Venice to Shylock (IV.1) seems more straightforward: the duke will pardon Shylock his life providing he makes a gift of his remaining property to his daughter. But this, too, would warrant further study: the duke first tells Shylock, "I pardon thee thy life before thou ask it," as a gracious contrast to the Jew's insistence upon contract, but then later sets Shylock's gift to Jessica as a condition to his pardon.

Chapter Three

1. AN, JJ252, 33^v–34^r, letter of remission, dated Feb. 1536/37, for Marguerite Vallée, widow of Jacquemin Valenton.

2. Though I will suggest below (see also note 13 to this chapter) some differences in the representation of women's anger and aggressiveness in the nineteenth and twentieth centuries, Jean Harris's report of the death of Herman Tarnover in 1980 makes remarkable reading next to the pardon tale of Marguerite Vallée. (Jean Harris, *Stranger in Two Worlds* [New York, 1986], especially pp. 111–42.) She insists she went to his house only to kill herself out of despair and depression, and she says nothing of anger at him for anything he did, including hitting her that night. She felt "hurt and frustrated, because the script wasn't working out the way I expected it to"; he was the one who was angry ("I made him very angry"). Of course, there are important contrasts in the accounts: Marguerite remembers killing her husband in self-defense, Jean Harris says she does not know precisely how the man she loved was shot. Marguerite Vallée had been beaten often over the years; Herman Tarnover's ill-treatment of Jean Harris had been psychological.

3. AN, JJ248, 80^{r-v}, letter of remission, dated May 1535, for François Thorel of Anse in Lyonnais for the homicide of his wife Ancely Learin.

4. Heinrich Kramer and Jacob Sprenger, *The Malleus Maleficarum*, trans.

Montague Summers (New York, 1971), part I, question 6, pp. 43, 45; Ecclesiasticus 25:17. Calvin, *Commentary on Seneca's "De Clementia"* (cited chap. 2, n. 87), book 1, chap. 5, pp. 109, 117.

5. On women's vices see Ruth Kelso, *Doctrine for the Lady of the Renaissance* (Urbana, Ill., 1956), pp. 11–12, and p. 102 on the wife's anger; Ian Maclean, *The Renaissance Notion of Woman* (Cambridge, Eng., 1980), pp. 15–16, 51. On the disorderly woman, see N. Z. Davis, "Women on Top," chap. 5 in *Society and Culture* (cited chap. 1, n. 85). An excellent and wide-ranging recent thesis on images of women in sixteenth-century France is Sara F. Matthews Grieco, "Mythes et iconographie de la femme dans l'estampe du XVIe siècle français: Images d'un univers mental" (Thèse de doctorat du 3e cycle, Ecole des hautes études en sciences sociales, Paris, 1982), chap. 2, pp. 149–59, on Judith and "femmes fortes"; chap. 4, pp. 342–70, on "violences féminines"; forthcoming under the title *Représentations de la femme dans l'estampe du XVIe siècle français* (Paris, 1987). Charles de Bouelles, *Proverbes et dicts sententieux, avec l'interpretation d'iceux* (Paris: Sébastien Nivelle, 1557), 22^r: "Cheminee fumeuse, Femme rioteuse." A. J. V. Le Roux de Lincy, *Le Livre des proverbes français*, 2d ed., 2 vols. (Paris, 1859), vol. 1, pp. 219–32.

6. Louise Bourgeois, *Observations diverses sur la sterilité, perte de fruict, foecondité, accouchements, et maladies des Femmes, et Enfants nouveaux naix*, 2d ed. (Rouen: Widow of Thomas Daré, 1626), vol. 1, pp. 3, 25: "L'occasion la plus ordinaire qui fait accoucher les femmes, est la colere."

7. Laurent Joubert, *Erreurs populaires au fait de la medecine* (Bordeaux, 1578), book 2, chap. 4. Aristotle, *Nicomachean Ethics*, book 3, chap. 8, 1117a (*Basic Works of Aristotle* [cited Introduction, n. 6], p. 978) on the relation of passion to courage. Montaigne, following Seneca's *De Ira*, had great reservations about the uses of anger ("There is no passion that so shakes the clarity of our judgment as anger"), but said that "anger is always an imperfection, but more excusable in a military man, for in that profession there are certainly occasions that cannot do without it" ("De la colere" in *Essays* [cited chap. 2, n. 87], book 2, chap. 31, pp. 540, 543).

8. Joubert, *Erreurs populaires*, book 2, chap. 4; Bourgeois, *Observations diverses*, p. 2. Montaigne, "Defence de Seneque et de Plutarque," *Essays*, book 2, chap. 32, p. 548.

9. Davis, *Society and Culture*, chaps. 3, 5, on women's roles in grain riots and religious riots in the sixteenth century. Matthews Grieco, "Mythes et iconographie," pp. 149–59, on Judith. Marie de Jars de Gournay, *Egalité des hommes et des femmes* (1622), printed in Mario Schiff, *La fille d'alliance de Montaigne, Marie de Gournay* (Paris, 1910), p. 74, on Judith and the Maid of Orléans.

10. Christine de Pizan, *The Book of the City of Ladies* (ca. 1405), trans. Earl Jeffrey Richards (New York, 1982), book 1, chap. 14, p. 37; chap. 17, p. 43. The English feminist writer "Jane Anger" (perhaps a pseudonym) gave a defense of anger, though not violence, for women in a text of 1589: it was legitimate to "reprove men's filthy vices." "Our furie [is] dangerous because it will not beare with their knavish behaviors. If our frownes be so

terrible, and our anger so deadly, men are too foolish in offering occasions of hatred, which shunned, a terrible death is prevented" (*Jane Anger Her Protection for Women* in Moira Ferguson, ed., *First Feminists: British Women Writers, 1578–1799* [Bloomington, Ind., 1985], p. 63).

11. Benedicti, *Somme des Pechez* (cited chap. 1, n. 44), book 2, chap. 4, pp. 104–6. Benedicti also said that it was a sin for a woman to kill herself to prevent being raped or after being raped: the rape of her body was not a sin for her so long as she did not consent to it.

12. J. G. Bellamy, *The Law of Treason in England in the Later Middle Ages* (Cambridge, Eng., 1970), pp. 87, 228. Of course, it was still permitted to women in England to kill their husbands in self-defense. Papon, *Arrests notables* (cited chap. 1, n. 1), book 22, title 9, p. 1247.

13. On the expression of women's anger and aggression in their writing in the nineteenth and early twentieth centuries, see Carol Christ, "Aggression and Providential Death in George Eliot's Fiction," *Novel,* 9, no. 2 (Winter 1976): 130–40; Patricia Meyer Spacks, "Women's Stories, Women's Selves," *Hudson Review,* 30, no. 1 (Spring 1977): especially pp. 29–30; Elaine Showalter, *A Literature of Their Own: British Women Novelists from Brontë to Lessing* (Princeton, N.J., 1977), especially chap. 6 and pp. 180, 213, 263–64; Jane Marcus, "Art and Anger" (discusses Virginia Woolf), *Feminist Studies,* 4, no. 1 (Feb. 1978): 69–98; Sandra W. Gilbert and Susan Gubar, *The Madwoman in the Attic: The Woman Writer and the Nineteenth Century* (New Haven, Conn., and London, 1979), especially pp. 360–61 on *Jane Eyre*; Elissa D. Gelfand, *Imagination in Confinement: Women's Writings from French Prisons* (Ithaca, N.Y, and London, 1983), pp. 20–30. The older Freudian view on the relinquishing of female aggression can be found in Helene Deutsch, *The Psychology of Women* (New York, 1973; first pub. 1944), vol. 1, pp. 256–57.

Margaret Ann Doody says there is rather little attention to motive and states of mind in the *Old Bailey Sessions Papers* of the eighteenth century. She suggests they reflect a moment of transition between the spiritual perturbations of seventeenth-century criminal motive and the scientific explanations of the nineteenth century ("'Those Eyes Are Made So Killing'" [cited Introduction, n. 7], p. 64).

14. AN, JJ237, 1^r, letter of remission, dated June 1524, for Marguerite Panete from a village in the Bourbonnais ("emeue et irritée"); JJ253B, 60^{r-v}, letter of remission, dated June 1540, for Monde Millete of Lyon ("emeue et rechauffée," "didn't know what she was doing").

15. AN, JJ248, 137^{r-v}, letter of remission, dated Sept. 1535, for Françoise Pounet of the village of Beaumont in the Maine ("toute emeue et eschauffée"); JJ247, 138^v–139^r, letter of remission, dated Paris 1534, for Marguerite Petit of Paris ("perturbée et de collere"); JJ257C, 7^v–8^r, letter of remission, dated Jan. 1546/47, for Bonne Cessier of Choqueuse ("en la collere," "seullement pour le corriger").

16. AN, JJ236, 332^v–334^r, letter of remission, dated Jan. 1523/24, for Vidalle Bayonne for the homicide of Catherine Bonnamente. AN, JJ258B, 122^v–123^r, letter of remission, dated Oct. 1548, for Jean Bourriau, mer-

chant apothecary of Tours for the homicide of his wife and of the merchant Jean Estienne, her lover. A village surgeon named Claude Bousture killed his wife during a quarrel that started, so he said, because she called him "jealous," which he denied he was (JJ257C, 53^v–54^r). Rabelais, *Tiers Livre,* chap. 28, on Hans Carvel, and chap. 33, on the married men doing service to the goddess Jealousy (in *Oeuvres complètes* [cited chap. 1, n. 83], pp. 432–33, 449–50). And compare the undoing of Shakespeare's Othello in Act III, Scene 3, as Iago makes him jealous.

17. AN, JJ257C, 111^v–112^r, letter of remission, dated Apr. 1546/47 before Easter, for Jeanne de Francastel, widow, for the homicide of Guillemette Pasquiere, daughter of plowman Antoine Pasquier and his washerwoman wife.

18. AN, JJ236, 687^r–689^r, letter of remission, dated Nov. 1524, for Jeanne, widow of Etienne Mayet, of Montbazon in the Touraine, in connection with the homicide of Jean Muye, her son-in-law.

19. Maclean, *Renaissance Notion of Woman,* pp. 78–79; Paul Ourliac and J. de Malafosse, *Histoire du droit privé,* 2d ed., 3 vols. (Paris, 1971), vol. 3, pp. 135–36. On the subject-wife plea, see Nicole Castan, "La criminalité familiale dans le ressort du Parlement de Toulouse," in A. Abbiateci et al., *Crimes et criminalité en France, 17e–18e siècles* (Cahier des Annales, 33; Paris, 1971), pp. 91–107. This plea seems to have been used more systematically in English defense than in French (see N. Z. Davis, "Women on Top," p. 146 and n. 39, and especially Beattie, *Crime and the Courts* [cited chap. 2, n. 125], p. 414). The one example I have found of a woman using the subjection defense is the peasant Jeanne Domecourt, accused of the imposture of Charlotte Lebel in order to acquire the inheritance of a fief. She explained in her June 1545 letter of pardon that as a young woman she had become the servant and concubine of a canon of Saint Quentin, that the whole scheme was his idea, and that she could not rightly disobey him ("estant lors sa servante et concubine et auquel elle ne pourroit bonnement desobeyr"). The letter also used the formula "la fragilité de sexe feminin," adding that she was in the "puissance" of her master. The Parlement of Paris ratified her letter and ordered a trial of the canon (AN, X2^A 98, 31^r–36^r, Apr. 6, 1545/46).

20. AN, JJ238, 23^r–24^v, letter of remission, dated Jan. 1524/25, for Louis Desmaroys, miller aged about 21 years, and his wife Jacquette, aged about 16 or 17, living in Orléans, for falsely retracting testimony about an intruder in their landlord's house. JJ258B, 39^v–40^r, letter of remission, dated June 1548, for Michel Alin and Marie Picart his wife, "pauvres gens de labeur," about 40 years of age, living in the village of Villefleur en Dunois, for the homicide of Jean Alain. Other examples of supplications from both husband and wife: JJ237, 5^{r-v}, letter of remission, dated Sept. 1524, for Etienne Aport and his wife (not named), "simples gens de villaige," for killing Etienne's brother in a fight about how they were treating their mother; JJ249B, 118^{r-v}, letter of remission, dated Oct. 1536, for carpenter Gilles Gallart and his wife Mathurine Ginault living in a village in the region of La Rochelle, for the homicide of a woman who had insulted Mathurine;

JJ258B, 73^v–75^r, letter of remission, dated July 1548, for Jean de la Ruelle, sergeant at Ribemont in Picardy, and his wife Bonne Bougin for the homicide of her son-in-law (married to her daughter from a first marriage) in a property dispute; JJ258B, 135^r, letter of remission, dated Nov. 1548, for Perrine Chicherelle and her husband Pierre Le Compte, locksmiths of Nantes, for the homicide of a cabinetmaker who was trying to kill another woman.

A young barber of Angers began his remission with a "maternal remonstrance." His mother complained to him of the ill-treatment she suffered from her stepfather because of a woman of ill-repute whom he was maintaining, and asked her son to go scare the "paillarde" away from her husband. He never did find the woman, but rather killed a man in the house where he was looking for her (JJ238, 63^r–64^r, letter of remission, dated Apr. 1524/25, for François Bachelier of Angers). It would have been interesting to see how he constructed his mother's role in the affair if the "paillarde" had been the victim.

21. The following precentages on women's presence among those prosecuted for homicide are given to be suggestive only, for the studies cover different time spans and jurisdictions, and some include infanticide among homicides and some do not. James Buchanan Given, *Society and Homicide in Thirteenth-Century England* (Stanford, Calif., 1977), pp. 134–36: 8.6 percent. Barbara Hanawalt, "The Female Felon in Fourteenth-Century England," *Viator*, 5 (1974): 257 and appendix 1: 7.3 percent. Schnapper, "La justice criminelle rendue par le Parlement de Paris sous le règne de François Ier" (cited chap. 1, n. 23), p. 271, table 7: 11.7 percent, including infanticides. B. Boutelet, "Etudes par sondage de la criminalité dans le bailliage du Pont de l'Arche (16e–17e s.)," *Annales de Normandie*, 12 (1962): 249: "La criminalité féminine est mince au XVIIe siècle comme au XVIIIe siècle; elle reste dans le rapport de 1/8 environ masculin." Porphyre Petrovitch, "Recherches sur la criminalité à Paris dans la seconde moitié du XVIIIe siècle," in Abbiateci et al., *Crimes et criminalité*, pp. 234–35. Beattie, *Crime and the Courts in England, 1660–1800*, p. 83, table 3.1, p. 97: women make up 9 percent of those indicted for homicide at the Surrey assizes, but when indictment for concealing a birth and presumptive infanticide is added in to all homicides (pp. 113–16 and table 3.6), they make up 23 percent. Nicole Castan gives a detailed portrait of female criminals in the eighteenth and early nineteenth centuries in Languedoc and information from other jurisdictions as well in *Criminels de Languedoc* (cited chap. 1, n. 43), pp. 25–36. Her tables for female criminality show the percentage of female crimes of *all* crimes, including theft, violence, and others; the percentage for the period 1760–90 ranges according to the region from 8.1 to 22.9 percent. Back in the first half of the sixteenth century in Arras, Robert Muchembled has found that just under 15 percent of *all* crimes judged were committed by women (*Popular Culture and Elite Culture in France, 1400–1750*, trans. Lydia Cochrane [Baton Rouge and London, 1985], p. 119).

The percentage of women accused of various forms of homicide in the United States from the end of the 1950's to the middle of the 1970's has been about 15–16 percent. Rita James Simon, *Women and Crime* (Lexington, Mass., 1975), p. 40, Table 4–5; Lee Bowker, *Women, Crime, and the Criminal Justice System* (Lexington, Mass., 1978), p. 5, table 1-1 and see tables 1-2 and 1-3 for variations in individual states. In France the percentage of murders reported as committed by women was 11 percent in 1955, 8 percent in 1960, 15 percent in 1965, and 12 percent in 1972 (ibid., p. 263, table 9-1). A new review of the literature for the contemporary period is Meda Chesney-Lind, "Women and Crime: The Female Offender," *Signs,* 12 (Autumn 1986): 78–96.

22. Certain registers of the JJ series I examined start to finish, remission by remission, simply looking for women: JJ236, 237, 238, 245B, 247, 249B, 253B, 255B, 256B, 256C, 257B, 257C, 258B, 260B, 265, 266. Out of 4,189 letters in these volumes, I found only 37 women receiving remission in 35 different letters. I may have missed a few, but even then the figure is not high. (Five additional female supplicants were found in registers that were not searched page by page for women's remissions, thus bringing my total pool to 42.) The figures from the Conciergerie of Paris are from APP, A^{B1}–A^{B6} (see chap. 2, n. 63). There were no women among the recipients of the 40 letters of remission ratified by the Sénéchaussée of Agen in the seventeenth century (Hanlon, "Les rituels de l'agression" [cited Introduction, n. 4] and private letter of Aug. 21, 1986) and none among the 21 letters ratified by the Parlement of Navarre from 1752 to 1784 (Desplat, "La grâce royale" [cited Introduction, n. 4]).

In England the situation in regard to pardons for women was quite different from that in France: of 495 pardons for felonies given to persons convicted on the Home Circuit during the reign of Elizabeth I, about one-quarter went to women. Some of them had previously had their penalties delayed because of pregnancy, and then this was extended into a pardon. (Cockburn, *Calendar of Assize Records* [cited chap. 2, n. 124], pp. 121–23, 128, and appendix 8). Women were also favored in pardons in eighteenth-century England (Beattie, *Crime and the Courts,* p. 438). In accounting for this difference, it should be stressed that English pardons were granted for a wider range of offenses than in France, many of them going for theft and other property crimes.

23. It could be that more women than men accused of homicide were being acquitted or given lesser penalties by the courts or on appeal, and therefore a remission request was not in order. Cockburn found English courts more lenient in dealing with women accused of felonies than with men (*Calendar of Assize Records,* p. 114); a study of this for sixteenth-century France would be most useful.

24. Alfred Soman, "Décriminalisation de la sorcellerie" (cited chap. 1, n. 62), especially pp. 188–96: of 265 persons appealing death sentences for witchcraft to the Parlement of Paris from 1540 to 1587, 12.1 percent were condemned to death, 34.3 percent were released, and 34.3 percent were sentenced to be tortured to see if they would confess. Of the last group, virtually all of them got through the torture without making an avowal that led to a death sentence. See also Jonathan Dewald, *The Formation of a Provin-*

cial Nobility: The Magistrates of the Parlement of Rouen, 1494–1610 (Princeton, N.J., 1980), p. 320, for a report on the disposition of twenty witchcraft cases appealed to the Parlement of Rouen: seven executed, two released, the rest given lesser sentences.

25. AN, JJ261B, 96ʳ–97ʳ, letter of remission, dated Mar. 1551/52, for Anne Bachet, merchant of Lyon, his wife Claudine Troignat, his mother-in-law, and his son-in-law for the homicide of Philiberte Guillon, whom they accused of bewitching Bachet's young son and who refused to lift her spell. See the remission for Pierre Marion, described in chap. 1 and the re-missions described below and in n. 63 to this chapter. Soman gives many examples of the lynching of witches ("Décriminalisation de la sorcellerie," pp. 180–85).

26. See Beattie, *Crime and the Courts*, p. 113 n. 84, on the usefulness in a broad legal study of distinguishing between the homicide of a baby newly born or under a few weeks old and other forms of homicide of children. For the purposes of pardon tales, it is also important to distinguish three categories: the homicide of a newborn; the killing of a child at the breast by "overlaying," that is, suffocating it in one's sleep; and other kinds of killing of children up to the age of eight or nine. The first type is distinguished from the second in the confessor's *Summa* of Jean Benedicti (*Somme des Pechez,* book 2, chap. 4, p. 109), both being mortal sins, but the former much more seriously reproved; the first type is the subject of special royal legislation in Feb. 1556/57, as we shall see; and the first and second types have a different history in regard to penalty, the killing of the newly born being a capital crime that for some centuries generated remission requests, the suffocating of a nursing infant in bed being given lesser penalties. The essential study of Yves-B. Brissaud, "L'infanticide à la fin du Moyen Age, ses motivations psychologiques et sa répression," *Revue historique de droit français et étranger,* 50 (1972): 229–56, is based on letters of remission and concerns only the killing of the newly born. Remissions for the third cate-gory were given when the claim could be made that the death was acciden-tal (AN, X²ᴮ 106, Feb. 18, 1580; ADR, BP444, 212ᵛ–215ᵛ, letter of remis-sion, dated Nov. 1558, for Jean Bas dit Grandes, boatman of Lyon, for the accidental shooting of the three- or four-year-old son of another boatman). For important studies especially concerned with suffocation of nursing babies, see Richard C. Trexler, "Infanticide in Florence: New Sources and First Results," *History of Childhood Quarterly,* 1 (1973): 98–116; Richard Helmholz, "Infanticide in the Province of Canterbury During the Fifteenth Century," *History of Childhood Quarterly,* 2 (1975): 380–90. For a study on infanticide that includes material on the homicide of children up to the age of eight, see Peter C. Hoffer and N. E. H. Hull, *Murdering Mothers: Infan-ticide in England and New England, 1558–1803* (New York and London, 1981).

27. On infanticide and its remission in the medieval period, see the ex-cellent article by Brissaud, "L'infanticide à la fin du Moyen Age," especially pp. 235–41. Guérin, *Recueil des documents concernant le Poitou,* vol. 11 (cited chap. 2, n. 6), pp. 334–37 (JJ197, 142ᵛ), 343–46 (JJ197, 140ʳ), 86–89 (JJ200, 72ʳ). Paul Guérin and Léonce Celier, *Recueil des documents concer-*

nant le Poitou, vol. 12 (for 1475–1483), vol. 41 of *Archives historiques du Poitou* (1919), pp. 148–50 (JJ206, 229ᵛ), 296–97 (JJ205, 181ᵛ), 240–41 (JJ205, 59ʳ).

28. Philippe de Vigneulles, *Gedenkbuch* (cited chap. 1, n. 75), pp. 124, 144–45, 291–92. On the hardening of sentiment against infanticide in Flanders in the late fifteenth century, see Myriam Greilsammer, "The Condition of Women in Flanders and Brabant at the End of the Middle Ages" (Doctoral dissertation, Hebrew University of Jerusalem, 1984), pp. 490–515.

29. Nicolas de Troyes, *Le Grand Parangon des Nouvelles Nouvelles* (cited chap. 1, n. 75), no. 32, pp. 92–95. Kasprzyk, *Nicolas de Troyes* (cited chap. 1, n. 75), p. 86.

30. Isambert, ed., *Recueil général* (cited chap. 1, n. 13), vol. 13, pp. 471–73: Edict of Feb. 1556/57, registered by the Parlement of Paris Mar. 4, 1556/57, and repealed in 1791. For a similar hardening of the law in England in the last half of the sixteenth century, see Hoffer and Hull, *Murdering Mothers,* pp. 6–20. This culminated in a statute of 1624 (pp. 19–20) very much like the French one in making the concealment of the birth presumptive evidence for murder, except that it was confined to unwed mothers, whereas the French law applied to "toute femme." In the eighteenth century English courts began to take "a softer line" in regard to infanticide, and convictions under the statute of 1624 declined (Beattie, *Crime and the Courts,* pp. 118–24). Again a subject warranting full treatment for France.

31. The earliest of the registers I have examined in the series JJ is 1523 (JJ236; for complete list of registers searched for remissions for women, see note 22 to this chapter). The publication of all medieval letters of remission concerning the Poitou made by Paul Guérin and Léonce Celier goes up to 1502 (Léonce Celier, *Recueil de documents concernant le Poitou,* vol. 14 [for 1486–1502], vol. 56 of *Archives historiques de Poitou* [1958]). The latest pardon granted for an infanticide in the Poitou series is Jan. 1478/79, letter of remission for Marguerite Moricelle of Louin, JJ205, 59ʳ (Paul Guérin and Léonce Celier, *Recueil des documents concernant le Poitou,* vol. 12, pp. 240–41; see also pp. 148–50 for a Feb. 1476/77 remission granted to a father and son who, "to safeguard the honor" of the daughter of the family, abandoned her new baby at the almshouse, where it was found dead).

Bernard Schnapper notes regarding the eighteen infanticides (thirteen killings of a newborn, two abortions, three unspecified) judged on appeal by the Parlement of Paris in 1536 and 1546, "Il est étrange de constater qu'aucun des infanticides que j'ai relevés n'a donné lieu à lettre de rémission." He suggests that the Parlement's "indulgence" (some of the women who had come up from lesser jurisdictions with death penalties were given whipping and banishment instead) made it unnecessary for women to seek letters of remission (Schnapper, "La justice criminelle," p. 272 n. 51, p. 274). But such discrimination in penalty did not prevent people from seeking letters of remission—and thus pardon without penalty—for involuntary homicide in other kinds of cases.

32. See the preamble to the Feb. 1556/57 edict against concealing pregnancy for a description of the courts' difficulties in dealing with infanticide

cases (Isambert, ed., *Recueil général,* vol. 13, p. 472). Alfred Soman, "Les procès de sorcellerie au Parlement de Paris (1565–1640)," *Annales. E.S.C.,* 32 (1977): 797, figs. 3 and 4: in a sample of over 200 cases of infanticide, two-thirds of the women appealing were condemned to death. Schnapper, "La justice criminelle," p. 21, table 8: of eighteen cases of infanticide or abortion appealed from lower jurisdictions to the Parlement of Paris in 1536 and 1546, thirteen were appealing death sentences, and five, sentences to be tortured. The Parlement decreed eight sentences to death, three to torture to see if the accused would confess, and six whippings followed by banishment. An example of one of the reduced sentences is the case of Didiere, wife of Ennoy Bazard, living in the village of Longprez in the Nivernais. Condemned by the local prévôt to be hanged for the "homicide par elle commis à ung sien enfant nouveau neay" and to have all her goods confiscated by the Duchesse de Nivernais, she appealed to the Parlement of Paris. The Parlement ordered her questioned under torture "to know from her own mouth whether the child was alive when it was born"; she stuck to her story of stillbirth. Her appeal was denied nonetheless, but her sentence was reduced to being beaten at the crossroads of Longprez for three days and then banished from the seigneury of Longprez forever (AN, X²ᴬ 98, 167ʳ, May 12, 1546).

See also Jonathan Dewald, *The Formation of a Provincial Nobility: The Magistrates of the Parlement of Rouen, 1499–1610* (Princeton, N.J., 1980), p. 320. The Parlement of Rouen was harsher in this matter than that of Paris: out of twenty infanticide appeals examined from a twenty-year sample, eighteen were executed; Dewald found the Parlement of Rouen more severe in judging infanticide than any other crime, including witchcraft. See further his discussion in "The 'Perfect Magistrate': Parlementaires and Crime in Sixteenth-Century Rouen," *Archive for Reformation History,* 67 (1976): 284–300.

Alfred Soman has told me of a remarkable and exceptional remission for infanticide during the reign of Louis XIII. In Jan. 1613, the eleven-year-old king was returning from hunting when a servant, being led to the Conciergerie of Paris, threw herself at his feet asking for grace. She had been condemned to death for infanticide at Senlis and was appealing her sentence to the Parlement of Paris, insisting that her child had been stillborn and was dead when the neighbor women arrived. Deeply moved and pointing out that there was no proof that the child had been killed by the young mother, the king persuaded the queen-mother to give her grace. This was done and the letter was ratified by Parlement in Mar. 1613. (Letter of Feb. 17, 1987, transcribing BN, ms. fr. 4024, 275ᵛ; APP, Aᴮ21, 32ᵛ; AN, X²ᴬ 975, Mar. 7, 1613; X²ᴬ 184, Mar. 7, 1613.)

33. Cotreau, *Commentaires . . . exposans les dix Commandemens* (cited chap. 1, n. 45). 172ᵛ: "La femme desbordée fait mourir le fruict de son ventre." Benedicti, *Somme des Pechez,* book 2, chap. 4, p. 109: "Helas que sera ce de ces mal-heureuses femmes lesquelles apres avoir abandonné leur pudicité aux ruffiens viennent à desfaire leur propre fruit pour eviter le deshonneur du monde." *Les larmes de repentance d'une jeune fille Prisonniere,*

dans le Prisons de Lyon, qui a pery son fruict (Lyon: Pierre Roussin, 1606). *Discours pitoyable, sur la mort d'une damoiselle, âgée de quinze à seize ans, Executée dans la ville de Mantouë, le Samedy sixiesme jour de Mars, 1599. Avec les regrets qu'elle fait avant sa mort* (suyvant la coppie Imprimé à Paris, 1599). Seguin lists an edition of this same pamphlet with an execution at Padua in September 1607 (*L'Information en France* [cited chap. 2, n. 93], p. 71, no. 15). The English legislation also stressed the "lewdness" of its targets (Hoffer and Hull, *Murdering Mothers*, p. 22).

On increased religious and civil action against illicit sexual behavior in the early sixteenth century, see Jean-Louis Flandrin, ed., *Les Amours paysannes (XVIe–XIXe siècle)* (Paris, 1975), pp. 207–15, and Robert Muchembled, *Popular Culture*, pp. 172, 192.

34. AN, X²ᴮ 106, letter of remission, dated Feb. 1580, for Marie de Soullier, 20-year-old servant of Bonny-sur-Loire, ratified Feb. 18, 1580. JJ249B, 65ʳ, letter of remission, dated Apr. 1535/36, for Suzanne Mathieu Legrande, 29-year-old linenmaker, wife of a mason, the two of them "chargez de petits enfans." Of 42 women involved in 39 letters of remission in JJ, X²ᴬ and X²ᴮ, one was unmarried, one was a concubine, 24 were married, 15 were widowed, and one was of unknown status. The precise age was given in 19 cases: the median age of female recipients was 30.

35. On the high legal connections of Marie Quatrelivres, see chap. 2, n. 68.

36. AN, JJ247, 166ʳ, letter of remission, dated Nov. 1534, for Nicole, widow of Lorin Lamer from a village in the Vermandois, for the homicide of her servant Louis Boutier, provided she pay 10 livres for alms to pray to God, 100 sous to the "pauvres mendians" of Paris, and 100 sous to the "filles pentitentes," that is, the reformed prostitutes of Paris. JJ255B, 56ʳ⁻ᵛ, letter of remission, dated May 1541, for Antoinette, widow of Etienne Beauvois, aged 60 and servant of a priest in the diocese of Troyes.

37. On female self-definition in the sixteenth century, see N. Z. Davis, "Women in the Crafts in Sixteenth-Century Lyon," *Feminist Studies*, 8, no. 1 (Spring, 1982): 46–80.

38. *Les Evangiles des Quenouilles,* ed. Madeleine Jeay (Paris and Montréal, 1985), "Introduction," p. 27, and p. 79. Also see note 43 to chap. 1 of this book on women making up songs about their neighbors' antics. On women as privileged "frame narrators" of fairy tales, see the essay by Karen Rowe, "To Spin a Yarn: The Female Voice in Folklore and Fairy Tale," in Ruth B. Bottigheimer, ed., *Fairy Tales and Society: Illusion, Allusion, and Paradigm* (Philadelphia, 1986), pp. 54–74.

39. Platter, *Autobiographie* (cited chap. 1, n. 76), pp. 20–21, family information, some of it from his mother. Jeanne du Laurens, "La Généalogie de Messieurs du Laurens," in Charles de Ribbe, *Une famille au XVIe siècle d'après des documents originaux,* 3d ed. (Paris, 1879), pp. 35–99. For further discussion of the genre of family history, see N. Z. Davis, "Ghosts, Kin and Progeny" (cited chap. 1, n. 43), especially pp. 96–100, and "Gender and Genre: Women as Historical Writers, 1400–1820," in Patricia Labalme, ed., *Beyond Their Sex: Learned Women of the European Past* (New York and London, 1980), especially pp. 161–65.

40. Benedicti, *Somme des Pechez,* book 4, chap. 5, pp. 647–48. Jean de Coras, *Arrest memorable du Parlement de Tholose. Contenant Une Histoire prodigieuse d'un supposé mary, advenüe de nostre temps* (Paris: Galliot du Pré, 1572), p. 21; Davis, *Return of Martin Guerre* (cited chap. 1, n. 24), pp. 68–69. Cellini, *Life* (cited chap. 2, n. 77), p. 313.

41. AN, JJ248, 137^{r-v}, letter of remission, dated Sept. 1535, for Françoise Pounet, widow aged about 35 with two children, servant for a peasant family in the Maine. Another gap in Pounet's story is suggested by a strange remark about her reputation: she has always lived "in honesty," etc., but she says she was so afraid of the soldiers in the vicinity that she didn't know what she was doing and because of this, "she might have a bad reputation and people might say she conducted herself badly."

42. AN, JJ238, 240^{v}–241^{r}, letter of remission, dated Dec. 1525, for Claudine, wife of Jean Fouyn, laboureur of Courtenay, a village in the bailliage of Sens, for the homicide of Michau, the "varlet" of her husband.

43. Philippe de Vigneulles, *Cent Nouvelles Nouvelles* (cited chap. 1, n. 46), no. 40, pp. 183–85. See also Bouchet, *Serées* (cited chap. 2, n. 89), Quatriesme Serée, vol. 1, pp. 136–37: "Vous sçavez . . . que les masques ont de grands privileges . . . et . . . bien souvent soubs l'ombre et nom de masque, il se fait des marchez bien cornus."

44. Christine de Pizan, *City of Ladies,* book 1, chap. 10, p. 26. Anatole de Montaiglon, *Recueil de poésies françoises des 15e et 16e siècles,* 13 vols. (Paris, 1855–78), vol. 6, pp. 171–78, "La vengence des femmes contre leurs maris à cause de l'abolition des tavernes" (Paris: Etienne Denise, 1557); pp. 179–89, "Le plaisant Quaquet et resjuyssance des femmes pour ce que leurs maris n'yvrongnent plus en la taverne"; vol. 2, pp. 223–29, "La reformation des tavernes et destruction de Gormandise, en forme de dialogue." Nicolas de Troyes, *Le Grand Parangon des Nouvelles Nouvelles,* no. 105, pp. 215–18, a cheerful tale about two goodwives who get drunk on wine. Bouchet, *Serées,* Premier Serée, vol. 1, pp. 13–16, the company debates whether women get as drunk as men. Benedicti, *Somme des Pechez,* book 4, chap. 13, p. 370: "As for the sin [of drunkenness], it is all the more indecent in women than in men, for she who is 'prise de vin' is exposed to many dangers." *Discours veritable de Toussaint Letra, lequel a esté bruslé tout vif dans la Ville d'Aix le 26 d'Aoust 1618 pour avoir violé sa fille* (Lyon: François Yvrard, 1618).

45. AN, JJ257C, 135^{v}, letter of remission, dated May 1547, for Jérôme Turpin, tissotier of Lyon, for the homicide of his wife Anne Destroit. Turpin had been invited to the country feast by a woman and had left his wife behind. He does not comment on why she was so cross when he got back home. Another meal preparation fight: JJ248, 11^{v}–12^{v}, letter of remission, dated Jan. 1534/35, for Pierre Guillot, peasant in the Orléanais, for the homicide of his wife, who refused to prepare dinner for him and his carter when they returned from a long morning's work doing customary services.

46. AN, JJ253B, 118^{v}, letter of remission, dated Oct. 1540, for Bonne Goberde of Arnay-sous-Vitteaux, for the homicide of her husband. See Appendix A for a transcription of this text in French.

47. AN, JJ257C, 6^{r-v}, letter of remission, dated Jan. 1546/47, for Jeanne

Regnart, widow of Jean Foucart, laboureur in a village near Coucy in Picardy.

48. AN, JJ258B, 110^v, letter of remission, dated Sept. 1548, for Barbe Milly, wife of a laboureur of Jully-le-Château (now Jully-sur-Sarce) in Champagne, for the homicide of Michel Motin, who was loading his wagon with her widowed mother's goods. JJ258B, 73^v–75^r, letter of remission, dated July 1548, for Jean de la Ruelle and his wife Bonne Bougin, cultivators of Ribemont in Picardy, for the homicide of Bonne's son-in-law Charles Poirier (married to her daughter by her first marriage) in a quarrel over a property that Bonne had let them use as an "oeuvre de charité," and which the young couple tried to "usurp," claiming the daughter had inherited it from her late father. This letter was challenged by Poirier's children, and two years later, the couple, still in prison, obtained another letter of remission (JJ260B, 45^{r-v}); here Poirier is no longer referred to as their son-in-law, but as a man "de mauvais gouvernement" who had seized their property, to which he had no right from the moment Bonne (or Peronne as she is called in this letter) made her second marriage.

JJ247, 127^{r-v}, letter of remission, dated Sept. 1534, for Jeanne, wife of sergant Jean Galzy, and Katherine Reberbelle, a 25-year-old widow, of Saint Victor in the Rouergue, for the homicide of a young village man who they believed had stolen their belongings, including the shirt of Jeanne's husband. JJ257C, 7^v–8^r, letter of remission, dated Jan. 1546/47, for Bonne Cessier, widow, for the homicide of her son Jean Hommart, a taverner, who claimed she and his brother, a priest, had defrauded him of his inheritance. When he began to break an entrance into her house, claiming he had a right to it, she seized him by the hair and ears and hit him with her cane "in anger . . . only to correct him."

49. AN, JJ249A, 40^v–43^r, letter of remission, dated Sept. 1536, for Etienne Mechault, carpenter and cabinetmaker of Lyon, for the wounding of his wife Anne Fantier and the homicide of her lover Jean Danjou; he opens by talking about how Danjou came to Lyon from Paris three weeks before and began to frequent his wife. He said he attacked the two of them in the act on Sept. 20, when he returned from doing craft errands in town; the remission was signed within the next few days. Whether Anne subsequently lived or died is not known. JJ256C, 30^r, letter of remission, dated Apr. 1543/44, for Antoine Vigier dit Le Blanc, chaudronnier of Freix-Anglards in Auvergne, for the homicide of his second wife, the sixteen- to eighteen-year-old Antoinette de Coue. He had forbidden her to associate with Michel Messergnolles; in January they had a fight about her seeing him and he hit her "in fury and in chaude colle" with a sword.

The account of Jean Bourriau, merchant apothecary of Tours, opens with his inviting his wife's sister and her husband and the wife of another neighbor to supper and "to make good cheer together." The wife excuses herself after a whispered message from the daughter saying she must relieve herself ("aller à ses affaires"), and when she stays away too long, he goes after her, becomes suspicious at a locked door, breaks in and finds his wife "doing an immodest act" with merchant Jean Estienne, "notwithstanding the fact that he had previously forbidden her his company." "Troublé en son esprit," he killed them both (JJ258B, 122^v–123^r, Oct. 1548). Jean Manigault's killing of his wife is a Twelfth-Night tale. A 60-year-old peasant of Fontaine-Chaalis, he opens with the good cheer of their drinking to the Twelfth-Night King at his son's house, but then he went off on his own and got drunk. Returning home, he found a man with his wife and killed her (JJ236, 480^v–482^r, Apr. 1524).

50. AN, JJ252, 112^v–113^r, letter of remission, dated July 1537, for Simon Guy, barber-surgeon of Lyon, for the homicide of his wife Benoîte Benique.

51. L'Estoile, *Journal* (cited chap. 2, n. 57), pp. 151–52 (Sept. 1577), 217 (May 1579). Unfortunately, Villequier's letter of remission could not be found in the Parlementary records, so that we are unable to compare his story to that reported by L'Estoile. Since the crime was committed in the chateau of Poitiers during the king's residence there, it was probably judged on the spot by the Prévôt de l'Hôtel rather than by the Parlement of Paris. (I am grateful to Alfred Soman for his comments on the location of the Villequier documents.) The wife of the Protestant Sire de La Bobetière was rumored to have had sexual relations with her lover while the husband was imprisoned with other Huguenots in Lusignan, a timing that made the ambush in the garden by the aggrieved husband all the more understandable. Papon reports this sentence and execution as part of his discussion of when husbands are or are not to be pardoned for killing an adulterous wife; he names the man the Sire de La Bellantiere rather than La Bobetière (*Arrests notables,* book 22, title 9, p. 1265).

52. AN, JJ247, 138^v–139^r, letter of remission, dated Sept. 1534, for Marguerite Petit, wife of a gardener of Paris, for urging her son to kill a journeyman visiting a woman lodger in her house whom she suspected of being a prostitute. When he refused to leave, "in great anger . . . like a woman speaking lightly and without thinking, she said, 'Traitor, whoremonger, you're making a brothel of my house. . . . Kill him for me, kill him for me,' without however meaning that any wrong be done."

53. Two men telling of attempts to get sexual favors from women portray themselves as beginning with insults and/or physical threats. AN, JJ259, 38^{r-v}, letter of remission, dated 1548, for Me Vincent de Saint Ayon, aged 25 or 26, bachelor of law of Toulouse: going about with two other men, he saw some women known as "macquerelles" and said to one, "'I know you well, whore . . .'" and other verbal insults and "pretended he was going to hit her, without however touching her, just intending to frighten her." JJ236, 473^v–475^r, letter of remission, dated Apr. 1524, for Jean Fiadet dit Garnier, laboureur: on Pentecost, he went with another man to the house of a woman described as "living lubriciously," and, when she would not open the door, broke it down and hit her. On collective rape by youths and the humiliation of their victims, see Jacques Rossiaud, "Prostitution, jeunesse et société dans les villes du Sud-Est au XVe siècle," *Annales. E.S.C.,* 31 (1976): 289–325.

54. AN, JJ255B, 53^v, letter of remission, dated May 1541, for Agnès

Fauresse, wife of Heliot Clergeon of La Rochefoucauld. Also JJ260B, 104ʳ, letter of remission, dated Aug. 1550, for Marguerite Banoyre, wife of Pierre Vallot of Naillat in the Comté de La Marche: she was walking along the street when a man from the priory of Naillat shouted "putain" at her from the entrance of the blacksmith's shop. She called him a "larron" (thief), and after further exchange, he hit her with his chain-mail sleeve and she, bleeding and offended by his words, struck him with her little bread knife.

55. On "gay cultural expression" among the medieval clergy, see John Boswell, *Christianity, Social Tolerance, and Homosexuality: Gay People in Western Europe from the Beginning of the Christian Era* (Chicago and London, 1980), chaps. 7–9. Emmanuel Le Roy Ladurie, *Montaillou, village occitan de 1294 à 1324* (Paris, 1975), pp. 209–15, for the "homosexual" Franciscan Arnaud de Verniolles and his pupils. A sixteenth-century Protestant attack on the Catholic clergy as Sodomites in [Pierre Viret], *Le Manuel, ou Instruction des Curez et Vicaires de l'Eglise Romaine* (Lyon: Claude Ravot, 1564), p. 137: "ces vilains putiers, ie n'ose pas dire Sodomites, comme ils le sont pour le moins une grande partie." Catholic canon law against clerics involved in sodomitic acts became stronger in the sixteenth century, especially with the papal bull of 1568, *Horrendum illud scelus,* discussed by Benedicti, *Somme des Pechez,* book 2, chap. 8, pp. 148–50. Offenders were to be deprived of their office, degraded of clerical status, and, Benedicti says approvingly, "delivered over to the secular justice to have them die by the ordinance of secular law."

56. The many examples of the use of the term given by Edmond Huguet in his dictionary of sixteenth-century French usage all pertain to a person claimed to be doing literal sodomitic acts (*Dictionnaire de la langue française* [cited chap. 2, n. 7], vol. 1, pp. 646–47). In a careful examination of insults in cases before the Parlement of Paris, Alfred Soman shows that "bougre" loses some of its specificity by the mid-seventeenth century. (I am grateful to Dr. Soman for letting me read his unpublished essay on "Injures," based on material collected for his soon-to-be-completed thèse d'état, *Sorcellerie et magie devant le Parlement de Paris, 1540–1670.*)

57. AN, JJ257B, 67ʳ⁻ᵛ, letter of remission, dated May 1546, for Jean Le Bon, priest and religious of the order of Fontevrault, living at Bezu-le-Guéry for the homicide of Ezan Garnier. In another interesting account, the sodomitic insult is made by a wife against a Piedmontese merchant, who she suggests by her details had designs on her husband: AN, JJ253B, 60ʳ⁻ᵛ, letter of remission, dated June 1540, for Monde Millete, wife of Me Jean Odet Balle of Lyon. Her husband was sick in bed and summoned the merchant, Jean-François Gros, to do an errand for him. They were such good friends that they called each other "brother" ("frere"). On returning from the errand, the Italian ignored the wife and her neighbors supping at the table, went to the bed, and said very low, "Bonsoir, frere." The husband suggested he greet the company, the Italian said to the wife, "I have nothing to do with greeting a villaine like you"—"putain, paillarde"—he'd "cut her nose." "Upset," she called him "bougre," he hit her with his fist,

and, "outraged in the presence of her husband," she struck him in the side with a supper knife. It should be added that the Italians were the other major group in France accused of sodomitic practices and tastes.

58. Christine de Pizan, *City of Ladies,* book 1, chaps. 16–20, pp. 40–51. The image of the Amazons by the Poitiers poet Catherine des Roches, "Nous faisons la guerre / Aux Rois de la terre" ("we wage war against the kings of the earth"), is cited by Tilde Sankovitch, "Inventing Authority of Origin, The Difficult Enterprise," in Mary Beth Rose, ed., *Women in the Middle Ages and the Renaissance: Literary and Historical Perspectives* (Syracuse, N.Y., 1986), p. 235. See also Celeste Turner Wright, "The Amazons in Elizabethan Literature," *Studies in Philology,* 37 (1940): 433–55.

59. Du Fail, *Propos Rustiques,* pp. 71–73. Of the word "vesse," Rabelais has Pantagruel say, "In my country you can not offend a woman more than in calling her that" (*Le Quart Livre,* chap. 9 in *Oeuvres complètes,* p. 565). Although "vesse" is translated today as "fart," "slutbag" comes closer to a sixteenth-century meaning. On the ridiculousness or perceived unimportance of women's quarrels in the Agenais in the seventeenth century, see Hanlon, "Les rituels de l'agression," p. 259: "Les chocs entre femmes étaient considérés comme moins sérieux, relevant du burlesque, car elles maniaient rarement des armes, infligeaient très rarement des blessures conséquentes"; and in the Vivarais in the eighteenth century, see Mallen, "La criminalité dans le Comté de Crussol" (cited chap. 1, n. 78), p. 53, quoting a male witness: "Il ne se rendit pas à la voix parce qu'il luy fut dit que c'etait des femmes qui se battaient."

60. AN, JJ249B, 118^{r-v}, letter of remission, dated Oct. 1536, for Gilles Gallart, carpenter, and his wife Mathurine Ginault, living in the bailliage of the Grand Fief d'Aulnoys for the homicide of Jeanne Gaultiere, who insulted Mathurine as "vesse, putain, excommuniée" and said she went "chez les prestres." JJ255B, 52^{v}, letter of remission, dated May 1541, for Catherine Carry, wife of Bon Duet of the village of Manicamp, for the homicide of Comete Guillebert, who insulted the supplicant and threw excrement and a milking stool at her. Alfred Soman's essay on "Injures" gives the range of insults used against women, with "putain" being the most common. Nicole Castan provides eighteenth-century examples in *Criminels de Languedoc,* pp. 163–64.

61. AN, JJ260B, 119^{r-v}, letter of remission, dated Sept. 1550, for Robinette, widow of Robinet Rubin, in service in a village in Normandy, for the homicide of Katherine, wife of Michel Le Maire.

62. If we consider a fairy tale like *Mélusine,* which existed in printed editions and which also was recounted at peasant veillées (du Fail, *Propos Rustiques,* p. 37), we note that the major quarrel described among females is that between Mélusine's mother Pressine and her three daughters when the girls avenge their mother's ill-treatment by their father and are in turn punished by Pressine. Jean d'Arras, *Mélusine* (based on the 1478 edition; Paris, 1854), pp. 21–24. In her excellent correction of "gender-related biases" in the indexes of tale-types and motifs in folktales, Torborg Lundell does not report physical strife between females in Western European tales except in regard

to "cruel mothers" and Gretel pushing the wicked witch into the oven ("Gender-Related Biases in the Type and Motif Indexes of Aarne and Thompson," in Bottigheimer, ed., *Fairy Tales,* pp. 150–63). For the representation of the violence of mistresses toward their servants, and especially of Sarah beating Hagar, see Matthews Grieco, "Mythes et iconographie," chap. 4, pp. 347–49.

63. AN, JJ256C, 30ʳ–31ʳ, letter of remission, dated Apr. 1543/44, for Jeanne Pasquellet of Lyon. For earlier steps in the case, X²ᴬ 89A, sentences of Apr. 29 and May 14, 1540 (I am grateful to Alfred Soman for transcriptions of these two sentences). Another effective tale pits two young women against a witch in Auvergne: JJ258B, 45ʳ⁻ᵛ, letter of remission, dated June 1548, for Anne Falgouze and Agnès Chavaliere, wives of plowmen of Fayet in the diocese of Clermont, for the homicide of Jeanne Andrade. This account, opening on the Saturday before Carnival, combines many women's motifs. The two wives were washing their sheets in the stream when old Jeanne Andrade came to cross it on a plank. She had lived her youth in lubricity and now her old age in "sorcellerie." The wives, because of an illness they had and because of the death of six or seven of their children, had the "fantaise" that Andrade had bewitched them out of hatred. They asked her to lift the spell, and when she "in derision" would not answer and tried to run away, they beat her and left her bleeding by the stream. She died nine or ten days later, they say, perhaps from their blows, perhaps from old age. They explain that it is customary in their region to give witches blows "to make them afraid and force them to lift their spells." Fearing the rigor of justice, the women fled. They were granted remission provided they paid 50 sous in alms.

64. AN, JJ237, 1ʳ, letter of remission, dated June 1524, for Marguerite Panete, wife of Mathieu de La Faye of a village in the Bourbonnais.

65. Du Fail, *Propos Rustiques,* p. 37, lists "De cuir d'Asnette" as one of the stories recounted in the Breton veillée. Geneviève Massignon describes *Peau d'Ane* as "one of the earliest recorded in French folklore" (Geneviève Massignon, ed., *Folktales of France,* trans. Jacqueline Hyland [Chicago and London, 1968], p. 274).

66. ADR, 3E540, 261ᵛ–263ʳ. AN, X¹ᴬ 9215, 51ʳ⁻ᵛ, Sept. 18, 1540. [Conrad Gesner], *Tresor de Evonime Philiatre des Remedes Secretz* (Lyon: Balthazar Arnoullet, 1555), aa3ᵛ, dedication of Barthélemy Aneau to Simon Guy: "I've always known how adroit were his hands." Archives municipales de Lyon, CC1174, 16ᵛ. ADR, 3E4542, spring 1566; 3E4062, June 13, 1571.

Of course, not all pardoned men did so well as Simon Guy. Etienne Dolet kept getting into trouble and, after one more letter of remission, was finally burned for heresy in 1546. Gilles Crespin of Angers got a letter of pardon for the homicide of a priest in March 1538/39 and then was condemned to death several years later for blasphemies against the honor of God. The Parlement of Paris dismissed his letter of pardon and reduced his sentence to life in the galleys (AN, X²ᴬ 98, 104ᵛ–105ʳ, Apr. 20, 1545/46). In 1562 a sergeant of Senlis was back in front of the criminal chamber of the

Parlement of Paris on a new charge not long after a letter of remission was ratified (Guérin, "Déliberations politiques" [cited Introduction, n. 10], pp. 22–24).

67. Philippe de Vigneulles, *Gedenkbuch*, pp. 220–21.

68. *Histoire sanguinaire, cruelle et emerveillable, d'une femme de Cahors* (1584; cited chap. 2, n. 94); *Histoire cruelle et sanguinaire: D'une femme de Cahors en Quercy, desesperee pour le mauvais gouvernement et mesnage de son mary, et pour ne pouvoir appaiser le famine de ses enfans elle massacra inhumainement ses deux enfans, et puis son mary. Avec la remonstance qu'elle fit publiquement devant tous les assistans, sur le devoir des hommes mariez envers leurs femmes et enfans* (Lyon: François Yvrat, 1643), date of execution, Apr. 5, 1643.

69. See, for instance, Seguin's bibliography of crime pamphlets in *L'Information en France*, pp. 69–82, nos. 5–8, 18–19, 48. *Discours tres-veritable, de deux meurtres* (cited chap. 2, n. 94): a seigneur kills his wife in fury because she insists upon separation from him in goods and body; a lady has her husband killed by men who frequent her house "par une fausse concupiscence ou autrement." Jean Papon included several cases of wives consenting to or aiding in the slaying of their husbands by their lovers in *Arrests notables*, book 22, title 9, pp. 1247–48. All the women were executed, except in a case which came on appeal before the Parlement of Bordeaux in Apr. 1527. The wife was condemned to be beaten in public, and the penalty was remitted for Good Friday. Cotreau, *Commentaires*, 172^v: the wife has the husband killed "pour vivre à son plaisir."

In England there was much interest in the conspiracy of Alice Arden of Kent in 1551 to have her husband murdered so she could marry her lover. For the story and its later dramatic representations, see Catherine Belsey, *The Subject of Tragedy: Identity and Difference in Renaissance Drama* (London and New York, 1985), chap. 5.

70. Marguerite de Navarre, *Heptaméron* (cited chap. 1, n. 11), end of nouvelle 35 to introduce nouvelle 36, p. 261.

71. Ibid., Prologue, p. 10. The copious notes of Michel François to this edition of the *Heptaméron* sort out the various historical and literary sources of the nouvelles. Tetel, *Marguerite de Navarre's Heptameron* (cited chap. 1, n. 76), pp. 193–97.

72. AN, X^{2A} 98, 486^v–487^r: the Parlement of Paris reviews the criminal case brought by the baillif of Perche at the request of the Queen of Navarre, Comtesse du Perche, against Gillet Verdrier and Jeanne Berrast, his wife, for the homicide of Thoinnecte Lamyer dit Gatienne (July 23, 1546).

73. AN, JJ236, 332^v–334^r, letter of remission, dated Jan. 1523/24, for Vidalle Bayonne, wife of Blaise Sere of the village of Montgazin, for the homicide of Catherine Bonnemate. Vidalle described herself as about 25 years old, having been married to Blaise for ten or twelve years and with several children.

74. *Heptaméron*, end of nouvelle 37, as Longarine introduces nouvelle 38, her story of the wife of Tours, p. 269. Vidalle Bayonne's serious account of her jealous violence also contrasts with the comic treatment of a fist fight between two wives of Metz in the Burgundian *Cent Nouvelles Nouvelles* in

the mid-fifteenth century. They quarrel over a kerchief given them by a canon with whom they had both had intercourse (*Cent Nouvelles Nouvelles* [cited chap. 2, n. 101], nouvelle 92, pp. 240–42).

75. On the importance of "ambiguity and dialogue" in the *Heptaméron,* see the interesting discussion of Tetel, *Marguerite de Navarre's Heptameron,* chap. 4, and on the introduction of epistemological doubt in the *Heptaméron* through suggesting an uncertain relation between what people tell about and what people really do and feel, see Philippe de Lajarte, "*L'Heptaméron* et la naissance du récit moderne. Essai de lecture épistémologique d'un discours narratif," *Littérature,* 17 (Feb. 1975): 31–42.

76. *Heptaméron,* nouvelle 8, p. 47. See also the distinction among saying angry words, feeling anger, and acting upon anger in Montaigne, *Essais* (cited chap. 1, n. 49), book 2, chap. 31, pp. 691–98, "De la colere."

Conclusion

1. *Heptaméron,* Prologue, p. 9.

2. Montaigne, *Essays* (cited chap. 2, n. 87), book 1, chap. 31, "Of cannibals," pp. 151–52.

3. See the discussion of oral tales in Peter Burke, *Popular Culture in Early Modern Europe* (New York, 1978), pp. 124–48. I am making a stronger claim for novelty and inventiveness in the supplications than he is for the oral tale, though admittedly remission tales are told in a distinctive setting and with collective authorship. Nonetheless, with proper qualification, they should be added to the folktale as an index for storytelling skills.

4. Montaigne, *Essays,* book 1, chap. 51, "Of the vanity of words," p. 223.

5. On the medieval sources of the reality claim, see Dubuis, *Les Cent Nouvelles Nouvelles* (cited Introduction, n. 7), pp. 25–33 and *passim.* On the definition of the nouvelle as in part "une relation fournie par une société à propos d'elle-même," see the magisterial study of Pérouse, *Nouvelles françaises du XVIe siècle* (cited chap. 1, n. 43), Introduction, chaps. 1–2, and p. 554. On Philippe de Vigneulle's "contract with the reader to narrate 'real' events" in his *Cent Nouvelles Nouvelles,* see Kotin, *Narrative Imagination* (cited chap. 1, n. 75), pp. 84–85. On "the fiction of truth and the truth of fiction" in Marguerite, see Tetel, *Marguerite de Navarre's Heptameron* (cited chap. 1, n. 76), chap. 6. Marc Fumaroli, "Jacques Amyot and the Clerical Polemic against the Chivalric Novel," *Renaissance Quarterly,* 38 (1985): 22–40. On the claim of fiction writers for the importance of the *vraisemblable* versus the claim of history writers to the "truth," see Nelson, *Fact or Fiction* (cited Introduction, n. 6). Lennard Davis, *Factual Fictions: The Origins of the English Novel* (New York, 1983), chap. 3: "News/Novels: The Undifferentiated Matrix"; the "novel" he discusses is the longer form of the eighteenth century, rather than the short nouvelle of two centuries before.

6. Rabelais, *Pantagruel,* chap. 34 in *Oeuvres complètes* (cited chap. 1, n. 83), pp. 312–13.

7. Shakespeare, *A Midsummer Night's Dream,* Act V, Scene 1, lines 430–37; *The Tempest,* Epilogue. Stephen Orgel's essay on Prospero would sug-

gest that the magician himself had considerable need to be pardoned, "Prospero's Wife," *Representations*, 8 (Fall 1984): 1–13. See also the Epilogue to *All's Well That Ends Well*, where the King speaks ("The king's a beggar, now the play is done") and the Epilogue to *King Henry IV, Part Two*, where a Dancer comes "to beg your pardons."

8. Renaissance rhetorical theory does not include asking pardon among its "Figures for ending" (see Sonnino, ed., *Handbook to Sixteenth-Century Rhetoric* [cited chap. 2, n. 92], p. 255). Quintilian's *De Institutione Oratoria*, concerned exclusively with a lawyer's pleading before the judge, says in passing in the section on the peroration that "some think this part should include prayers and excuses," but they would be for the client, not for the lawyer and his speech (Quintilian, *Institution Oratoire*, 4 vols., trans. Henri Bornecque [Paris, 1933–52], vol. 2, pp. 287–317, book 5, chaps. 1–2). It would be interesting to explore Renaissance epilogues more generally with this question in mind.

9. Thomas M. Greene, *The Vulnerable Text* (cited chap. 2, n. 50), especially p. 103, where he talks of the vulnerability of a poem as a source both of risk and of power.

10. Rabelais, *Le Quart Livre*, chaps. 5–8 in *Oeuvres complètes*, pp. 551–61. See the interesting discussion of the comic features of this episode and also of that in which Gargantua drowns 260,418 Parisians in his urine in Gregory de Rocher, *Rabelais' Laughers and Joubert's "Traité du Ris"* (University, Ala., 1979), pp. 59–68. Montaigne, *Essais* (cited chap. 1, n. 49), book 1, chap. 38, "Comme nous pleurons et rions d'une mesme chose," pp. 229–31. On Calvin, see above, p. 61. Benedicti, *Somme des Pechez*, book 5, chap. 2, p. 624.

Index

Index

171nn13 and 15, 172n22 (Abbeville), 175n51, 190n19, 191n20,
198n48, 201n60; medieval letters
of remission from, 194n31
Pizan, Christine de, 81, 84, 92
Plaidoyers, 18, 24, 164nn62 and 63
Plausibility, see Truth; Vraisemblance
Plots, pardon, 12, 14, 64, 68
Poisoning, 5, 85, 102, 108
Poitou: supplicants for remission
from, 40, 155n19, 170n11; execution for homicide in, 96
Politian, 16
Premeditation: in homicide, 49, 75,
96, 98n; in poisoning, 85, 108
—and pardon narratives, 28, 33,
43–44; about adultery, 95–96;
about battered wives, 94; in
Romeo and Juliet, 72–73
Priests: in letters of remission, 21,
23, 25–26, 40, 87–88, 190n19,
198n48; and sex, 21, 23, 97–
98, 190n19, 200n55, 201n60,
203n74; as supplicants for remission, 27–28, 97–98, 160n42; as
victims of homicide, 28, 43,
177n65, 200n54; in *Heptaméron,*
68, 106–7; in *Romeo and Juliet,*
71–72, 74–75. *See also* Clergy
Printers, 6, 57; in craft fights, 6,
51, 161n46; as supplicants for remission, 8, 23, 50f, 178n66; and
crime pamphlets, 60, 180n82; as
victims of homicide, 161n46
Privy Council, 152n9, 176n58
Processions, 28, 30–31
Property, as source of quarrel, 26,
65, 94–95, 172n18. *See also* Inheritance; Trespassing
Propos Rustiques, 43, 69–70, 98,
101
Prostitutes, 1–2, 47, 105, 196n36,
199nn52 and 53
Protestantism: quarrels about, 28,
33, 40, 42–43, 155n19; and par-

don, 60–62; and execution,
60–61, 96
Provence, 108n. *See also* Aix

Rabelais, François, 32, 66–67, 83,
113, 184n110, 190n16; *Quart
Livre,* 14; *Tiers Livre,* 31, 41,
66–67, 83, 190n16; *Pantagruel,*
46, 113; *Gargantua,* 184n110,
205n10
Rape: in canon law, 81, 189n11;
used as excuse for homicide,
88–89, 96–97; in *Heptaméron,*
106
Ratification, *see* Letters of remission
Reality effect, 45, 64–65, 66. *See
also* History; Vraisemblance
Reformed Church, 8, 60–62, 139,
152n9
Repentance: in letters of remission,
37, 85; in crime pamphlets, 60,
64, 87, 105; after infanticide, 85,
86, 87
Revenge: in letters of remission,
57, 175n53; in duels, 57; in
literature, 68, 184n102; in *Heptaméron,* 106–7, 108–9
Rhetoric: Renaissance views of,
3–4, 63, 111–12, 147n6; judicial, 4, 18, 24, 164nn62 and 63
Ricoeur, Paul, 3, 174n39
Riots, *see* Tax riots
Romeo and Juliet: anger, homicide,
and pardon in, 70–76, 185n114;
version by Matteo Bandello,
185n114; by Pierre Boaistuau,
71–72; by William Shakespeare,
72–75
Ronsard, Pierre de, 24, 53
Rouen: Little Chancellery at, 8, 15;
Church of, 52. *See also under*
Parlement
Rouergue, *see* Guyenne
Roussillon, supplicant for remis-
sion from, 166n79